PN 6231 .W4 W34 1988

Walker, Don D., 1917-

The adventures of Barney Tullus

THE ADVENTURES OF BARNEY TULLUS

THE ADVENTURES OF
BARNEY TULLUS

DON D. WALKER

UNIVERSITY OF NEW MEXICO PRESS

ALBUQUERQUE

Library of Congress Cataloging-in-Publication Data

Walker, Don D., 1917–
The adventures of Barney Tullus / Don D. Walker.—1st ed.
  p.   cm.
ISBN 0-8263-1046-X
1. West (U.S.)—Anecdotes, facetiae, satire, etc.
2. Western stories—Anecdotes, facetiae, satire, etc.
3. Criticism—Anecdotes, facetiae, satire, etc.
4. Parodies. I. Title.
PN6231.W4W34   1988
814'.54—dc19   87-33420

© 1988 by Don D. Walker.
All rights reserved.
First edition

*For Marjorie,
who alone understands
how a cranky scholar,
a dreamy cowboy,
and a loving husband can
be the same person*

CONTENTS

Preface   ix

Genesis: A Cowboy and His Critics   1
The Rise and Fall of Barney Tullus   3

Adventures: The Cowboy Modus Vivendi   13
Talking Point   15
A Conversation with the Author   20
The Milk of Human Kindness   23
La Belle Sauvage   31
The Western Verité   41
The Metawestern: A Further Conversation
  with the Novelist   53
A Visit from the Novelist   61
The Romance of Allis Chalmers   64
The Devil and Barney Tullus   72
The Singing Cowboys   90
The Western Experience   100
The Exhibitionist   113
The Evaluation   125
Cowboy Culture   134
The Blue Saddle Blanket: The Novelist
  and the *Nouveau Western*   143
The Bunkhouse Murders   149
Afterword: Some Critical Reflections on the
  Work Just Concluded   236

PREFACE

Unlike the cowboys of much western fiction, Barney Tullus did not ride in off an actual range into the awareness of his author. Thus the search for his prototype may be long and difficult and fruitless. To be sure, in the beginning there were some actualities. Until she was sold into an unknown future, the patient bay mare kept herself fat and matronly on my grasses. Her full name was Brunhilde, but we usually called her Hilda. On a warm summer day the author actually overshot the summit of her back, to fall into the earthly dust and into a creative thesis. The cowboy to whom the final critical appeal was made did live within riding distance. His name was not actually Jim, but before I took up that character-building task myself he did shoe Hilda and he did refer to my pinto gelding with a feminine pronoun.

But Barney himself cannot be discovered in the world of actuality. If the author rose and fell, he is not therefore an autobiographical Barney. No, Barney Tullus was conceived out of rhetorical necessity. (As Barney himself might say, what a hell of a way to be conceived.) The occasion was an academic symposium. The subject was Western literary criticism. The author's motive was to satirize the strained excesses of that criticism. The result was a straight-faced paper titled "The Rise and Fall of Barney Tullus." The paper was well received, in laughs and in thesis approval. It was published and republished. For some literary pundits it seemed the *Pooh Perplex* of Western American literature.

Luckily—and perhaps ironically—Barney survived his strange conception. Whatever the anguish of Western literary criticism, he seemed comfortable in his imaginative world. When he could stop trying to fit into three-part sentences, triangular structures, and stylistic delicacies of one sort or another, he found a simple,

Preface / ix

stubborn, comic way of being. The Pulley ranch became a home, and in the company of Sill and Burt and Mont and the cows they tended, the ranch became a world, a place where act and talk, thought and feeling had a coherent center. Barney himself would put the proposition less grandly. "We don't need any goddamn philosopher," he might have said, "to justify the way we live as cowboys."

The academic critics of course would need to go on writing. If Barney and his friends didn't carry guns and didn't save blue-eyed maidens from the perils of stagecoach robberies, in the logic of higher criticism they must be anti-heroes, cowboy conceptions designed to deflate stereotypes and myths and any other sort of popular wrenching of the mundane realities of the historical range. As Barney himself might have said, "It sure as hell is hard to get started as a cowboy. First you get conceived this way, and then you get conceived that way. Reminds me of that old Hereford cow who couldn't decide if she wanted to get romantic with an Angus bull or wait until somebody brought in a Charolais or one of them even more fancy breeds."

But if Barney was not an actual cowboy riding in from the range, where did he get the name Barney Tullus? We could of course leave the question to the scholars, but for the fun of it let the author play with the problem. A friend, in apparent seriousness, once asked, "Was Barney named after Marcus Tullius Cicero?" It is easy to answer "No," but such an easy answer ignores a fact of literary history, that writers, particularly in the South, had a fondness for classical names. Barney is not from the South, but his author has read a lot of Southern works. No doubt a considerable number of classical names rattle around in the name bin of his mind. However, a more likely source—if one must have a source—is a name list of Texas cow people. Sometime after Barney had begun to ride his own way through my stories, I reread J. Frank Dobie's *Cow People*. When I saw the name Barnes Tillous, I paused, letting memory associations sort themselves out if they would. They wouldn't. Tillous (the name is spelled Tillus in *The Longhorns*) was boss of the Quien Sabe outfit on the Plains and thus no character prototype of the cowboy who rose and fell. However, Dobie did give a bit of story with a line that can be turned to my own advantage (or disadvantage). A buyer of polo ponies followed Tillous to his camp, hoping to buy

x / Preface

a colt named Possum. Approaching Tillous, the buyer said, "My name is Savage." Tillous retorted, "I can't help what your name is. I didn't give it to you."

Whatever the name I gave to Barney, whatever the pieces of ranch actuality I have used to thicken his world, I prefer to think of him as *sui generis*. But since the only *sui* Barney has probably ever heard is *sooey*, a sound used in talking to cows and pigs, my special personal apology to Barney for allowing myself to become so damn pedantic. Pedantic or professorial, the term fits: Barney is his own kind of cowboy. Historians and sociologists and demographers may have a hell of a time making any generalizations out of him. But the author hopes the reader will nevertheless find a special pleasure in his uniqueness. Put Barney with those other unique cowboys, Sill, Burt, Mont, and Andy, and you have a porchful of humanity, but you still can't abstract much general truth from that small outfit. No matter, if the reading's fun.

A literary license from the author to the reader: the following pieces cover a wide range of matters in a variety of voices and tones. They deal with the struggle of a Western novelist to keep his work timely in theme and method. They tell the stories told by that novelist when happily his cowboys issued alive and free and unscarred from the creative chute. The reader has the author's permission, if he or she feels so inclined, to skip the struggle and jump right into the action at the J. G. Pulley Ranch and Feedyard.

Notes of thanks go to many who helped the author along the literary trail: to compañeros at academic roundups who listened, laughed, and hoped for a book; to Josette and Irene, who processed my words so efficiently; to Beth Hadas and her staff at New Mexico, for making the words become a book; and finally, to all the cows who listened to my typewriter and wondered what the hell was going on.

Don D. Walker
Flying W Ranch
May 1987

GENESIS
A COWBOY AND HIS CRITICS

"A cowboy story has to start at some point. What better point than the cowboy himself. Then the critics can come along and try to figure out what the hell he is up to."

—A. D. Light,
Prolegomenon to Matters Western

THE RISE AND FALL OF BARNEY TULLUS

Late in the spring of 1962 a small novel issued from the presses of an Eastern publishing house. Coming as it did rather late in the critical season, it attracted little attention from the reviewers. The *Times* simply noted that it had appeared; the *Wednesday Review* gave it a three-line summary; and the *American Saddle and Bridle Gazette* allowed it one substantial paragraph, noting particularly that the saddle mentioned on page 104 seemed to be a genuine Peotone Rider, with leathers hand-shaped over the seat and side bars of the tree hand-formed with a drawing knife.

The Rise and Fall of Barney Tullus, however, was destined for a more serious and extended critical consideration. Early in the winter of that same year scholars in Western American Literature apparently discovered it. There followed a series of full-length critical essays, explicating *Barney* from various points of view. By the end of 1964 he was in quality paperback, and when the academic year opened in September 1965, he was required or recommended optional reading in a dozen classes at a dozen different colleges and universities. Just a few years later one can say that *The Rise and Fall of Barney Tullus* has become a minor classic in American letters. And one can predict with considerable confidence the ultimate appearance of a work entitled *The Art of Barney Tullus* or perhaps *Barney Tullus: Text, Sources, and Criticism.*

A critical history of *Barney Tullus* of course remains to be written, although earnest graduate students may already be at work on such a project. However, while waiting for the completion of such a study—a more definitive analysis and a more complete summary of critical discoveries—we can usefully survey briefly some of the major interpretations that have demonstrated the novel's importance.

Since some readers may not know the book, let me quote in full a key episode, the one from which the novel seems to have derived its title and upon which the critics have chosen to focus.

Barney slowly sat up and sleepily reached for his boots. The warm afternoon air had partly dried his socks, but after he had pulled on the left boot the right boot stuck, and he thought again, as he had thought so many times, why does one goddamn foot have to be bigger than the other? Or why can't a man go into a store and say, give me that little boot and give me that big boot and put 'em in the same goddamn box?

The exertion stirred the old beer again. He could feel it rumble beneath his broad belt buckle. He wished now he had saved the fourth bottle for another time.

Booted at last, he rose unsteadily. He tipped backward; he tipped forward; he caught himself in a gentle sway. He spread his legs; the boot heels dug deeper into the soft earth; he stood solid at last.

It can't be the beer, he thought. It must be the sun.

He pulled the rag of a handkerchief from his left rear pocket, wiping his sweaty face. "Goddamn," he said. "Even a man's dainties stink of horse sweat and dust."

Lifting the coil of rope from the dry juniper limb, he squinted toward the watering trough a hundred yards away. They were still there all right, the mare stirring the dust with her big feet and brushing black flies with her tail. Even with the flies, they'd just as soon wait awhile, he thought.

The saddle lay dumped where he had dropped it a couple of hours ago, the blanket still damp with the morning's sweat. I've come to the crossroads of life, he thought: I can pack this stinking saddle all of the way down to that horse, or I can lead that stinking horse all of the way back to this saddle.

He chose the second way. That way didn't look any easier, but he could put off the hardest part a little longer. Maybe he could carry himself and the rope those hundred yards, but if he had to put that saddle on his own back he'd be dead. He'd be down in the brush before he'd stumbled a hundred feet, let alone a hundred yards. And it wasn't the brush he hated so much as the goddamn itchy June grass.

So he took a quick aim and launched himself. The sagebrush wavered hotly around him; the steel blue sky seemed too bright to look at; he stumbled weakly across the tilting world. But he spread his arms like balancing wings; he spread his uneasy legs across the hot earth; he moved steadily again. My legs are already too short, he thought; I need to be up there to see where the hell I am headed; but even if my ass does drag the brush, I'm still going.

He reached the mare, and she stood for him, her tail still steadily sweeping her rump. He reached the rope around her neck and turned a half hitch over her nostrils. I'm pooped again, he thought. I couldn't lift that saddle even if it hung right now on my strong right arm. If I had that fourth bottle, which I should have saved, I'd drink it now to give me strength. The tail continued to swing.

Barney was at the crossroads again. He could either stumble back through the brush with the mare on the end of his rope, or he could make a gigantic effort to lift himself across her bare back. It'll be sweaty either way, he thought. But one way she'll do the sweating; she'll do the sweating, even if it does end up on me.

She was a tall mare; Barney was a short man; it would truly take a gigantic leap. Even with a stirrup, he thought, it's a long way up. Every time he had stretched his left leg and felt the denim tighten across his crotch, he thought, maybe they ought to put those goddamn rivets in other places too.

Now he placed his boots solidly for the leap. With his left hand he fastened a sweaty grip on her withers. For his right hand there was only the fat back and slick hair, but if he could get an elbow on the other side he could hang in balance; he could kick himself upward; at last he could spread his legs and sit as a man was made to sit: astride, man and horse become the centaur.

The warm earth gave him strength. He leaped upward. He pawed the air and the ungrippable hair, hung like a kicking sack for an instant upon the apex, then tumbled headdown to the earth again. His head struck the pile of dung; his legs

The Rise and Fall of Barney Tullus

flew loosely into the sagebrush; he lay face upward, the delicate dung dust settling about him, his boots a yard apart in the twisted gray green branches. He could look up and see the old teats of the mare, black, slightly wrinkled and unused. She hadn't moved. She hadn't even stopped stirring the flies.

"Goddamn," he said to himself gently. Then he thought, maybe I'll just stay here until the sun goes down.

One of the first to note the real complexity of *Barney Tullus* was Professor Ernest Dewlap of Two Forks Junior College. In an article entitled "Style and Structure in *Barney Tullus*," he developed the thesis that whatever its seeming indifference to literary design, it is in reality a highly complicated, closely wrought text, with a great many literary devices functioning effectively to deepen and heighten meaning.

"Structurally," writes Professor Dewlap, "the story is a triangle, an isosceles triangle, with one side the rise, one side the fall, and the base the horizontal earthly experience of the hero. The title of course makes this clear. However, even without the title, the triangularity of the design would be strongly revealed.

"Consider the first description of Barney as he stands 'booted at last.' 'He spread his legs; the boot heels dug deeply into the soft earth; he stood solid at last.' Barney thus becomes a human triangle, and in his triangularity he becomes strong upon the earth. The same image is picked up a bit later, and again Barney is able to order his experience. 'He spread his uneasy legs across the hot earth; he moved steadily again.'

"Note, too, that the mare herself is a triangle in her relationship to Barney. Her withers are both the apex of her own solid structure and the high point of Barney's rise. And as he lies prostrate looking up at her, he in a sense completes the form which gives her strength.

"Furthermore, in the development of such structural design, the style functions with special effectiveness. Note the three-clause shape of a great many sentences, and note that in many of these sentences the third clause binds the form. Steadiness, control come in the very design of the sentences. An already quoted passage illustrates this stylistic feature: 'He spread his legs; the boot heels dug deeper into the soft earth; he stood solid at last.'

Note, too, that even the alliteration moves in threes: 'broad belt buckle,' 'still steadily sweeping,' and 'delicate dung dust.'

"The triangularity of design is thus clear. However, lest the reader take this for mere mechanical contrivance, the imposition of rigid forms upon the naturally amorphous human experience, note the way the form really reinforces the ambiguity of the human predicament. The apex signifies aspiration, perhaps hubris, but it is also the point of fragile balance and fall. And in the fall, which may be the failure of aspiration, is a return to that which may be mundane but that which is the plane of strength. All of this is imaged also in the figure of Barney himself: his head, which is the human apex, becomes giddy at times but becomes steady in its dependence on the legspread grounding to the dusty earth."

Still another dimension of the novel was revealed by Professor Alister Outlook, writing in *The Balsam Review*. In an essay entitled "Mythic Patterns in *Barney Tullus*," Professor Outlook argued convincingly that the real power of the novel comes from its evocation of great mythic themes. "The first evidence," he noted, "comes in the word *gigantic,* in 'he could make a gigantic effort to lift himself across her bare back,' and repeated shortly after in 'it would truly take a gigantic leap.' Now Barney is clearly not a giant in any strictly physical sense, yet an aura of the superhuman begins to surround him. Thus when he falls in weakness and lies close again upon the earth, we say to ourselves at once: this is not Barney Tullus; this is Antaeus. And we can be certain, though the novel does not tell us explicitly, that Barney will regain his strength and rise again.

"Less immediately obvious is another mythic allusion. As he makes his way to the horses, Barney moves through a field of sagebrush. After his fall he lies with boots 'a yard apart in the twisted gray green branches.' Now it is never clear whether this is black sagebrush (*Artemisia nova*) or big sagebrush (*Artemisia tridentata*), but in either case it is *Artemisia*. And, as everyone knows, Artemisia derives through association with wormwood and mugwort from Artemis. Although Barney is probably not a virgin in any strictly physical sense, he is nevertheless a hunter. And thus the relevance of the myth becomes overwhelmingly clear."

If Professor Outlook suggested that Barney will rise again in all of his old strength, Professor L. B. H. Fescue seemed to have his doubts, though he did not state them in a direct and dogmatic manner. In an article entitled "Barney Tullus as American: An Old Theme Restated," he saw the hero finally as a changed man. "If Barney goes up one side of the mare an innocent," he wrote, "he comes down the other side a fallen man. This realization takes us at once from the dung dust of the West deep into the central development of American self-awareness—or lack of self-awareness. If Jonathan remains a hick, Manly has never been one; yet in his pompous goodness—indeed his manliness—he has no insight into his own nature. If he comes out well in other conflicts, he will do so by good luck, the good luck of the cultural circumstances which save his kind of nature—or should we say allow for it. His heroism is ambiguous, or at least let us say that his creator has an ambivalent attitude toward him. In one sense, he—that is, the hero—is a barbarian, and we suspect that if he were to take his Americanness to Europe a century later, although he would have little patience with the Anglomaniacal Dimple, he would nevertheless prefer a shiny, well-preserved Da Vinci to a faded and cracked one. And certainly were he to encounter Newman, who, as Leslie Fiedler so aptly points out, might well have come upon that other innocent barbarian, the conversation would fail, not merely because a century lies between them but also because for one—that is, for Newman—at least one wall, the outer wall to self-discovery, has been penetrated. Yet even Newman, as he stares too eagerly up at the masterpiece he wants to know, is substituting—or at least trying to—an American frontier energy for the reflective awareness that is the knowledge and burden of centuries-old traditions. And even as he turns finally to see if the little paper is in fact consumed, he has played the game to the end in his own way. As Mrs. Tristram must point out to him, it is his remarkable good nature that has saved *them*, as it has saved *him*, kept them a facade of innocence as it has kept him the real purity of his moral intent." Thus concludes Professor Fescue.

So far the school of authenticism had not been heard from. However, at last the word got around that here was a novel about a cowboy. "We'll see," said Dr. Angus McFrisby, Professor of English at the Upper Pahvant College for Girls and one of the leading authenticators in Western letters.

"There is some evidence here," began Dr. McFrisby, "that the author of *The Rise and Fall of Barney Tullus* knows something about the real West. At least he has read widely. Although his sources may be difficult to identify with satisfactory scholarly precision, one can be confident that if necessary he can provide a solid bibliography and a comforting foundation of specific notes.

"Having said this, we are sorry that we must object to a few matters which make uncertain the complete authenticity of this account of Western life. Reference is made in the story to the mare's brushing black flies with her tail. We assume that these flies are black-bodied gnats of the dipterous family *Simuliidae*. If this assumption is correct, then within the limited historical context of Barney's experience these flies may be slightly anachronistic. Let us consider the time of Barney's rise and fall. The author mentions the extreme heat; indeed the hotness is the dominant climatic note. He mentions the itchy June grass, which we take to be cheatgrass (*Bromus tectorum*). Now June grass is itchy only when it is ripe, and it ripens only in late June or early July, with the possibility, when the spring is long, wet, and cool, of reaching maturity only in mid-July. The heat and the itchy June grass (one does feel more comfortable calling it *cheatgrass*) do thus seem to belong together. But what about the black flies? As everybody knows, the larvae of the black gnat are aquatic. They thus develop only in the wetness of the late spring, coming to their most vicious maturity by mid-June. Dates will differ here, according to latitudes, elevations, and particular circumstances of weather patterns, but it is my personal observation that the black flies have passed out of the picture by June 29 or by July 2 at the latest. In short, if one scratches his legs in June, he probably scratches the bite of the black fly. If he scratches in July, he probably scratches the cheatgrass caught in his socks. Although he may possibly scratch both in the same period of time, such simultaneity would, I believe, be highly unusual.

"Furthermore, we are sorry that we must add that some signs of a phony literary West still flaw the book. It is good—indeed it is delightful—to have dust and sweat and stink in the story, but we are more than mildly troubled about the word *dung*. Dung it must be, to be sure, but haven't literary conventions won out here? Hasn't the author given in to the temptations of the pleasantly alliterative 'd' and the poetically euphonious *ung* when he ought to give way manfully to linguistic realities? To sum up, for the writer about the West a spade must be a spade, or, to paraphrase slightly, a horse turd must be a horse turd."

This completes my survey of formal criticism, but one more critic ought I think to be included in this brief study. I know an old fellow who sometimes reminds me of Barney, in the little things he sometimes does, in the little things he says, even in the way he looks. I have to be careful about fusing reality and fiction here because this old guy is in other ways unlike Barney. He sometimes shoes my horses, and although he seems to insist on calling my gelding a mare, I still have confidence in his horse sense. In a certain way he is a cowboy. I reasoned that he would do as an informed lay critic.

When his wife met me at the front door, she said, "Jim's in the basement watching television." I knew that if I announced boldly that I wanted her to tell him that I wanted him to read something, he'd spook and probably climb out a window. "Tell him to come up a minute," I said. "Just tell him I want to ask him something." She opened the door to the basement stairs and yelled down. "Someone wants to see you." "What about?" I heard him say. "Come on up and see," she said. I could hear him growling, so I walked across the room to the door and yelled down in my own way. "Come on up a minute, Jim. I need your opinion on something." "Okay," he answered, "as soon as I slip on these goddamn boots."

When he saw the book, he did spook. But I had him trapped. He couldn't do anything but sit down at the table and read the pages I shoved in front of him.

"That's pretty rough language for a book," he said.

"Never mind that," I said. "Just get to the part about falling off a horse."

He read slowly, smiling slightly.

"Well, what do you think?" I finally said.

"What do you mean, what do I think?" he said.

"I mean, is it true?"

"How the hell should I know?" he said. "I don't know the guy."

"I mean, does it seem true? Could it happen?"

"Sure it could happen," he said. "Happened to me once."

There was a bit of silence; then he added, "But I wouldn't write a book about it."

---

10 / The Rise and Fall of Barney Tullus

I think I understand why my friend Jim would not write a book about falling off a horse. The books he knows simply do not give attention to such seemingly unimportant human experiences. However, there is no good reason why the writer should not write about falling off a horse. Perhaps it would be difficult to make such an experience one of the major experiences, but if that experience, trivial, unexciting, unromantic, or whatever it may seem to Jim, can function with other experiences to define and illuminate something important about a man, then clearly it can have a rightful place in the story. The rightness will depend upon the understanding and skill of the writer. Some writers cannot make falling off a thousand-foot cliff important; Henry James could make taking off a glove important.

A part of that skill may well be a close attention to the sound of words, the rhythms of sentences, the patterns of imagery, the larger structures of chapters and sections and of the short story or novel itself. At his best, and when he has the active cooperation of an intelligent and sensitive reader, these things, these devices, should function in the fictional persuasion without the help of the critic. After all, a novel should be read as a novel, and this goes for *The Sound and the Fury* as much as for *David Copperfield* or *The Man of Property.* If as readers we come armed with or prepared by maps, genealogical charts, handbooks to this and that, we are no longer reading a novel. We are playing an academic literary game. But perhaps I make reading too simple. Obviously some young readers need help in developing the kind of awareness, those habits in which the skills of the writer can really have their say. But obviously, too, critics can help too much. Innocent readers can still, I believe, read Cooper with pleasure. College juniors and senior English majors, trained to quiver at the least exquisite twist and turn of a phrase, have their difficulties.

Furthermore, a part of the understanding and skill involves an awareness of the mythic dimensions of human experience, although *awareness* may be misleading here since what is meant is not just the central controlling consciousness but the unconscious as well. So in the long view, I don't object to relating Barney to Antaeus, providing the pattern of mythic allusions does really illuminate the *human* dimension of Barney. The trouble with Professor Outlook is that he is not really interested in Barney.

The Rise and Fall of Barney Tullus / *11*

And poor old Barney will do better carrying that stinking saddle than toting all that classical pedantry.

    With one exception, I really have no quarrel with the critical assumptions of the eminent men I have quoted. I confess that McFrisby stirs me up. For the real enemy of Western American literature, in my opinion, is the high priest of authenticism. He thinks he is a literary critic, but he is not really a critic, for he has none of the qualities of mind that make a critic. He is really a bastard type, fathered by a third-rate historian and mothered by a retarded lady who never got over the shock of learning that Shakespeare *lied* when he added those years to young Prince Hal. What can he know of the acts of the creative imagination, when he has none of his own? He is convinced that Western American literature began—and perhaps ended—with Andy Adams and *The Log of a Cowboy*. He says to the young writer, get those cows in there and rub a little shit on their hides, when he ought to be saying, keep reading Andy Adams because he can teach you honesty, but don't forget to read Hawthorne also and even Henry James. He discovered a cardboard literary West and learned to call it phony. Indeed *phony* is his favorite word, but he really doesn't understand what makes it phony. He assumes it is phony because it has too many guns, too many women, not enough cows and too many horses. He thinks Taisie Lockhart is phony because she is a woman, when a woman doesn't belong on the trail. But the critical truth is that Taisie is phony because she isn't a woman. She is a cardboard doll. And no supply of footnotes could have given her life. Only a novelist's imagination could have done that.

ADVENTURES
THE COWBOY MODUS VIVENDI

"I've known the cowboy to do some damn fool things."

—Ezra Pinker, sometimes known as the Plutarch of Pinville

TALKING POINT

My name is Andrew Monroe Pickens. Just call me Andy. Two or three times in my short uneventful life somebody somewhere has given my name the full space it needs on a piece of paper or the full time it needs in the listening air. My mother must have liked the sound of it when she told my father what she had decided to call me. I think he got to name the horses and dogs, and she got to name the kids. But I don't know that she ever wrote it down. I did see my full name in the paper once, in the society column of the *Pinville Post*, after a big going-away affair for Professor Covington at the end of his visit. And I heard it once in a church that was being used for a court of law. When a fellow is being charged with murder, the bald-headed bailiff or whoever is making the announcement likes to get as much as he can out of the names, as if he is reading the winners in a foot race to hell itself. I once thought of starting my own herd, having my own brand, with my initials about three inches high to burn on their hides. But when I scratched it in the dust alongside the loading chute and was thinking that even in the cow-stained dirt it had a certain elegance, like the sign above a barroom door, my friend Mont came along, studied the marks in the dust, and said, "I've seen that word in some funny places, including the inside of a rusty John Deere, but I've never seen it up plain on the ass-end of a beef cow." That didn't bother me much, but I got to thinking what other funny stuff would come my way. I could hear some cattle buyer looking at that brand and saying, "What do you feed 'em to put that charge into 'em? If you eat some of the beef, does your hair start to stand on end?"

All of this doesn't really matter. Most of the time I'm just a plain old pronoun. You can say I'm the "I" in the stories that make up this book. If the "I" sounds like *eye,* that's all right. I'm the one who has been in the middle of things, who has seen and remembered all of the sad and crazy damn fool things that can make a cowboy sweat with pride or wish he had joined the navy before the cows came home. Hearing is part of it too. Sometimes most of it. I've sat on Sill's front porch in the evenings with my eyes shut or my hat pushed down over my face and heard enough things to fill a hundred books. Some of it true. Some of it not true. Some of it bull. Some of it just as solemnly serious as a well-built hand of poker. Somebody once told me that somebody told him that the "I" is just a grammatical fiction. If I could locate the shorthorn thinker who said that, I would tell him that this "I" is sure as hell not just a fiction. He may not always be grammatical, but he sure as hell is not just a fiction. Ask Barney or Sill or Burt and Mont, any of the fellows who have heard me swear when I get a burr in my boot, or watched me squinch when my levis fit too tight, or feel the roughened scab under my rope-burned fist.

You could say that the bunch of us are cowboys—if you don't haul in too much fancy stuff when you use that word. We work with cows when the need arises, but much of the time when we work, when Mr. Pulley gives the orders, we dig postholes, string barbed wire, rassle bales of hay, and stir around some to give the place the look of being busy. We spend some time in the branding corral, but our favorite work place is Sill's warm kitchen or his cool front porch. We can put Pulley's brand on his calves. We can cut up an ear with the Pulley mark. We can pull the balls out of a little bull. But we're not much into roasting and eating the oysters. We don't believe that old shit about the manpower they give, and we have an old habit of preferring almost anything that comes hot out of Sill's old cookware. We keep a few horses and ride them on occasion, but we prefer the pickup, even when we have to make our own road through the greasewoods and sagebrush. We like a good shoot-out, especially when the gunplay starts out even. We would have liked it better if Henry Fonda had at least got nicked in his boot and if Gary Cooper had at least been grazed on the knuckles. It wouldn't have even needed to be his shooting hand. Barney keeps an old .30–.30 leaning in a corner of the bunkhouse, but I can't remember his cleaning it or putting a shot of oil down the barrel. If there is anything small enough to live down that hole, that critter must be happy with the smooth way things always seem to be going.

Aside from the cows and a few horses, there are five of us living here at the Pulley Ranch, not counting a few crows and jack rabbits and of course a wandering bedbug or two. The place sure as hell isn't your ordinary Ponderosa, but we like it. A few old poplar trees would touch the place up a bit, maybe make a roosting place for a set of kingbirds or a pair of curious owls, but we can get along without the shade. Sill's front porch is cool enough if you move down the wall ahead of the sun, and besides it's close to the coffee Sill keeps steaming on his old wood stove. We don't need the trees for hangings. Poplar's pretty brittle, and besides we're not much into hangings. In Pinville I once saw a book with a hanging tree on the cover. It sure as hell made a nice cover, but that sort of tree would look out of place around here. On the book it seems mostly dead. Probably chopped down and cut up into arm-size pieces, it would make a good steady fire in Sill's old stove. Probably save us the hard work of hauling oak and juniper all of the way from the Cricket Mountains.

Aside from Sill's kitchen with its wide front porch, there is a bunkhouse just a rock-toss away and your basic outhouse back up a low-slung hill. Besides these comforts there is a feed yard with a poled-in place for hay, and just to one side an all-round shed, with a junk rack of old saddles, bridles, half-used rolls of barbed wire, rat's-nest coils of saved-up baling wire, and in the middle just enough room for the old John Deere, or whatever four-wheeled critter we happen to be enjoying at the time. In a normal course of events, Mr. Pulley might have built himself a big sprawling ranch house, with an acre of Indian rugs and a fireplace he could throw the whole butt of a granddaddy juniper into. Mr. Goodnight is his model. Even though Mr. Pulley will never own as many cows as Goodnight, he admires the grand style of the old Texas cowman. The trouble is that times are changing. Pinville isn't exactly the Rome or Paris of our desert valley, but at least it has a garden club and a newspaper with a social column. Mrs. Pulley knew from the beginning that she has her cultural rights. If her husband wants to think of Charles Goodnight as his model, she doesn't have to think of Barbara Stanwyck as hers.

Talking Point / 17

How many miles is it from the ranch to Pinville? Hell, I don't know. I've ridden over the road in the saddle, in the cab and in the bed of a pickup, even in the sidecar of Turley Sinker's Harley, but I still can't give more than a guess at the distance. Sometimes the road seems short. Sometimes it seems as long as the twisty road to hell itself. Depends on the weather. Depends on how many ruts the mud has left in the late spring sunshine. Depends on the state of mind. If I'm thinking of a cold beer in Pinville, the trip can seem short. If I'm wearing home a head-busting hangover, it can seem like a ride to the end of nowhere and all of the way back again.

I once heard about a writer who made a map of his county. I suppose I could make a map of mine. But what the hell good would it do? Suppose I put on the map that it's nine miles from where we're keeping the cows to where old man Barnes is keeping his Angus bull. What's that going to mean? Suppose I show on the map that you ride east to get there. What's that going to matter? Out at Pulley's place we aren't much into living by maps. If you're riding a horse some place, it's the seat of your pants that's going to measure the distance. If the horse is spavined in the left hind leg and doesn't like to break into anything faster than a soft jog, there may be a lot of miles in it. A map can't show a thing like that. Mr. Pulley could probably make a check on the speedometer of his pickup, but he don't give a good goddamn about the miles or inches. He just wants to get out there as fast as he can to start the herd milling and get his hard-working cowboys pointed up the true and proper trail. He doesn't need a map to tell where that is.

Map or not, we pretty much know where we are, even if we sometimes don't know where we're going. But maps don't give that kind of information anyway. There's a pinched little old lady in Pinville who uses the palm of your hand to map the future. But anybody who has seen the hand of cowboy knows you can't read much for certain there. I don't know what that little old lady can see in my palm or Barney's palm. Maybe she can see a tall redheaded woman wearing a tight black dress that would drop right off if she suddenly sucked in her breath. But I doubt that she can see a future like that. She doesn't look like she's much into seeing tall red-headed women. As for me I can't tell the future any better than I can tell the past. I'm sure as hell not trying to be

18 / Talking Point

some sort of all-wise historian. About all I could say if I studied the inside of Barney's fist would be some simple advice: The next time you ride your rope down to that calf, wear your goddamn gloves. Or one of these days you're going to end up scratching yourself with a thumb nail.

A CONVERSATION WITH THE AUTHOR

Some time after the publication and critical success of *The Rise and Fall of Barney Tullus,* I sought a quiet occasion when I could question the author about his literary philosophy and creative methods. I was particularly curious to learn what other writers had influenced him, what works had perhaps been his models, and what his readers could soon expect from his pen. I knew little about the author, but I supposed that since he wrote westerns his tastes would likely be western. I could not imagine him sipping tea, but I could see him chewing on sourdough pretzels shaped like little brown horseshoes. With my notebook in one hand and a fifth of eight-year-old Black Bull in the other, I knocked at the door of his log-covered study. I felt a high sense of mission. I hoped to illuminate the present and future hopes of Western American letters.

I'll not attempt to describe him, nor will I detail the furnishings of his place of work and inspiration. I do recall a general dustiness, a certain tang of juniper chips, mouse dung, and shut-in air. He moved a couple of well-used glasses into position, and I poured a pair of shots from the bottle of Old Black Bull. "You need a little ditch," he said, "there's a cow trough just over to the right of the outhouse. The wasps don't seem to mind when you move them." I said straight would be just fine.

I opened with some of my questions, and he seemed glad to talk around some answers. However popular *The Rise and Fall* had become, I could guess that the literary columnists for *Time, Newsweek,* and *The New Yorker* were not calling in great numbers. I ventured an observation, "I would guess that being a western writer is sometimes a pretty lonely business."

"You're damn right," he answered.

"It's sort of like riding point, isn't it?" I said. I wanted him to know that I was up on matters western.

"A writer's got to find new ground," he answered. "I could say, fresh literary pasture, but I'm not going to say that."

"You've got to explore new frontiers," I said, feeling he shared my sense of mission.

"I'm not going to say that either," he answered. "We talk too damn much about frontiers. We talk too much about places where the Indians begin. We talk too much about places where the buffalo roam."

"You mean there really aren't any frontiers left?" I said.

"I didn't say that," he answered. "I just mean someday we've got to stop writing about those goddamn buffalo."

I decided to change our ground a bit. I poured another round of Old Black Bull. Without the ditch it was pretty fiery stuff.

"What about the critics?" I said. "I assume you read the critics."

"Some of them," he answered. "Some of them just talk to themselves. I knew an old miner once who did that. Sometimes when he was down in his hole, his answers would bounce around from wall to wall. Sounded like a whole goddamn committee."

"Do the critics ever help you find the new ground you are looking for?"

"I don't know how often is ever," he answered. "Most of the time they just stir me up. Most of them are so puffed up with rules and ideas and theories they can't see a story when they're staring straight at it. You can't make a novel out of that kind of stuff. You can't tell a writer what's right and what's wrong. He's got to find that out when he gets deep down into the thick of things."

"I'll bet you sometimes get hold of a good antithesis," I said.

"I wouldn't know how to get hold of one of those critters," he answered. "I wouldn't know whether to grab it by the horns or by the balls."

"But you do make counterstatements?" I said.

"I don't make statements," he answered. Then he grinned for the first time. "I guess I just made one. You fellows are good at making us writers make statements. I guess that's your line of work, just as writing novels is supposed to be mine."

"Then you do sometimes try to do in your writing what the critics say you shouldn't do?" I said. "You do deal with that which is not important according to their rules?"

A Conversation with the Author / 21

"Hell, yes," he answered. "As I said, they stir me up. I work up a real creative sweat trying to get around their rules. Let me show you what I mean." He put down his glass of Black Bull and pulled a book from his bookshelf. He opened it at a place marked by what seemed to be an old boot lace. "Let me read you something," he said. "'The significant relationship is not between men and cows, but between men and men and men and women.' That was written by some professor, who probably can't tell a cow's tit from a turnip, but I don't have any big objection to what he is saying. But where does it leave me? I can't get into men and men. The Australians have already proved up on that ground. And I can't get into men and women because most of the time there aren't any women to get into, unless you count the garden club and maybe that set of ladies who keep the night air of Pinville smelling like whiskey and roses. That leaves me with men and cows."

"And you've got to have a significant relationship," I said, wanting to show I understood his literary problem.

"Yes, it won't be enough just to put a brand on a hip or open a new bale of hay in the feeder."

"But I can see that you're working on it," I said.

"Oh, I'm working on it," he answered, "I sure as hell am working on it."

THE MILK OF HUMAN KINDNESS

We had tamped the dusty dirt around about a thousand posts that summer day, and all that hot dirty endless work on foot made a man mean as well as hungry. Sill, the cook, had just dumped the first cup of beans on Barney's plate when Barney spoke up, "How come you put all those grass seeds in the pot?"

"They aren't grass seeds," Sill said. "All them specks and sprinkles and bits of different color are herbs and seasoning."

"How come you don't just leave the beans all by themselves?" Barney added. "A bean ain't got nothing to be ashamed of."

"Adds flavor," Sills answered. Then he reflected a moment. "Besides, it quiets 'em down."

With all that late afternoon heat on the outside and all those beans on the inside, even if Sill had quieted them down some, we were working up a sweat just trying to find a place to cool off in. We had looked as far as the shed where Burt was supposed to keep the tractor when Barney blew a sigh like a winded range cow and said, "I'm going to drop my butt right down beside this bale of hay." The iron on the roof was still hot enough, as Mont said, to warm a cold whore's heart, but there were only two sides to the shed and the breeze came through. The air had a lot of hay dust and gnats and itchiness in it, but it was moving, and you could drop down against the hay, put your hands together behind your head, and feel the coolness come into your arm pits. Barney cocked his boots up on a nearby bale. "Don't bother to wake me," he said. "I'm going to settle down here a long long time. And maybe I'll have myself a nice wet dream."

It was about then that we first heard her, a quarter of a mile or so away, just a sad bawling every part of a minute or two. We waited, all our ears turned now in her direction.

"She don't even take time to listen," Mont said. "If her calf was bawling back right smack in front of her, she wouldn't hear him." Then the bawling got louder, and we knew she was moving our way. We stopped talking and gave our whole time to listening. We could almost see her, with each step or so along the south field road giving a breathy bawl, barely slowing to suck in air. By the time she nosed up to the pole fence just beyond the open side of the shed, we were all watching, and when she turned in the evening light you could easily guess why she kept on bawling.

"She couldn't hear that calf," I said, "because there likely isn't any calf. He probably went and got himself hung in that old field fence."

"That's that old cross cow Wilt used to have milked," Mont said. "Said she had a bigger bag than some. Said we needed the milk. Said it would keep our teeth from falling out."

"Why'd he quit?" I said.

"He didn't quit," Mont answered. "The milkman did. Said he didn't come out west to milk no cow. Chopped up his milking stool one morning and walked off up the road."

The cow continued to bawl.

"Barney," I said, "how would you feel if your bag was full up tight with milk?"

Barney grunted, and that's the first we knew for sure that he wasn't still into that old-time dream.

"Somebody's got to go over there and milk her," Mont said. "I can't because I never learned how to milk a cow. My old man said if we didn't have enough milk in us when we were weaned it was just too bad because he wasn't going to keep no goddamn milk cows around to draw the flies."

"This time," I said, "it isn't a matter of needing the milk. It's what you might call a hurry-up humanitarian cause."

By then I could tell that Barney was fully awake. So I said to him, "Barney, that cow is trying to appeal to your humanity."

He answered, "My humanity ain't appealed to by no goddamn milk cow."

"Come on," I said. "Just listen to her. Just look at her. Let your heart be moved. I'll go find a bucket. All she needs is a few good pulls."

---

24 / *The Milk of Human Kindness*

"I don't even want to touch her," he said. "I ain't milked a cow in twenty years, and that's twenty years too soon."

"It'll be nice and soft and warm and wet," Mont said.

Barney grunted like a cornered badger.

"Besides," Mont added, "you can wear your gloves. That old cow is so full and ready she won't even know the difference."

We had Barney, and he knew it. All he could do was go ahead and save that cow from further bawling. And we were all willing to help, providing help didn't mean doing the milking. Mont got his rope. However much that cow had been milked before the day that fellow ran up the road, she was still a range cow, and range cows don't usually know the milking side from a shut barn door, and when it comes to which foot is up and which is back you usually take your chances. Turned out we really didn't need the ropes. This old cow was a true blue lady. Either that or she was so puffed out she didn't care. She was so sweet we could have rolled her on her back and let the milk squirt up instead of down.

Barney wouldn't use a stool. Said he wasn't going to be there long enough to really sit down. So he hunkered on his heels and went to work, and I guess he would have got off to a good clean start if he hadn't taken Mont's advice and pulled on those stiff old gauntlets he had used for stringing wire. However ready the old cow was, she wasn't going to put up with anything like that. Barney didn't even have a chance to get the leather wet before she lifted one hind leg, right or left doesn't matter, and tapped Barney sharp against his knee cap. It wasn't much—maybe she was tickled instead of angry—but it tipped Barney off his heels and sent him back flat into the dust.

"Goddamn," he said. Then he added that he was through. Said if he had a milk stool he would chop it up right then and there and beat the hell up the road, any road would do.

We let him snort and blow a bit. Said he couldn't run off like that, especially since he didn't even have a milk stool to chop up first.

"It's those gloves," Mont said. "That was my mistake."

"Take 'em off while you milk her," I said. "Then you can put 'em on when you're through. That way you can get the milk out, and you won't have to smell it on your hands afterwards."

The Milk of Human Kindness / 25

Barney grunted a sound that didn't quite become a word, but he squatted down again, this time without the gloves, and when he had finished, or when the cow had taken all she could, he had about two quarts. I peeked over and looked in the bucket. It might have looked good to that hung-up calf or maybe a starved cat, but I began thinking about then that my teeth were as tight and solid as they'd ever been.

The old cow sort of backed out of position, turned to look at Barney, and then walked away. He was still squatted on his heels, holding the bucket between his legs, staring at that mess of faintly foamy milk.

"You want to save that milk in a pan," Mont said. "Then you can skim the cream, and when you get enough, you can put it in a churn and we can have fresh butter."

Barney looked up with what you could call an unhappy grin. "First I get worked into milking a cow," he said, "and now I'm getting worked into turning out a goddamn square of butter."

"He didn't say square," I said. "A round piece would be just as good. The main thing's it's fresh."

The whole affair could have ended right there. For Barney's sake, maybe it should have. But next morning it started up again. Sill stacked a pile of sourdough pancakes on Barney's plate and said, "Now you've gone full swing into the milk cow business, I can use about four quarts of milk, a pint of cream, and a couple of pounds of butter. That's tomorrow's order. After that, I'll let you know from day to day. And eggs. You going to carry some eggs too?"

"Sill," Barney answered, "the only eggs I'm going to carry is up your big smart ass."

Even Sill would have dropped it in a day or two. He would have got tired of ordering whipped cream and cottage cheese and egg nog and gone back to pouring strong coffee and shoveling pancakes. But the old cow wouldn't let go of it. She was back next day about the same time, still bawling every other step of the way to that same pole fence.

Barney said, "We got to find something or somebody that sucks."

But that was just a wasted wish on his part, because we didn't have anything extra that sucked. Every calf had his cow, and there wasn't any point in switching around, playing a game of musical tits because there would always be four left over, and if they didn't hang down from that old cross cow they would hang down from some other cow. We would be right back where we started. So Barney kept on milking.

"Besides," Mont said, "that old cow has taken a special liking to you. I'll bet if I was to go out there carrying a bucket, she would look at me in a lonesome way, leave off bawling, and head back down the road again."

"I'll bet a small goldplated cow turd," Barney answered, "you ain't willing to try it."

"Like I said," Mont easily went on, "I never learned how to do any of that dairy work. They say you got to build up your wrist muscles while you're still quite young."

The milk piled up in every old coffee can, honey bucket, lard can until there wasn't a thing left that was hard and empty except Burt's old piss pot he kept under his bunk for cold winter nights.

"Somebody's going to have to start drinking milk," Mont said, "or we're in real trouble."

Sill said, "Maybe we ought to lay in a set of pigs. That'd take care of the milk and one of you fellows could carry out the potato peelings when you took out the milk. Save me some time and work."

"I'm not about to save you work, Sill," Mont answered. "What work you do in this kitchen wouldn't put sweat on a bedbug."

"It's not beating the batter that wears him out," I said. "It's having to throw those peelings far enough out so the wind won't blow 'em back in before he gets the screen door shut."

"Especially," Mont went on, "I'm not about to carry a potful of peelings out to any damn pigs. Even if we do have a dairy, we don't have to start up a stinking pigpen."

So I guess Barney was beginning to get us. He wouldn't stop milking. He wouldn't give that old cow a chance to dry up. Sill said if he didn't soon stop, we'd all drown in the milk of human kindness. For saying that, for putting our misery in such a poetic way, Mont wanted to sneak up and cut the ropes on Sill's hammock where he usually dozed between dinner and supper.

As long as that old cow showed up, Barney kept right on milking.

"By god," Mont said, "now he's got his wrists built up again, he don't seem to want 'em ever to go back to being weak again."

"Either that," I said, "or he's come to love the feel of all those milk-warm tits."

"Either that," Sill added, "or he's grown so stubborn he don't know when to quit. He's like a goddamn parsnip that don't know when to let itself be pulled up out of the ground."

So the milk piled up. And the smell of sour and souring milk seemed to hang like a cloud over the whole damn ranch. Then one night we sat down to supper and Sill fed us nothing but thick chunks of cold canned beef and some of that tough old bread he had stored away for emergencies. He said you never could tell what might happen. The dough might die in the crock, or it might decide to move into what Sill called fission.

"Where're the beans?" Mont said.

"Can't have beans without a pot," Sill answered.

"Then where's the pot?" I said.

"Full of milk," Sill answered.

Mont exploded. "By God, that's the end. That the absolute end. If I have to try to please my tired old gut with cold boiled-up bull, then I'm through. I'm heading up the road."

But if we thought we had a crisis now, we soon had a worse one. Somehow Mr. Pulley got the word in town—maybe he could smell that cloud of sour milk. He jumped in his pickup and came roaring down the road. Sounded like he didn't even bother to shift out of second gear.

"By God, Tullus," he yelled, "you've got to break it off. You've got to stop pulling that old cow's tits. I can't have my good men heading up the road. In the meantime I can't afford to take any chances. One of you men get out there and chop up his goddamn milk stool. And the rest of you help me find that cow and get her loaded in this truck. After giving all that milk, she may not be worth a damn as beef meat, but I can't take any chances. I got to get her away from here."

That pretty much brought an end to the whole affair. Next day we had beans for supper, hot as it still was, but when we went outside to hunt for a cool place we knew that shed was safe. We knew there wouldn't be any bawling cows—at least we hoped there wouldn't be any. We knew we could smell that good old dust again instead of all that stinking milk. Things looked good again. Barney stretched out against a bale of hay and let his sweat-stained hat slide slowly down his nose.

"Barney," I said, "what the hell you going to do these nice evenings without that old cross cow to milk?"

Barney grinned a wide old inside grin. "I'm just going to slip down here and rest a long, long time. Give these wrists a chance to get as soft and bendy as an old felt shoe. And maybe, if the ghost of that old cow don't come bawling back, I'll have me a chance to finish up that old wet dream."

LA BELLE SAUVAGE

"Women! they're made of whimsies and
 caprice,
So variant and so wild, that, ty'd to a God,
They'd dally with the devil for a change.—
Rather than wed a European dame,
I'd take a squaw of the woods, and get
 papooses."
—Lieutenant Rolfe, in
The Indian Princess, 1808

About the only thing we had left around the ranch to remind a fellow of Indians was Burt's fancy saddle blanket. That was made in Mexico out of cotton and the hairs of cattle, horses, and donkeys, but Burt said it had a Navajo design. Burt didn't know a damn thing about Navajo designs, and we knew just about as much, so we went along with thinking it was some kind of Indian blanket. He could have said it was a bedspread from a Dodge City whorehouse, and we would have gone along with that too.

Burt had the blanket hanging on a stretch of baling wire high up in the bunkhouse. He said, "Any mouse that wants to piss on that blanket has got to walk a tight wire at least two feet. If he slips he's going to wish he had some wings like one of those unnatural squirrels." Hanging up there high kept it safe from horses too. Kept it from getting sweat-stained and dirty. "Someday," Burt kept saying, "somebody important is going to ask me to lead a parade, and by god I and that blanket are going to be ready."

Looking up at that blanket, Barney said, "Whatever happened to all them cowboys and Indians?"

Sill said, "Some of them Indians bit the dust, some of them

struck oil and made it rich, and some of them took up choice lots out on the reservation."

"The cowboys, that's us," Mont said. "We're the last living remnants."

"Especially you, Barney," I said. "Anybody can tell in a minute that you're a remnant. Even that old sorrel horse can tell you're a remnant."

"I ain't no living remnant," Barney answered. "And even that old sorrel horse can tell it."

"I read this book once," Sill said.

"One thing we already know for sure," Mont said, "that sure as hell wasn't one of them cookbooks."

Barney said, "That where you learned all about them seeds?"

"About Indians," Sill finished.

"Sure," I said. "The Indian women go around in the bushes and gather up the seeds."

"Tastes like ground-up cockle burrs to me," Mont said.

"Goddamn," Sill said. "It wasn't a cookbook."

Mont said, "Sill, we already knew that."

Sill lifted and spread his hands in an empty sort of way. Then he groaned like an iron pot sliding on a hollow rock. "Getting anything straight around here is like trying to shove a cow turd down a bent gun barrel."

"What do you want to do that for?" Barney said.

"Only they weren't called Indians," Sill went on.

"Probably seed gatherers," I added.

"Children of nature," Sill said. "That's what they were called."

"Who's he?" Barney said.

"Who's who?" Sill answered.

"Nature," Barney said. "Who's nature?"

"He their ma or pa?" I said.

Sill groaned again. "It's what they call a figure of speech."

"We know that, Sill," Mont said. "Now tell us who he is."

"Who who is?" Sill answered.

"That figure, goddamnit."

This was enough for Sill. He was already showing signs that it was time to get back to the kitchen and set some beans to soak. "Just like poking a cow turd down a bent gun barrel."

Barney said, "I still don't see what you want to do that for."

La Belle Sauvage / 31

When Sill left, that was the end of talk about Indians for that night. And that might have been the end of talk about Indians for a whole year if something hadn't suddenly come up. How suddenly we knew the next morning when, even before we had finished the third round of Sill's sourdough pancakes, we heard the roar of Mr. Pulley's pickup.

"You ain't milking another cow, are you, Barney?" Sill said. "Even with the dutch oven empty now, I still got enough milk to last me eight or nine months."

We didn't bother to listen to what Barney had to say, because by then we could see the pickup making the last turn down the ranch road. Even the big plume of dust was having a hard time trying to keep up. The truck swung around and nosed up to the door, which by then Sill had already opened, and we could easily see that Mr. Pulley's jaw was set as hard as it would be if he was trying to bite a half-inch oak root into two short pieces.

We didn't even have time to say there wasn't a milk stool in the whole damn section when Mr. Pulley yelled, "Where were all you hardworking cowboys when that tribe moved in?"

We just stopped waiting for a chance to make answers and listened for the next words. We didn't have a glimmer in hell about what tribe had moved in, but we knew he'd tell us faster if we waited.

"A couple of you cowboys get up off your breakfast butts and get out there and tell them they've got to go. Tullus, by god that's a good job for you. There may not be any milk in it, but the ride will sure as hell tighten you up some."

"Ride?" Barney said while Mr. Pulley paused to suck in steam.

"Ride," Mr. Pulley said. "Ain't that what cowboys are supposed to do? If they don't stop spooking the cows away from Seepyhill Spring, we won't bring in enough beef to make a starving man's stew. Takes grass *and* water to make beef. Got that, Tullus?"

Barney had it all right. He still didn't know what the hell had moved in, but he had it all right.

It turned out that the other half of Mr. Pulley's couple of cowboys was me. He didn't say I needed tightening up some, so I suppose any other cowboy would have done as well. I just happened to be there in the line of sight when his finger stopped. "See that Tullus holds his ground" was all he said to me. Then just before he banged the pickup door, he added, "And by god don't let him stop to milk any cows. It's beef we want, not butter. Got that, Tullus?"

Barney had it again.

We saddled up early that same day and headed out to Seepyhill Spring. We knew where the spring was, even though we didn't know what the hell had moved in. Once we got there, I reckoned we would find out soon enough.

All Barney said was, "They must be a dumb son of a bitch to move in there."

I had to agree. I knew the spot because I had pulled up there many times to let my horse drink from the long iron trough Burt had put in on Mr. Pulley's orders. The spring pushed out in the grassy mud back on the hillside and then trickled down through a bunch of willows. There wasn't a hell of a lot of water in the first place, and if you let just any dumb cow critter come right up there and put her hooves down where the water was supposed to come out, you wouldn't have enough clear water to wash a small and dirty dabber wasp. As Burt said, "A spring that ain't nothing but a thousand wet cow tracks ain't no spring at all." First he put a little fence around the spring itself, sort of corraled the place where the water bubbled out, but that just moved the tracks on down the hill. Any water that finally got past that string of thirsty willows had been stepped on so damn much, it must have been the flattest-tasting water ever to run downhill. So Burt got Mr. Pulley to haul a load of pipe out there in the pickup, shovels too. The fellows sat in their saddles until Burt had unloaded the pipe. Then Burt said, "All by theirselves these shovels ain't going to dig that pipe a hole." Barney said he wasn't any goddamned plumber. But they laid the pipe anyway, though a low-backed snake could have crawled along that trench with some of his belly showing. Now the water could run the whole way without getting stepped on. If some cow wanted to mix her feet in it, she had to crawl between a set of poles that stood like a long frame around a trough that looked for all the world like a twenty-foot bathtub. But you could drink that water where it first poured out, cold and good and a whole lot wetter than a pool-hall beer.

We pulled up just where the trail crossed a low ridge, and we could look down a stretch of maybe thirty rods and see that skinny row of willows and the bleaching whiteness of the aspen poles.

"Whatever moved in," I said hopefully, "has gone, or else they don't show big enough to see from here."

"I can't see a goddamned thing," Barney said.

"Maybe it was just a swarm of bees," I said.

"Or just a tribe of piss ants," Barney added.

There wasn't a cow in sight. And there wasn't a thing we could see moved in to spook a cow away.

"Wait," I said. My eyes were getting back their focus after all that ride and all that staring at the rump of Barney's sorrel. "Wait," I said again. "There is something. It's hanging on the upper pole."

Barney squinted now. "It's just a rag or maybe somebody's old white sock."

We spurred into a hard trot, and when we got closer we could see a bunch of other rags, three or four pieces anyway, colored enough to sort of hide against that watering trough. I centered in on the brightest piece, the one we had seen from the top of the ridge, but when I got up close enough to reach out and touch it with my boot, I suddenly knew what it was, even though I couldn't believe it was that anymore than I could believe it was the national flag of China.

Barney said, "That sure as hell ain't no rag."

It was a pair of ladies panties calmly drying in the sun.

"No wonder those cows are forgetting to get thirsty," Barney added.

I said, "A sight like that could make an old bull blush."

We studied the sight a while.

"There's something missing," I said.

"You mean," Barney said, "that old black cow that always hung around here?"

"No," I said. "I mean one of those other contraptions. One that looks like a couple of mush bowls tied together with strings on each end."

"Goddamn," Barney said. "You're right. There sure as hell ought to be one of those things here too."

We paused in deep thought. But we didn't even have time to wonder how a pair of pinkish panties could have walked out there all by itself and snuggled up around that pole. We didn't even have time to check out all those other rags when right behind us this nice voice said, "Hey, you guys, those things belong to me. I'm using your old pole fence for a clothes line."

We both turned then, not waiting to swing our horses around, just wrenching our heads, necks, and shoulders so we could see. She stood back up the slope about thirty feet, a plumpish girl in a dress as plain as a sack. But even maybe before you saw the sack, you saw the top and bottom of her, the long dark hair pulled and tied on each side of her head and above her forehead a band with a feather in it, her bare legs and feet, the toes half hidden in the deep brown dust.

She had us. The truth was we didn't know what the hell to say. We were surrounded, on one side the panties quivering in the sun, on the other side the Indian maiden who would have been wearing them if they hadn't been back there behind us clinging to that pole. When we got back to the bunkhouse that night, I filled the whole thing out a bit. "We heard this war whoop," I said, "and when we turned around there was this savage with an eagle feather as tall as a mean mule's ear. Old Barney he pulled his hat down until his eyes were barely showing. He didn't want that Indian to see his hair."

Burt said, "Damn poor scalp that hair would make."

"Besides," Sill added, "I hear it's not just the hair they like to cut off anyway."

So she had us. Finally she must have noticed Barney's mouth still open in surprise. "Haven't you guys ever seen a girl before?"

"Yes, mam," Barney answered.

We'd seen a girl before all right, but I guess we'd never been surrounded in quite this way.

"You live around here, miss?" I said. That was a silly question, but it was all I could come up with. Of course she didn't live around there. There wasn't a house within fifteen miles, let alone a town with women in it.

"Of course I do," she answered. "You go on past those willows and around that little hump of a hill and you'll see our tents."

"Our tents?" I said.

"Of course our tents," she answered. "You didn't think I'd be out here all by myself, did you?"

I said, "You mean a bunch of you were passing through and decided to camp over there for a day or two?"

"Oh, no," she said. "We may decide to stay here a long time."

I heard Barney say a soft "goddamn," not to her, just to himself. "You mean live here, mam?" he added.

"Of course I do, silly. What else would we do?"

"He means settle down," I said. "He means start farming or chasing cows or digging gold or working in some way." I was about to add "or making rugs," but I cancelled that before it got out.

"Oh, we wouldn't do any of those things. We wouldn't do anything to make money. We don't believe in money."

She had us again.

"Miss," I said, "I'd sure like to be able to get along without the stuff too. The trouble is I like to eat, and if I don't buy a new pair of pants once in a while this saddle gets mighty close." I should have made my point without those pants, but we were too surrounded to clearly think things out.

"Oh, I wouldn't need to wear any pants at all. Not really," she said. She came down and stood alongside the poles. When she leaned back and locked her arms like wings across the top line of aspen, her breasts lifted up and out against her sack-like dress. "I don't wear a bra at all. I think it's more natural that way, don't you?" She said this last straight at Barney.

"Yes, mam," he answered.

About then I knew damn well we'd about earned our pay for that day. "Barney," I said, "tell her what we came for."

"I thought you came to see me," she said. "I thought *he* did anyway."

"In a way I guess we did," I said. "I guess *you* can take the message."

Right then Barney would have preferred giving a message to a gelded bobcat. But he pulled the cinch tight around his reluctant duty and spoke up.

"Mam," he said, "we've got to ask you to leave this place. You're scaring the cows away from this here water."

"We need the water just as much as they do," she said.

"But the cows were here first," I said.

"You own this place?" she said. "You didn't put a fence around this land."

"No, mam," Barney said. "We just got a right to use it. The cows got a right to come here."

"Oh, they can still come," she said. "I wouldn't want them to stay away. I like cows. They are so soft and peaceful when they chew their cuds. Besides they have such soft and pretty eyes."

"Yes, mam," Barney said. "But they ain't used to coming when there's people here. They ain't used to seeing things up on the poles."

"Oh, you mean my panties," she said. "Silly, did you think I was going to leave them here for good?"

"No, mam, I guess I didn't," Barney said.

"Well, you tell the others they've got to go," I said. "You tell them this is rangeland. You tell them to find another camping place."

"That's mean. That's real mean," she answered.

"Maybe it is, miss," I said, "but you tell them anyway."

She had us out on pretty shaky ground. Mr. Pulley didn't own this land any more than he owned the moon. He had something called the range rights, but that didn't exactly say that a bunch of people couldn't range there too. I could see him driving his pickup up to the BLM office the same way he drove up to Sill's kitchen. "By god," he would say, "what the hell's happening to this country anyway? Used to be the government protected the stockmen. Now they let a bunch of goddamned Indians take over and make a man's cows go thirsty. And they ain't even Indian Indians, just a bunch of trashy whites who couldn't work their way out of a greased pipe, even if that pipe was sloping down a steep hill."

"Miss, you tell them anyway," I said again.

Some of the sassiness seemed to go out of her. For a minute I was beginning to think she was kind of pretty after all, even in that sack. And about then I decided it was time to yank my horse around and get the hell on back toward home. So I couldn't see what Barney did. When I had a chance to look back, he was loping along in the wake of my dust. I reined up at the top of the slope to let him catch up, and when I looked back past him to the trough, I could still see her. Barney pulled up and stopped too. We were both watching when she lifted something from the top pole and waved it like a flag or maybe a tiny scarf. I guess she meant it for the both of us.

La Belle Sauvage / 37

When we rode in, the fellows were waiting. You couldn't have hung a saddle on the back side of an outhouse door without seeing their faces looking for an answer.

We played it slow to stir them up a bit. I even got an old sock and started to dust my saddle. But Burt wasn't about to stand there and let me go through that game.

"All right," he said, "what was it?"

"What was what?" I answered. My face was as sober as an empty passing plate.

"What moved in!" he exploded. "Holy hell, what moved in!"

"Indians," Barney answered. He said it quietly, like he was announcing the birth of a new skunk in his old dresser drawer.

They all kind of blinked. Then Sill said, "Well, I'll be goddamned."

"The real thing," I added. "War paint, tomahawks, bows and arrows, the scalp of the governor's wife."

I was all right until I got to that last. That was too much. "Bullshit," Sill said. And that wiped out the whole thing. We stuck to our story, but they wouldn't take a word of it. As far as they were concerned, whatever was out there by that spring wasn't a bunch of Indians. A wagon load of picnicking Republican ladies maybe, but not a bunch of goddamn Indians.

That could have been the end of it. But two days later, we didn't even get into the third round of Sill's pancakes when the pickup came tearing down the road. And the dust wasn't even keeping close this time. "The old boy's got a cockle burr under his tail this time for sure," Sill said. We could hear him rumbling even before the motor slowed down and started panting, and when he kicked the door open, he was halfway through his opening speech. "And by god they're still there. Tullus, I told you to get out there and move 'em off. I didn't ask you to go all of the way out there and lick their butts. I didn't ask you to smile once, not once, Tullus. By god I should of sent my wife."

"We told 'em," I said.

"Told 'em what?" he roared. "Told 'em to plant their butts in that ground and grow like a bunch of goddamn trees?"

"We asked 'em to leave," I said.

"Then by god, Tullus, you get out there and ask 'em to leave again. Because they're still there. You hear that, Tullus? They're still there."

"Yes, sir," Barney answered.

"Just you, Tullus," Mr. Pulley added. "It don't take more than one good man to take a message. But by god he ain't worth a soft cow turd in a big rainstorm if they don't know he means it when he says it."

I was beginning to feel the cyclone had passed me by.

"You two hard-working cowboys probably got out there and told each other to leave," he threw in as a final word. Then he kicked the starter, stomped the accelerator, and backed into an angry turn.

Beneath the noise of the pickup, I heard Barney say, "The bossy old bastard."

Barney was gone the biggest part of the next day. Long before his dust rose into sight we were getting restless. Burt allowed that Barney had decided to hell with Pulley and his goddamn cows. Burt allowed he had already joined up, picked up a crow's feather somewhere, and was right now laying in a tent watching the camp smoke climb the sky. Sill wasn't so sure. But he figured it would all work out right anyway. He figured they had already scalped Barney and would have to get out of the country, because now we would come hell bent for revenge and maybe a few scalps of our own. But before we could get any closer to the facts of the case, here comes Barney's dust down the trail.

But he might just as well have been scalped, butchered, and dropped in a hole for all we could get out of him.

"See any Indians this time?" Burt said.

"Run right into a whole goddamn tribe of them," Barney answered. "Chased me over every goddamn hill between here and Texas. Why I been gone so long."

"How come there ain't much sweat on that sorrel? He don't look like he's moved past a jog the whole damn day."

"He don't sweat much," Barney answered. "Gets that from his mother. She was a big mare used to belong to old Moss Peters. Moss had a small place about twenty or so miles from here. Kept a jenny with one short ear along with several mares."

"We don't give a goddamn about Moss Peters," Burt said. "What about those Indians?"

"Moss said it was because she didn't drink much," Barney added. "Said she was just like a goddamn camel."

La Belle Sauvage / 39

We couldn't turn him around. We tried but we couldn't. We couldn't find out a thing.

But I guess I should add that I found one thing, even if I didn't find it out.

I was passing Barney's chaps where they sometimes hang on a big nail in the bunkhouse. Peeping out of the top of the pocket on the right leg was a touch of white or maybe pale pink, just a spot of cloth no bigger than a mouse's ear. Against the greasy grey it stuck out, almost shining in the dust-speckled light. I stopped long enough to have a look. But I didn't even need to lift the flap the whole way and pull it out to know what it was. The feel of it got me at once. If you're used to nothing but denim and leather, the grab of that soft stuff was like the tickle of sparks on a dry cat's back.

Now I needed to know how it got in that pocket. Maybe he picked it like a ripe peach right off that pole, just reached out and took it. Or maybe he got it some other way. But I guessed I would never find out for sure. I wasn't about to ask. I wasn't about to get mixed up with that damn mare that didn't sweat. I'd had enough of that.

Two days later we got the news that the camp was gone, just disappeared one day, leaving a few holes where the fires had burned, a leather sandal with a broken strap, and a page from a paper called *Good News from Mother Earth*. We don't know why they left. It doesn't figure that Barney drove them off, but we couldn't ask him that either, not unless we could somehow get around that sweatless mare. Maybe they got tired of talking to cowboys. Maybe they decided to let those cows fill up. Maybe the chief decided if they didn't get the hell out, he'd have Barney for a son-in-law or whatever you get to be in an outfit like that. Anyway it's over. Barney's got a chunk of soft cloth sewed together in a pretty way, and we've got an undying itch to find out how he got it.

We're working on it all the time. Keeps us from worrying about the spiders that swing from the bunkhouse ceiling. Some day we'll get around that goddamn mare and come up on Barney before he can think of another way out. It may take some doing, but we'll do it.

THE WESTERN VERITÉ

"A pot is a pot is a pot."
—Grenadine Stone,
  Thoughts and Other Sweet Reflections

"The trouble with you fellows," Sill announced, "is that you just put down your heads and eat. You don't pay any attention to the pot the beans come out of."

We all stopped shoveling beans at the same time. Our heads all came up in one big look of wonder.

"Barney," Sill went on, "I'll bet you don't even know how many legs there are on a dutch oven."

"Sill," Mont said, "who the hell cares?"

"Do you, Barney?" Sill persisted.

Barney answered, "I don't even know many hairs on a bedbug's ass."

"And you other smart cowboys don't know either," Sill went on. "You're not even sure the pot's black and not some other fancy color, like some of those French cook pans."

"Goddamn," Mont said. "Sill, will you back up. Will you tell us what the hell difference it makes."

"I saw this movie the other night," he answered. We knew he had gone into town on a Saturday night, but up to now he hadn't said a damn thing about a movie. "There was this one bit when the camera moved up real close to the cook's fire. For about five minutes all you could see was his dutch oven. It filled the whole damn screen. Must have been about twenty feet across. Biggest goddamn pot I ever hope to see. I almost felt like crying."

I said, "What kind of movie was it? I thought they just showed cooking movies to girls in high school."

"It was a western," Sill answered. "Can't you tell that?"

A week or so later we had forgotten about this bit of crazy talk, when along about sundown this car about as long as a hayrack comes sneaking down the road. It was a convertible with the top down. Twenty rods or so before it pulled up alongside the porch, where we were still sitting in the shade, we could see the dude at the wheel was wearing some kind of big dark glasses.

"Sure hope he can still make out this house and this bunch of real active cowboys," Mont said. "I'd sure as hell hate to be run over by a steamboat with the top down."

He must have seen us all right because he stopped, let the engine ease down, and then turned the ignition key with a fancy throw of his best right hand. Even through all the dust that crowded up around him, we could tell he was somebody who thought he was pretty important. At least we could tell the car was.

"Howdy," he said.

We nodded some of the same.

He opened the door then and stepped out, pulling off the glasses and poking them quickly and neatly into the breast pocket of his blue sport coat.

"I assume," he said, "that you men are cowboys."

"Either that," Mont answered, "or this is the Sunday meeting of the Skunk Creek Bible Society."

The guy laughed easily, ending up with a sort of fixed grin, what we usually called a shit grin. "That proves it," he said.

"Proves what?" I said.

"Proves that you men are cowboys," he answered.

He had us. Our looks must have showed it.

"I mean you have a keen sense of humor. And everybody knows that the real cowboy has that. I mean the keen sense of humor."

At that point we gave him what you might call a group scowl.

"No, really," he went on.

"You come all the way out here to tell us we got a sense of humor?" Mont said. "What you call a keen sense of humor?"

"No," he answered. "I'll come right to the point."

"That sure as hell would be fine," Mont said.

"We can always use a little point," I said.

"There ain't nothing better than a point," Sill added. "It don't even have to be a big one. It can even be a little one, about the size of a piss ant's pizzle."

Barney said, "I'll agree to that. And I'll raise you five."

We had him, but he was such a slick dude that he was trying not to show it.

"The point is I'm a film maker. I want to make a new film about the West."

"A what?" Mont said. Mont knew as well as anybody what the dude was talking about, but we sure as hell weren't about to let him off that easy.

"What you probably call a movie," he said.

"Then why the hell didn't you call it that?" Barney said. "If I had a cow I was talking about, I wouldn't go around calling her a bovine lactatus."

"A what?" Sill said, his poker face all loosened up in quick surprise. We had all turned from looking at the dude to looking at Barney. I could tell that some of that milk he had been milking had soaked through his skin and gone straight to his brain.

"But you see there *is* a difference," the dude went on.

"You mean between a cow and a movie?" Barney said. "Everybody knows that."

"No, I mean between a film and a movie," he said. "You see, a film is an art form."

"Well, I'll be goddamned," Mont said.

When the dude finally got up off the pot, it turned out he wanted to make a fancy kind of cowboy movie, on location, as he kept saying. He didn't want no dolled-up bunch of Hollywood actors tending the cows. It turned out that Mr. Pulley's place was a location and that we were genuine cowboys, or at least as close as he was about to come short of putting a hell of a bunch of pages back on the calendar. "It's the real thing I want," he kept saying. "The real thing. That's the new western cinematic art." I guess you could say that we didn't give a damn about the new western art until he got around to saying he would pay us. That was the pill that pulled the plug. I knew damn well he could probably get Sill's dutch oven to act for nothing, but if there was money for cowboys in the business, we weren't about to set around while he took pictures of some goddamn bean pot.

It turned out he liked the looks of Barney, said he saw the real thing in Barney's face, said he wanted to give Barney what he called a feature role. Barney said he wasn't about to call himself an actor, but the dude said that didn't matter. He didn't want acting, he wanted reality. We all studied Barney when he said that, trying to see reality, but all we could see was the big ears, the skin as brown as juniper bark, and the stubble his old razor always left showing. Well, I thought, he's paying for it. For what he's going to take out of the bank, his boot, his silk purse or wherever he keeps it, he's welcome to whatever he wants to see. If he'd been looking for halos, we'd have been willing to sell him a stack of them too. Brown ones, green ones, any damn color he wanted.

When he got back in the car and drove off, we watched the dust until he was out of sight. Then Mont said, "Well, I'll be goddamned." If Mont hadn't said it, Sill would have said it, Barney too. It was about all you could say at a time like that.

About a week later a string of trailers as long as a short cow train pulled in, dragging more damn dust than a colony of fresnoes. They circled in around a little grove of cottonwoods, and even before the dust had settled, a bunch of guys had a Delco squatted on the ground and running. That dude who hired us to appear in this movie—film I mean—didn't say anything about pulling ourselves together as a welcoming committee, but we were a friendly set of fellows anyway, so we were close by, smiling our ugly best, when the first trailer door opened and this tall dame with hair the color of a dirty rope stepped down onto the porch of her sleeping car and said, "Gawd."

"Howdy, mam," we said, more or less in unison.

"You, I suppose, are the natives," she said. "Though I should think even the house flies, if they had any sense, would have given up on this god-forsaken place."

"Ain't bad, mam," Mont said. "Once you get used to it."

She looked out across the country, right smack over the top of us. "And how, pray tell, does anyone get used to it?"

"Easiest way," Mont answered, "is to marry one of these romantic cowboys. That way you have love to sort of smooth the way. That way when the bedbugs start to crowd in you don't really mind. Cause all the time you're snuggled up to this real romantic cowboy."

"Gawd," she said again and backed up into her sleeping car. Turned out she was the voice coach. Turned out she had to teach us how to say our lines. Next day when we lined up to go to work, the son of a bitch in the dark glasses was riding point. He said the words we spoke were almost as important as the pictures he took. Said if we all sounded like a bunch of two-bit actors, the whole damn film would be phony. Said, too, we had to say the right words, the real living speech of the range. Said any western film that didn't have a lot of *goddamns* in it wouldn't have a chance with the critics. He said even old ladies didn't want to hear a string of *hecks* and *shucks*.

We listened while he went on like this, the voice coach waiting just back of him, her eyes hooked on us, her head jerking up and down in strong agreement. Finally, when we figured we'd listened about long enough to earn a good day's pay, he shut up and turned the voice coach loose. She sidled up a step or two, pointed her best ear so she could hear real well, and opened up the coaching.

"Mr. Tullus," she began, "say goddamn."

Now anyone who knows Barney knows he doesn't use words like that around the ladies, especially to their faces. A cow is different. But that dude who was paying the cowboys had him by the short hair, so to speak. Besides, you couldn't exactly be sure that this coach was a lady.

"Yes, mam," Barney said.

"Well?" she waited.

"Goddamn, mam," Barney answered.

She seemed to let Barney's word roll around in her head beneath that ropey hair, her eyes shut while she listened to it. Then she sighed as if the wind had gone all at once out of her pillow. "My good man, it won't do. It won't do at all. It's all wrong."

"Yes, mam," Barney said.

"It's the first syllable that matters," she said. "That's a big round vowel in the middle. One of the great vowels of our language. We've got to hear it. That *g*'s not important. An ape could say that. It's the *o*. That's the heart of it. You know, Mr. Tullus, that vowel may possibly be the heart of the most important word in our language."

"Yes, mam," Barney answered.

The Western Verité / 45

"Now try again," she said.

He tried, and it didn't come out much different, not to my ears anyway. But she heard some improvement. Thought she did anyway.

"Round your lips," she said. "Remember that *o* in the middle. Make the *o* with your lips as you say it."

He tried again, his cheeks bunched up, his lips pushed out like the ass-end of a farting yearling.

About then we had to get the hell out of there. Either that or suffer a set of broken ribs from all the held-back push of laughing. One of those trailers was probably a hospital, complete with everything from a bedpan to a dehorning saw, but if the nurses looked anything like that coach, we weren't about to get put in there, even if the pay went on for all that too.

We just sat in the bunkhouse and let the funniness shake out of us. By the time Barney came in, we had begun to sober up some. If any other trail had opened up, he would have likely taken it, even a path to that Indian camp, but he didn't have much choice. He opened the door, and all our stiffened faces turned toward him. But he stomped straight in and dropped down on the side of his bunk, as if he had just ridden thirty miles on a bouncing horse or tamped loose sand around a thousand fence posts.

"Goddamn," he said.

"Round your lips," we said in a chorus. And the laughing started all over again. If something didn't soon happen to give us the feeling of sadness, we were all going to end up in that hospital.

Learning to swear is like learning to throw a calf for branding. If you keep at it long enough, the time will come when some of the feet will stick out in the right direction. Barney finally got the thing mastered. Either that or the voice coach decided to hell with it. Anyway the film-making moved along to the first big scene. Funny thing, this scene didn't have any goddamns in it, just a bunch of giggling and swooshing of water in a big wooden tub.

The dude in the glasses set it up for us. "There's one scene every good Western's got to have. That's a bathing scene. I'll picture it for you."

We figured we could look. We got paid for that too.

"See this huge tub, big enough to water a freight locomotive. There are the whores over on this side, the cowboys fresh from the trail drive on that side. In between this tub. The wet wood shines in the gaslight. Ladies first. Bloomers fly around like sails on a windy day. Then in they go, rumps, tits, waves of water. Happy. Happy! That's the tone of it."

That part looked pretty good to us. What we could see of it, that is, through this dude's waving hands and the dust that kept blowing up around him.

"Now the cowboys," he went on. "Boots sail happily through the air. Long-handled underwear dances like ghosts in the half-light. Sometimes the whores are out. Sometimes they're not. It doesn't matter. Life mixes easily like that."

It was a great scene all right. Trouble was the cowboys didn't exactly want to do it. They didn't mind taking a bath. Cowboys are no different from anyone else. We knew as well as the next fellow that a good bath once every two weeks or so never hurt nobody. Might even stop the itching where the black flies bite. So it wasn't the water that held us back. It was that damn wooden tub. If a fellow lives the whole of his life worrying about getting a little saddle sore on his butt, he's not likely to want to leave a bunch of skin on the horns of some damn pine plank.

We told him so. Said we hated to spoil his great scene. Said, why didn't he use one of Burt's iron watering troughs? He said no. It had to be a wooden tub. Every great Western has a wooden tub. He wasn't about to deviate from proven artistic principles. We sure as hell didn't want him to deviate, but we kept our boots tipped back in the mud. Finally he said he didn't really need us anyway. He could use some stand-ins.

So after his trailer load of carpenters had nailed that damn tub together, he got the show going. Turned out it was the same damn carpenters that took the bath. Seemed since they built it, they didn't have no fear of it. Besides, I guess they hoped they could maybe jump in there before the whores got out. And you sure as hell can't tell a carpenter from a cowboy when he comes running through the dust in his long handles and scrambles ass-up into a goddamn tub of water.

We watched it all from the sidelines. And when it was all over and there was mud and bare foot prints over a whole damn acre, Mont said, "Here I've been wearing these boots my whole damn life, here I've been hugging cows for well on up to twenty years, and now I see I don't know a goddamn thing about being a cowboy."

The Western Verité

Sill said, "By god, we're going to have to get us one of those tubs and somehow learn to use it."

"What about the whores?" I said.

"Pulley's going to have a fit about that tub," Mont answered. "He sure as hell ain't going to want to lay in a set of whores too."

So we let it stop there. We still had couple of dozen of big calves to cut out and run down to the lower pasture. Mr. Pulley had said it loud and clear, "You cowboys can play these acting games on the side. I and these cows don't give a damn. But if you want your pay this Saturday, then by god you get my work done."

When we were saddling, Mont said, "It can't take a hell of a lot of practice to drive a nail straight. And a pile of sawdust sure does smell a lot better than a pile of something else."

"I was coming to the same point," Barney added.

"It won't work, Barney," Mont said. "You couldn't drive a nail up a bull's ass, even if he held still and you used a frying pan for a hammer."

We got the calves cut and onto new grass in time to squat in our old shade before the sun went down. The dry air felt cool on our seats where the sweat had thickened. We could hear the whores laughing in one of the big trailers. The coach came out once, holding a tall glass with some ice in it. She looked over at us and we smiled back. Her mouth said something we couldn't hear, probably goddamn with a rounded *o*. Then she went back in and shut the door.

"If you can't drive nails, Barney," I said, "maybe you can be a coach."

"Goddamn," he said.

"Round it," we all sang out together.

Finally the dude in the dark glasses got around to the main part. We supposed it was going to be a trail drive or something like that. In fact every time we had moved a cow in the last few days, we had kept her steadily moving north as if there wasn't any real stopping this side of Abilene. We learned to sit soft in the saddle for the long day's ride. Sill even began figuring how he could load his gear in the old wagon we hadn't used for a couple of years. "Damn wheels will probably fall apart the first mile," he said. "Spill beans and coffee and bacon around like shit from a loosened cow. One of you fellows better get those wheels soaked." "Maybe you could throw them in that goddamn tub," Mont said. I said, "Better get the whores out first."

But it turned out he didn't have a trail drive in mind at all. "Trail drives are out," he said. "Nobody wants to see a herd of cows walking across the country. There's no art in that. There's too much romance in that." Mont said afterward, "I missed that too. I missed all those whores in the wooden tub, and now by god it turns out I missed the romance too."

"It's the little things that count," the dude went on, "the little things made big. That's the new realism."

He had us with that. But when he began to tell us about this other film he was trying to beat, we began to get the hang of it.

"There was this great scene. This guy comes out into the night wearing a huge fur coat. Then you hear him give a mighty belch, not one of them, not two of them, but three. Three great belches coming into the dark night out of that great skin coat. I tell you it was a great moment for the film." He seemed to stop to think about it, to let those belches sound again somewhere behind those damn dark glasses. "It will be hard to beat," he added.

But we were catching on. We knew how he was going to beat it. We could already see Barney coming out into the night wearing the coat we knew must be hanging somewhere in another of those trailers. Then he would belch not just twice, not even just three times, but four times. It would take a lot of beer, but we knew Barney could hold it if one of those trailers had enough of it stocked away.

Turned out we were wrong again. Turned out that wasn't what he had in mind anymore than he was thinking of a trail drive. "That's been done," he said. "Already that's a cliché. This has got to be fresh and different, an entirely new touch."

"How about Barney sing 'Just an Old Justin Boot'?" I said. "That hasn't been done before."

You could tell by the look on the dude's face that he was paying us to act, not make suggestions.

It turned out what he had in mind wouldn't even take much

The Western Verité / 49

acting if Barney could do it. We all agreed at once that Barney had the natural talent—we had heard him use it many times—but the talent was really up to nature, not to Barney. I mean he couldn't just tell it to happen any more than he could tell hair to grow on the bald spot where the front end of his Stetson kept rubbing. Even that damn coach couldn't help with this one.

But nature wasn't the only one that had to be coaxed a bit. Barney said he wouldn't do it. Said he didn't mind belching, in fact would be glad to on occasion, but this other was a different matter. The dude in the glasses said he should think of it as art. Said nobody would be able to tell it was Barney anyway. It would be a night scene, and Barney would be wearing a slicker with his big hat pulled down. Barney said, "Why don't you get one of those damned carpenters?" The dude answered, "No, that tub part was peripheral as far as the theme goes. This is the center. We can't fake it. My integrity says I can't fake it."

Finally Barney's integrity said he could do it, or at least try to do it. He didn't care whether it was on the periphery, in the center, or on the short end of a long bull's tail. What mattered, when it got down to tying the rope, was that the dude added a few bucks. Mont threw in, "I'd rassle a strong-minded skunk for that much." Seems the dude still preferred the scene with Barney.

With Sill's help the scene was shot. *Aimed at* would be our way of putting it. Sill cooked up a big mess of beans, leaving out the quieteners. Barney stoked up, sitting all by himself, until he said he felt like a bloated calf. When the great moment came, he squeaked out a weak one, then another one that had no more volume than the popping of a ground-cherry pod. Barney felt bad, said he wouldn't take the extra pay, said nobody could count on a thing like that anyway. But the guy who was helping—said he was a sound technician—said Barney's work was fine. Said he could amplify what we had barely heard until it would sound like the shot of a cannon. Said when he got through with it, it would shake the whole damn screen.

Next day the whole outfit, carpenters, trailers, whores, and technicians all pulled out. Wasn't nothing left but a pile of bottles, a lot more dust, and the puzzled look on an old bull's face when he watched them go. We got our pay same as the dude promised. The first chance we got we would go into town, buy a few things, and maybe take in a John Wayne movie on the side. We couldn't wait for our movie—film I mean. The dude with the glasses said it would take a while to get it ready. Said it had to be edited, the sound track worked out, the whole thing shaped to a high conception. We guessed that meant, among other things, turning that squeak into a cannon shot.

So we forgot about that damn film. We stopped thinking about someday taking up the saw and hammer. We even stopped chasing Mr. Pulley's cows to Abilene. This last wasn't hard to give up, because nobody had wanted to pay us to do that anyway. In a month or so we got back to doing things as if nobody at all was watching.

Then one Saturday night Sill came back from town with a newspaper somebody had shoved off on him. Said it had a story we'd like to know about. Said if we didn't watch out, the whole damn bunch of us was about to become famous.

That pulled us all up. We sat around the bunkhouse like a bunch of yearlings looking for a new sack of chopped grain. Sill took his time, said there was no hurry, said it would read the same in an hour as it would in ten minutes. Maybe he couldn't find the story, what with all the space given to a couple of wars and some new evidence that drinking had cut the birth rate.

"Here it is," he finally said. Then he read some of it slowly. "New Western may win Academy Award. Critics praise the stark honesty, the dark beauty of Henry Puffer's new film. A first-time actor named Barney Tullus is almost certain to be nominated for best supporting performance."

"What the hell were you supporting, Barney?" Mont said. "Looked to me like the only thing on top of you was that old brown Stetson."

"Is that all?" I said.

"That's all," Sill answered.

"It hasn't said anything yet," Mont said.

"Can't say everything," Sill said. "You have to remember this is a family newspaper. It can't tell what Barney performed. It can't go right on as if nothing mattered and say right out loud, 'The finest fart in movie history.'"

"It wasn't a movie. It was a goddamn film," Mont said.

"I'll bet that dude is already planning up a sequel," I said. "Barney, you going to perform in that one too?"

The Western Verité / 51

"This time I'll bet they'll let you have the tub all to yourself. Keep pants on the carpenters the whole damn time."

"And maybe now you've become so famous, they'll throw in that voice coach instead of all those whores."

We had him.

"Goddamn," he said.

And we all yelled, "Round it! Round it!"

THE METAWESTERN
A FURTHER CONVERSATION
WITH THE NOVELIST

September and October came. The oaks turned golden, then a rusty brown. Snow began to whiten the bald places on the higher peaks. But something seemed missing from the season. The warped rawhide cover of one of my books reminded me: there had been no new work from the creator of Barney Tullus.

Pained by my sudden sense of the incompleteness of the season, I resolved at once to call on the novelist. My hope began to run upward, for I knew—at least I trusted with deep confidence in the creative spirit—that if I had not yet heard of the new work, it must nevertheless lie waiting for my expectant eyes, bound like *The Milk of Human Kindness* in some appropriate skin, perhaps this time the soft white belly of a yearling Hereford.

I was doomed to disappointment. In fact, I was doomed to a series of disappointments. The author of *The Rise and Fall of Barney Tullus* had fallen into a profound silence.

When I called at his study, again bearing the gift of a fifth of Old Black Bull, I discovered that my elixir was not needed. The novelist was already deep into a tall glass of bourbon and his favorite ditch.

"I hope," I began, "that you are celebrating the completion of another great work."

"I have swallowed the pill of failure," he said sadly. "I am trying to make it slide down a bit easier. I once swallowed a rabbit turd I thought was a raisin. Reminds me of that."

Although I was shocked by what I was hearing, I knew I could not rush him into telling me what had happened. In his present mood he was not about to go back to the beginning and work rationally forward.

"Let's just say I tried," he said. "Like the short-legged bull and the long-legged cow, let's just say I tried."

"Your admirers all know you have tried," I said. "If you haven't yet won the Nobel Prize, we at least know you're trying."

"Tried, not trying," he corrected. For a moment he was silent, studying the last finger of brown liquid in his waiting glass. "But how could I know?"

"How could you know what?" I asked gently.

"You mean you don't know either? Then by god the world is in a crapped-up state."

Again I held myself to a studied patience.

"You're smarter than some guys," he said to me. "At least you're not as dumb. Tell me, what would you write about if somebody tied you up to a pencil and said, get going?"

"I guess I would write about people," I answered, trying to go along with his game. "Maybe I would stick in a horse or two. And I might even throw in a cow."

"I take back what I just said," he cut in. "About you're being smarter than some. By god you're as dumb as the rest of them. You don't even get past me in the race for brains."

Again I chose silence.

"Only two things important," he said. "And neither one of these is people, let alone cows and horses."

I still waited.

"Racism and sexism. That's all there is. By god that's the whole shitteree."

I knew something had happened, maybe a conversion experience of irresistible power. He seemed like a man caught up in a religion he really didn't want to believe in.

"Who said that?" I asked.

"You mean you don't know?" he answered. "You mean the whole damn world hasn't heard that truth?"

I assumed a mild inquiring innocence. "The truth comes slowly to some of us."

"Then by god let me tell you about it. There was this jolly little fellow, dressed for all the world like a dusty priest. But he sure as hell wasn't no priest. Prophet maybe. Yes, when he uttered a truth, when he waved his fist and shook his little beard, by god it was like hearing the twelfth commandment. When he said, 'The western has only two themes, racism and sexism!' you could no more doubt what he was saying than you could doubt your father when he said, 'Get the hell out to the woodpile, and make the sticks short enough this time. Your mother is goddamn sick of having to leave the lids half off while the wood burns down!'"

I saw at once that I had to do a little supporting missionary work. Otherwise the very creative center of western letters was going to collapse in total despair.

"I don't know a damn thing about that *ism* or this *ism*," he went on. "I even tried a dictionary. That second son of a bitch wasn't even in it."

"You don't have to worry," I said calmly.

"I don't?" he said. "You can easily say that because you're riding way off there where these things don't matter. That little fellow doesn't have you by the balls."

"No," I went on. "You just write the books. Let the critics find the *isms*. After all, you've got to leave them something to do."

"But will they be sure to find them?" he said. "The racism and the sexism, I mean."

"Sir," I said, "you are a novelist of little faith. Trust the critics. Trust them to find whatever needs to be found. And they don't even have to be paid to do it."

"That's reassuring," the novelist said. "That's real reassuring. But I still don't see how they're going to do it."

"If I may presume," I rushed on, "let me suggest a way. You just said that fellow has you by the balls. Now suppose you had transferred that feeling to Barney. Suppose in a novel Barney had said it."

"Yes," he answered, "that could happen. Many's the time the world has had old Barney by the balls."

"All right," I said. "See what it means, see how ambivalent the situation is. It's a classic love-hate predicament."

A look of amazement was coming over the novelist's face, but the idea had me—well let us say it had me in its grip—and I wasn't about to stop. I knew I had to get western literature back in the groove—I mean back on the trail—well, anyway, going again.

"You see," I plunged on, "to the extent that he likes it, it means that he is homosexual. But of course he hates it, fears it, for it is an overt gesture of castration. His masculinity is clearly in immediate jeopardy. And of course you can't have a cowboy hero without that. I mean both the masculinity and the jeopardy." I held up for a moment. "Don't you see how easy it is?"

"Well I'll be goddamned," he answered, not in agreement but in pure amazement.

So then I thought I had him started, willing to write novels and let the critics take care of the racism and the sexism. A month or so later I decided to check back. If he would let me, I would look at the work in progress, point out a few bits of the necessary *isms,* and thus give him a fresh charge of confidence that he was on the right trail.

The tall glass was empty. In fact, it was the bottle this time that was getting down to around a finger or two.

I peeked about as best I could, looking for the manuscript that I figured ought to stack up at least an inch or two.

"There's a pile of paper over there," he said, pointing with the side of his glass, "but there's nothing on it. Not a goddamn word. I can't get the damn thing started."

"You still worried about those *isms?*" I said.

"Hell, no," he answered. "I'll let all that take care of itself. But that little fellow said something else."

Again I waited.

"Seems things change every time there's a president who gets a war going. By god now I've got to sit around and wait until we know which way we're going. Maybe he's going to put the damn army out to picking up a bunch of beer cans. Maybe he's going to march 'em off to keep the peace on Easter Island. Point is, we novelists have got to wait. We can't just sit down and throw a bunch of men and cows together. We've got to wait and see which way the national drift is going. A fellow might get halfway through a book and bang, the whole thing shifts like a load of hay that's all sides and no middle. Before he knows what the hell is happening, he's at the bottom of a ditch when he should be riding like a king on the highest pile. He goes along thinking he's writing a book like Henry Wadsworth Longfellow when bang, he should have been writing one like Tommy Wentworth Higginson."

I could see he had a problem.

"What we need is some kind of national ramrod to watch which way the bull is running. He could send the word down, and then by god we could get these novels going again."

"Wasn't this little fellow a kind of ramrod?" I said.

"Hell, no," he answered. "He's waiting too. He's no more riding point than I am. Course once he sees which way to follow, then he can tell us where we've gone. But just between me and you and a yearling steer, there's not a hell of a lot of comfort in that."

I started looking for a new way out of his problem. "Those other writers, did they wait too? Take old Owen Wister."

"A racist right to the bone," he answered.

"All right," I said. "At least he didn't have to worry about a central theme."

Clearly I had struck a responsive chord. "That's right," he answered. "By god what we need is another Teddy. He didn't go tippy-toeing around the world. He sometimes used more horns than brains as president, but at least he didn't leave old Owen wondering which way to jump."

"You sure old Owen even waited?" I said.

"By god I believe you're right," he answered. "Harvard didn't take old Teddy any closer to God than it took Owen. Even if Teddy did get to be president, old Owen could play the piano a hell of a lot better."

"Then why not take your chances?" I said.

"By god I think I will," he answered.

Having helped build up his trust in the critics and having made him see he couldn't wait around until another imperialistic war got going, I thought I had him back on the literary trail. I held back a month or two to give him a running start and then I knocked again at his study.

He met me with an unsmiling face, but I knew of course that he struggles with great complexities in his fiction. I knew I should not expect the bland happy look of a man who has just turned a sourdough pancake with little or no fallout. If there were lines on his face, they would be—or at least could be—the physical signs of an anguished creative spirit.

He was anguished all right. As if pointing he looked with tired eyes at his dusty old Underwood. A couple of steps allowed me to see that the sheet of paper was blank.

"Can't even find a title," he said sadly.

"That ought to be the easiest part," I answered. "The West is full of titles."

"Used to be, you mean."

"What's wrong with a good old-fashioned title? Something like *Sixguns at Sunset* or *Silver Spurs at the Lazy S.*"

"Won't do," he answered. "Won't do at all. We're past all that. Now we've got to strike a new note. And the title's got to get the whole thing going."

"How about *A Horse for All Seasons?*"

"A horse? Don't you know we can't say anything about horses?"

"Not even in a western?" I said with some surprise, if not with a touch of mild shock.

"Hell, no," he answered. "We're past all that. A couple of days ago, without thinking, I put down *The Cow Jumped Over the Moon*. Then I realized I had that damn cow in there. I didn't even look for an eraser. I just wadded her up and dropped her in the stove."

"I guess I'm old-fashioned enough to like a cow or two."

"But you're stuck back there with the old western. Now we've got something new. It's called the metawestern."

"The what?" I said.

"The metawestern."

"What's that?" I said. "And where did it come from?"

"I'll answer that second question," he answered. "But damned if I want to touch that first son of a bitch."

"No, wait," I said. "I'll take a guess. That little fellow with the sexism and the racism."

"You've hit the bull right square in the ass," he answered.

"You mean, don't you, that my deduction is valid."

"I mean," he answered, "that you've hit the bull right square in the ass."

"What did he mean?" I said. "What did he mean by meta-western?"

"If I knew," he answered, "I'd write one of the critters."

"Did you try the dictionary?" I said.

"Sure I tried her," he answered. "Trouble is she was written by some shorthorn named Webster. That little fellow didn't have a damn thing to do with throwing her together."

He knocked a pile of books aside and pulled out a dictionary. I could see the spine was broken. I could see that the corners were not only dog-eared but open to the mashed boards inside.

"Maybe you just need a new dictionary," I said.

"And maybe that little fellow just needs to slow down making words. Ain't no book going to keep up with a fellow as mouthy as him."

He opened the dictionary at about the middle. He didn't even bother to check the tabs.

"Been hanging over this place quite a bit," he said. "Kind of got it wore down to where it shows. *Meta*—she's Greek, you know—old as a goddamn rock. A new dictionary, even one of those as big as three Sears catalogues stacked on top of each other, ain't going to change all that. Prefix meaning in general *along with, after.* I say that's pretty damn general. Along with what? After what? Hellalmighty, a writer needs to know."

"What about those other words?" I said. "I once heard a preacher say *metaphysics.*"

"She's in here," he said, lifting the dictionary slightly. "And there's another son of a bitch that takes off from that word. *Metempsychosis.* Altogether they've got something to do with *beyond, transcending, higher.* I'd sure as hell like to write me a western that's beyond, transcending, higher, if I could only figure out how to get the bugger up there."

"Any more meanings?" I said.

"God, yes," he answered. "Seems that little Greek bugger can mean *change, transposition, transfer, trans.* As in *metamorphosis.* I tell you my mind's constipated with all these damn words. Metawestern. A western that changes. When Barney started milking that cow, things sure as hell changed. But I guess that's not what that little fellow means."

"He probably means the form, the style, the tone. You got to change things like that. Themes too. Except you got to stick with sexism and racism."

"It's enough to make a writing man hang up his saddle."

"Maybe that's what's wrong," I said. "Maybe you're still trying to write westerns in the saddle. Maybe you ought to change your whole life-style. Get out into the bigger world. Throw yourself into one of those new books about trading wives instead of cattle."

"They metawesterns?" he said. He was still stuck on that word.

"Could be," I answered.

"I'm beginning to feel like a mule who should have been a jackass. Or maybe it's the other way around."

"Wait," I said. "I've got a better idea."

"Than being a jackass?"

"No, I mean better than your trying to figure out about that

The Metawestern / 59

metawestern. First thing you've got to do is throw away that dictionary. Most of you novelists already know too many words."

"Maybe so," he answered. "But spelling 'em is another matter."

"You just write a novel," I said. "Let that little fellow play with his fancy words."

"Suppose it don't turn out to be a metawestern. Suppose it turns out to be just a plain old western. Those professors will have a fit. They won't even want to read it, once somebody says it's not along with anything, sure as hell ain't beyond, and doesn't have any more change than what comes with shifting from winter hay to green spring grass."

"I'll read it," I said.

"By god that's a start. Now if you can find one more dumb bastard, that'll make two readers. First thing you know we'll have a best-seller on our hands."

Already he seemed in a more hopeful mood. Still he had to write his own book, and no more preaching on my part was going to get him started any quicker. I left him then, waiting as I walked away to hear the quick, furious rattle of the old Underwood keys.

I didn't, but that was a few weeks ago. Maybe by now he will have got his novel under way. Unless of course he's been spooked again by something that little fellow said. That literary preacher sure said a lot, but one of these days there isn't going to be any more of his scripture to remember, or maybe the novelist will just forget the rest of it, let it fade out into the air like that newspaper recipe for herb-spiked biscuits he forgot without even getting around to gathering the leaves and the seeds.

And then—oh happy thought—maybe old Barney will ride again.

A VISIT FROM THE NOVELIST

I had just finished reading the latest story by Donald Barthelme. While my sensibility lingered lovingly over remembered bits of his style, I idly turned the pages of the magazine, and suddenly my eyes fell smack upon a high-crowned Stetson. I was startled. My first impulse was to swear off reading any more Barthelme. My second impulse was to turn quickly, almost violently back to the cover to see what the hell I was reading. It was *The New Yorker* all right. I felt steadied. Turning to the Stetson again, I let my eyes drop down the page. "The Texas Ranger," the words said. Then narrowing my focus to the smaller print, I saw the number 1,650.00. No dollar sign, just the number. But I could guess from that period in the middle that it was money that was being hinted about. I was about to say aloud, "$1,650.00 for a goddamn statue of a Texas Ranger," when I realized I was thinking somebody else's lines. Not more than half a dozen of us believe in Providence these days, so there was something uncanny in the fact that just as I thought those lines I heard an old car stop out front. I looked out my front window just as the driver with his back turned my way lifted a small square package out of the bed of a 1954 pickup. It seemed providential because when he walked up to my front door I recognized the unsmiling face of the author of *Barney Tullus*.

I hurried to invite him in, all of the time eyeing the package hopefully. There was nothing about it that said manuscript, but there was also nothing about it that said shirts or underwear or the folded-up part of a plastic tie rack. These last made no sense riding in the back of the truck and coming into my house, but I was trying to temper my expectations. More likely it could have been a ream of empty paper or an extra Sears Roebuck catalogue or even a bunch of back issues of the *Salt Grass Symposium*. I asked him to sit down. He said, "I've been sitting down too damn much already." I was out of Black Bull. I didn't even have a warm beer in the place. But it was only mid-morning and I figured he wouldn't be ready for that stuff anyway. "Would you like a cup of coffee?" I said. He flinched. "I got a lump of DiGel right here," he said, poking himself about the fourth shirt button down. "Big and hard as a goddamn rock. I doubt you got anything strong enough to melt it. But thanks the same." I was pleased. Now I knew for certain he had been at work again. Only being creative could give a man a lump like that.

So we stood, he holding the package which had to be a new novel, I with *The New Yorker* still in my left hand and the hat of that damn Ranger still showing.

"I decided not to wait," he said. "As soon as I got her finished, as soon as I hit the last period on the last damn page, I thought to myself, won't be five or six people in the whole damn world that will care, but one of them is the guy who's been bringing me that good Black Bull. So I threw her in the truck and came on over."

"There'll be other readers, I'm sure," I said.

"Oh, she's a good piece of work," he said. I waited for him to go on. "Maybe the critics won't know what to call her, but she's a good piece of work."

"Maybe the critics will just call her good," I said.

"And maybe the critics will piss up instead of down," he answered.

"I take it you broke new ground," I said.

"Plowed her all to hell," he answered.

"A metawestern?" I asked.

"Damned if I know," he said. "May not even be a western. Not a damn cow in the whole shitteree, not as much as a two-year-old yearling. You could run that pile of pages through a good meat grinder and you wouldn't come up with enough beef to make one good patty. Not a damn horse in her either. You could scrape that book with a sharp curry comb for a whole damn week and even if you came up with a hair, it wouldn't be a horse's hair. It would have to be a chunk of spider's web or a loose thread or a lock from some old cousin's hairpiece."

"Sex?" I asked.

"Sexiest damn book I ever wrote," he answered.

By then my literary appetite was ready. As soon as he gave me the package and drove away, I would sit right down and lose myself in the magic of his pages. Donald Barthelme would just have to be patient and wait his turn.

THE ROMANCE OF
ALLIS CHALMERS

About seven o'clock Sill called out through the screen door of the kitchen, "See him coming yet?"

We squatted along the south wall, having an after-supper smoke. It was still a little sunny. Mont had just got through saying, "The old man ought to put up a canopy or two. One of them orange things with green stripes and a row of yellow tassels."

"Nothing showing yet," I said. "Not even a good-sized cloud of dust."

Burt said, "You mean that thing is going to stir up dust? I figured for all old Pulley's paying for it, that thing will walk on air."

Sill came outside, shoving the door with his shoulder, still wearing the big dirty dish towel he used for an apron. He had rolled his sleeves back down and was trying to snap the cuffs. "Who the hell decided that cowboys have to wear snaps instead of buttons? What the hell's wrong with a good old button?"

"It ain't the button that changed things," Mont said. "It's the hole."

"Not more than four out of every five cowboys knows how to make a good buttonhole," Burt said. "And three of them makes the hole too big."

"It ain't the hole that's to blame," I said. "It's the skinning knife they use to poke it with."

Sill curved one hand across his forehead and took a long squint. "Sure beats me why he's taking so long. Even if that thing ain't starved for beef and beans, Barney sure as hell ought to be."

"God yes," Mont said. "If that thing don't come back fast enough, Barney'll tie it to a tree and walk in."

"I hear them things is damn near automatic," Burt said. "They can almost run themselves. All you got to do is set the son of a bitch with a knob or a lever and then get off and run ahead of it if you can run that fast."

"Except that last," I said.

"You mean the running," Mont said.

"I mean the running," I answered.

"Much as he loves my beef and beans," Sill said, "Barney ain't ever going to get that hungry."

Then we could hear it, first a sort of throbbing in the air, then a steady chugging. About then she broke into view, a chunk of reddish orange pulling along a cloud of dust where the road cut down the hill.

"By god," Burt said, "she does make dust."

Even at that distance we could make out the high square front of her, and then we could see the swollen pipe sticking straight up in the air, bluish smoke shooting out of the pinched-in end.

"By god," Mont said, "I believe she is running herself."

"Old Barney must have got that rope on the wrong leg and tied himself to the tree."

But when she pulled a little closer, we could make out the crown of the old brown Stetson.

"He's there all right," I said. "He may not be driving, but at least he's riding."

She came rolling through the gate and straight toward the kitchen wall. Just when we were thinking about climbing the nearest tree—except there weren't any trees—she slowed a bit and then she stopped, with her big square front end about four feet away and old Barney grinning over the top of her.

Mont spoke for all of us, "I'll be goddamned."

We still squatted on our heels. But looking up a bit we couldn't miss seeing the white *A* stuck there before us, plain as a red scab on a blond woman's ass. With a long arm and a short stick anyone of us could have reached out and touched it.

Burt said, "What is that *A* supposed to stand for? Seems to me if it means what I think it means it ought to be on the other end."

"It means Allis," Barney answered.

"Then she is a she," Mont said, "Up to now I wasn't sure."

"There's a *C* there too," Barney added. "That's for Chalmers."

"They brothers?" I said.

Sill said, "How come Alice gets her brand on top?"

But Barney was still filled with all that sweet air he'd breathed

The Romance of Allis Chalmers / 65

in at tractor school. As Mont had already said, pick a less than ordinary cowboy, take him to a railroad crossing that thinks it's a town, where there's a dude dealing in tractors when he should be dealing in poker chips, put that cowboy on a soft seat that adjusts to your weight and slides backward, forward, and up and down, and by god he'll come back acting like an old maid who's been smiled at by a buckle salesman.

"You going to leave her right there?" Sill said. "Or have you got a box to put her in?"

Sill went on before Barney had time to answer. "What's that 160 supposed to mean?" He was still the only one of us standing, so he was the only one who could see the number.

"Damned if I know," Barney answered.

"You mean you spent a whole long day loving up to this damn tractor and you still don't know what that 160 means?"

"Didn't tell me," Barney said. "Must not be important."

"Not important!" Mont said. "Why that's how much the driver's supposed to weigh." Mont was standing now, hunched just a bit to study the 160, white against black on both sides, high on the front above the wheels. "Didn't that fellow have you peel down to your undies so he could weigh you to see if everything would be all right?"

"Damn good thing you took in those seven or eight extra pancakes this morning," I said. "Otherwise you wouldn't have made it."

"Damn good thing I knew what was coming up," Sill said. "Damn good thing I put that extra handful of gravel in the batter."

Barney just sat, still holding the wheel, the grin changing slowly to the look on the face of a cat with an oversized turd. "Goddamn," he finally said. And we all laughed so hard that Burt slipped off his heels where he was sitting and fell over in the dust. "Goddamn," he said, for himself this time. But it was a good echo and it started us laughing all over again.

We knew right then that a tractor school can give a fellow a new layer or two of manners, like wetting an old board with linseed oil, but it can't make a come-outer out of a cowboy. When that dealer stripped Barney down to weigh him in, he must have been able to see that too.

That was the show for the day. Barney started her up again and drove her around the stack of old bales and into the iron-roofed shed. He had to run over a pile or two of liquid fertilizer getting there, and when he pulled inside, he damn near got knocked in the head by a rusty hame somebody had hung there a couple of hundred years ago. The shed wasn't exactly a box, but it was as close to one as Barney could come. "It's just a goddamn tractor," Mr. Pulley would say. "If it's going to spend its days digging around in the dirt, it sure as hell don't need no bed with sheets on to come home to."

But we knew Barney would work on it. Being a graduate of tractor school had to mean something. And even without that diploma, Barney had a kind of steadiness, like a porcupine walking on a hot steel rail. If he didn't have that old cow to give him purpose, he could show his stuff by taking special care of lovely Allis.

Next morning Barney was not around when we stood outside Sill's door and let his sourdoughs have some time to settle. Sill had hard rules about sitting in the kitchen. When the last pancake was turned and tossed our way, he was already getting ready to soak out the batter bowl. "This place is just for eating," he said. "That sign don't say nothing about a place to let the chuck sink in."

So we were not surprised when we heard Allis start up and soon come chugging round the stack, brighter than ever in the morning sun, little spurts of blue smoke shooting out that straight-up pipe. But when Barney pulled up close for our second look, we could see a special difference. The whole bottom of her front end bulged out at least a foot.

"By god," Mont said, "she's pregnant."

Barney eased her up and let her chug.

"Suitcase weights," he said. "Keeps her front end down."

"If you ask me," Burt said, "she's already had her end down once too often."

The graduate of tractor school went on. "Say you're pulling a stump as big as a steer's middle. Say you're plowing and hook onto a rock as big as a small house or a middle-sized haystack."

"It don't look like that at all to me," Mont said. "It looks like somebody ain't kept his old John Deere fenced in. Ought to have at least five strands of 12-gauge on a fence like that."

"Logs would be good too," I added. "Especially if you stand 'em up on end."

The Romance of Allis Chalmers / 67

But Barney had had about enough.

"Think it'll be twins?" Sill said. "One of each would be real nice."

"Goddamn," Barney said. "It's like talking to a herd of old women."

"Next time you talk to 'em," Mont said, "you better tell 'em about Alice. That's the kind of news they like to hear."

Barney hit the special foot throttle, jerked the wheel hard around, and Allis roared off full speed—damn near fifteen per—and we stood having the best laugh we'd had since that voice coach went home.

Without really meaning to, we were shoving old Barney back in upon himself. Himself and Allis. The more time we spent talking about Allis, the more time he spent with her back there in the shed. He'd shoveled and scraped the cow pies out of the way. He'd moved that rusty hame to another nail so it was harder to bump into. And he was using the right leg of an old pair of pants to wipe away the dust and grease that speckled her. But it was the white *A* that got the extra care. One day I took a load of posts down to the fence line along the piece that Barney was plowing. I drove the truck right up behind him so he didn't see me, and Allis was still chugging so he didn't hear me. He stood close in front of her, spit on his finger, rubbed the *A* hard, and then wiped it with his dirty glove.

Some of our talk was really trying to be helpful. Take the business of the boots for instance. Somebody must have invented the high-heeled boot to fit into the stirrup of a saddle. Or maybe he just wanted to make the little cowboys seem taller. But any resemblance between a saddle and a seat that adjusts to your weight and slides backward, forward, and up and down is about like the resemblance between a tin chamber pot and a white enameled toilet seat.

"It's not right," Mont said to Barney. "You better go back to that dude that runs that school and tell him he forgot to give you a pair of those shoes or slippers or leather socks it takes to run this thing."

"Maybe if you pulled the heels off," Burt said, "you could make those boots do. Your toes might point up some, but that wouldn't matter too much if you remembered to lean forward when you walked."

"You've seen pictures of those space cowboys," I said. "Ever see one about to go to the moon in a pair of high-heeled boots?"

"I ain't going to no moon," Barney answered. "Not unless I have to go there to get away from all this crap."

"Besides," Mont said, "how do you know Alice likes the feel of those boots? How would you like to have a pair of high hard heels shoving into your bare back?"

"Maybe you ought to try it barefoot," Burt said. "That ought to make her feel real good."

We didn't talk him out of his boots. Just as easy to talk him out of his feet. Those boots and those feet had been together so long you couldn't really think of one without the other. Whenever you saw Barney walk from the bunkhouse into the shower, which wasn't very often, you thought, there's something wrong about those feet. That cowboy walks like a tenderfooted mule with the string-halt.

Barney kept his boots, and as far as we could tell at first Allis seemed to like it. Or maybe it was all that rubbing in the right places with his fist full of that old right leg. Still it could be the boots that got her back up. At least we started to figure it that way. Barney wouldn't tell us, and when we finally dug Allis out of the haystack, there were so many leaves all over her parts that we couldn't be sure about anything.

You can sort of picture it this way. Barney was sitting up there in that seat that adjusts to your weight and slides backward, forward, up and down. He had a five-gallon oil can in one hand, a two-gallon water can in the other. Or maybe it was a bunch of red roses in one hand, a sack of mashed chocolates in the other. Anyway if he was using the hand throttle, he didn't have a hand left over to grab the black knob of the gear shift. All he had left over was that boot to stomp the clutch with, and you can guess he was kicking and pawing the air for fifteen feet around. Maybe he couldn't see the clutch for all that oil can. Maybe he was too damn new out of school to know how to find the clutch by guess alone.

All of this is a big guess, like wondering how that wagon got up on top of old man Spencer's barn. The hard facts are these: Here comes Allis full speed around the stack, taking out one gate post as smooth as scything a clump of bull rush. We heard the faint sudden crack of dry juniper, the tinny rattle of scrambled barbed wire, then Allis came swooping in a circle as big as a race track straight for Sill's corner. By then Sill was out waving her away with his dirty cloth, but she didn't slow down a bit, and Sill jumped back inside just as Allis wiped a big black streak of rubber along the whole damn kitchen wall. "He turned her. He turned her!" somebody yelled. And then we watched her safely, still chugging full speed, still swooping in that racetrack circle until she came full round and rammed whole hog smack into the middle of that stack of bales.

We dug her and Barney out. Barney was bent in a few places and dusted up a bit, but we didn't get to throw him onto the stretcher we made out of two skinny posts and a wornout quilt. Allis was messed up more. Her big square nose was pushed back and leaking, and that straight-up pipe with the pinched-in end was sticking straight out back.

Mr. Pulley came right out, tearing down the road in his three-quarter-ton pickup, throwing more damn dust than a team of tractors. He studied the situation for about four minutes, pushed back his old tan Stetson, and scratched his white bald head.

"We got about two choices," he finally said. "Maybe two and a half, but I'm not even going to think about that half."

We waited in respectful silence.

"We can send the driver back to school," he said. "Or we can go to another breed."

"I guess Tullus will live all right," he went on. "Might even do him some good."

So then Mr. Pulley climbed back in the pickup and drove off, and we marched into the bunkhouse and up to where Barney was supposed to be recuperating.

"Pulley thinks you're going to live all right," Mont said. "So now he's thinking about sending you back to that tractor school."

"You could say," I added, "to graduate school."

"You better give me a guess on what those bales scraped off," Sill said.

"Or what those bales rubbed in," Burt added.

"160 might be pretty hard to hit real close again."

Barney said, "I ain't going back to no goddamn graduate school."

That was the end of that. Mr. Pulley would just have to go to another breed.

---

70 / *The Romance of Allis Chalmers*

"I reckon it'll be one of those full-grown John Deeres," Mont said. "But like I was saying, you got to have at least five strands of 12-gauge."

"Or logs stuck up on end," I added. That last was only half serious because we didn't have enough logs within twenty miles to fence in a hill of beans.

It was kind of good to have Barney around again the whole time each morning, through the last sourdough and the last puff of the settling-down smoke. That tractor dude came out and hauled poor Allis away. I guess you could say she'd live too with a new part or two, some bending back, and a bucket of orange paint. I don't remember what the *A* looked like, but no doubt it got rubbed some by all those bales. Then Pulley showed up with a used John Deere, as green and ugly as a hungover dream. That big son of a bitch would do the work all right, but none of us, especially Barney, was going out there to rub his back with any old pant leg, right or left.

We were outside having our after-supper smoke. We didn't have anything special to watch for, so we squatted in the shade this time. With all his tractor troubles, Mr. Pulley hadn't got around to that canopy yet.

"Something I been wondering about," Mont said. "After you almost missed the kitchen, you still had half a racetrack to go. How come you didn't throw away those goddamn cans? How come you didn't do that and take hold of her?"

But Barney wouldn't talk. You had to guess about that too. Maybe he thought when he almost missed the kitchen she knew what she was doing and would almost miss the haystack too. Maybe when he heard us yell, "He turned her. He turned her!" he thought he had turned her, not with his hands, not with his boots, but with some sort of shove of his cowboy grit. Call it stubbornness, call it pride, call it any other damn thing that seems to fit. It was sad to see old Barney bleeding hay stems instead of blood. It was sad to see old Allis hauled away. But in the high moment of it, in the first wild explosion of Barney, bolts, and bales, it was a good show. Goddamn, there was something almost grand about it.

The Romance of Allis Chalmers / 71

THE DEVIL AND BARNEY TULLUS

"Nunquid Deo cura est de bobus?"
—St. Paul, quoted
by Reginald Scot

Using our bed rolls for pillows, we were taking it easy around Sill's fire while the stew came to its right kind of thickness. Sill, who usually stands fussing the fire and holding his long spoon like a club at the ready, had dropped into a squat. The spoon had gone limp in his hand. You could almost guess he had stopped worrying about the stew.

He said, "What if that pot suddenly got up and began to walk across the fire? What if it suddenly jumped about ten inches straight up into the air?"

It was a no. 14 dutch oven, as big around as a Mexican Stetson, with a deep lid heaped now with smoking coals. Whenever Sill lifted it from the fire, he had to throw out his left arm to keep his balance. We could remember a lot of times when he had got her set again, poked the coals around her, and then straightened himself up with a loud sigh. "You fellows think cooking is easy work. You think all a cook has to do is lift a handful of beans now and then, or maybe a cupful of ground coffee. But take that pot there. That's more work than rassling a green fence post. If you boys had any feelings for the man who brings happiness to your hungry innards, you'd help make his life a little easier."

This line of talk always brought out the best in us. Shifting his hips so they felt a bit less bony on the clay-hard ground, Mont opened with a suggestion. "I figure a fellow ought to be able to set a pole right there on the chuckwagon, run it out over the fire, make it steady with a couple of guy ropes, and then fasten on a pulley or two."

"A fellow could save himself all that trouble," I put in, "with a good skyhook. Wouldn't even have to be one of those fancy jobs. Could probably get by with one of those cheap ones from Sears."

"Sill is still going to have to pull that rope. And he's still going to give out that big sigh when he pulls it."

"You're damn right," Sill said. "I ain't no workhorse. And I don't intend to become one."

"No reason why you should," Mont went on. "Easy enough to tie that rope to the tail of Barney's old sorrel. You ought to be able to get that sorrel to start and stop at the right time. You ought to be able to get him to back up in the right direction and stop before his hams hit the fire. If he does get too close, you ought to be able to get him stopped before he jumps into the pond to put his fire out. Then if the rope hasn't burned in two while all of this is going on, you ought to have it smooth and easy."

"I said," Sill went on, "what if that pot jumped about ten inches straight up into the air?"

"We heard you," Burt said. "But I was wondering if you meant when it's full of beans or just sitting there warming a thick skin of gravy."

"Could be a bunch of beef chunks would make a difference," Mont added. "That might weigh her down some. Always makes me feel a little tighter to the ground."

"Reminds me of when old man Barnes used to fill his steers with wet hay before they hit the scales."

"Goddamn," Sill said. "Forget old man Barnes and get back to that pot."

"He's a funny old boy all right," Mont said. "But you do have to go along with the view that that wife of his has laid up her meat in just about the right places."

"I remember a time," Burt said, "I was riding past her yard when she was hanging clothes on a windy day. She went way over digging clothes out of the bottom of her basket and I damn near fell out of the saddle. If I had been that pot, I would have jumped about six feet, maybe more."

Sill never did get an answer to his questions. When he stopped asking long enough to hook the lid and let out some of the rich steam, we agreed unanimously that she was done. We got out our plates and went to work. If Sill still needed to know the answer, he didn't have any more time to talk about it.

We were camped about ten miles north of Sill's home ground. You could say we were on a trail drive, except that we weren't really following any trail and we were just moving a hundred head or so to a piece of range Mr. Pulley had leased for late summer grazing. The old man had said, "By god you just as well make a good thing out of it. Those fences up there are going to need a few days' work. You throw some posts and a couple rolls of wire into that chuckwagon and make a three- or four-day job of it." We could have said, "Don't have to bother about that, Mr. Pulley. A couple of us can run the cows up. The rest of the crew, along with those posts and wire, can jump in the truck. That way we can get the fences fixed and get back here for all the work that's going to need doing." But the old man would have said, "By god I ain't worried about all the work around here that's going to need doing. A man starts worrying about that, about all the sweat you cowboys are planning to sweat around this place, and he might just as well give his cows to his cousins and take up running a crap game for the Sunday School. There's more future in it." The trouble with old man Pulley was that he still believed that cowboys belonged on horses. He still believed there was nothing bigger than moving a large herd of cattle. In his thinking, Goodnight and Loving were only a little less important than Moses and his crew when they threw that herd together around Rameses. Even if a cowboy couldn't drive from Pinville to Haytown without hitting ten fences and fifty "no trespassing" signs, he still needed every chance he got to keep his butt in the saddle, his back on hard ground, his eyes full of hoof dust. Even when there wasn't much profit in it, there was a hell of a lot of character.

We never did get back to Sill's questions about that pot. As a matter of fact, he didn't ask them again. Probably he had already heard all the information he needed about old man Barnes and his prime-graded wife. He wasn't about to ask for anything more. So when we got settled around the fire the next night, even if that pot had started acting like it was going to get up and dance, Sill was ready to take up a new line of talk.

"I should have me a stool of some kind," he said. "A good

cook gets all of the way down on his heels. It leaves a lot of hard work getting back up to stir the beans."

"Could be the cook is getting old and lazy," Mont said. "Could be the muscles of his hocks are getting soft and flabby."

Burt said to Sill, "If we just hadn't chopped up Barney's old milking stool, you could strap that on with a couple of bridle reins. That way you could lift the pot with one hand and still have that other left to swat mosquitoes with."

But Sill finally settled down on his boot heels.

"Barney," he said, "you ever worry about not being?"

"About not being what?" Barney answered.

"About just not being," Sill said. "That's all of it."

"All of what?" Barney said.

"All of the question."

"What kind of goddamn question is that?" Barney said.

"You ever think about just being nothing?" Sill went on.

"Hasn't seemed to bother him so far," Burt said.

"God, no," Mont said. "Cows don't seem to care. Didn't matter a damn bit to that old milker. If her tits had been pulled by John Wayne, she wouldn't have looked happier."

"I mean do you ever think about dying?" Sill persisted.

"You keep that pot filled, Sill, and he's not going to bother about that one either."

"Ever know a cowboy who thought he was going to die?" Burt said. "Take Barney there. That time old man Pulley's big bay got tickled in the flank by a stiff bunch of wheat grass and tossed old Barney clear through the top of a dead juniper tree. Goddamn, there were enough sharp points in that tree to take the meat off a small jackass. Didn't even take Barney's hat off. Proves, don't it, you can't kill a cowboy."

"You thinking about dying, Sill?" Mont said.

"Hell, no," Sill answered.

"Course," I said, "what's true about cowboys ain't always true about cooks."

That ended the talk for that night. After Sill set the pot of beans off to one side, we shoveled in. And when we had filled up, we let the beans get comfortable inside while we had a goodnight smoke. It sure as hell didn't seem right to talk about dying when we felt so damn good. Then we rolled out the beds and lay watching the stars. Wasn't fifteen minutes before Barney began snoring.

I guess we all slept pretty hard, even if we didn't all join Barney in that tune he was playing. Anyway we didn't know anything strange had happened until we woke next morning and saw the hoof print about six inches from Barney's bed.

"Look at that," Mont said. "If he'd stomped ten inches more that way, he'd have mashed old Barney's gizzard clear down into the hardpan."

"How do you know it was a he?" Burt said. "Looks like a plain old cow track to me."

"The size of it," Mont answered. "Goddamn. Look at the spread of it."

We all gathered around for a close look, some of us still limping across the rough ground in our socks. It was a big one all right, damn near five by five.

"Don't see how that big bastard could walk right through the bedroom and not wake somebody up," Burt said.

"To do that he'd have to step on Barney," I said.

"You hear anything, Sill?" Mont said. "Like the close-up walking of a buffalo bull?"

"Didn't hear anything," Sill answered. "But I sure as hell felt it."

"Felt it?" we all said in a chorus.

"Yes, felt it," Sill repeated. "Like a sudden cold wind."

"So you woke up in the night and your bare butt was out of the covers. Now what was it made that track?"

"I said," Sill went on, "*like* a cold wind. I didn't say a cold wind made that track."

"I hope you didn't say that," Mont said. "Because up to now I've kind of believed you knew what was sand and what was water, what was a cow turd and what was scrambled eggs."

"Could be I smelled it too," Sill went on.

"Smelled it?" we all said a chorus.

"Yes, smelled it," Sill answered. "A lot like burning sulfur."

"You going to tell me," Mont said, "that cold wind smelled like burning sulfur? It don't take even a pint of good sense to know where that smell came from."

We studied the hoof print again. "Could be," I said, "it was there when Barney rolled in. Could be that old range bull went along here yesterday. Could be he stomped real hard just for the hell of it."

"Whenever it was," Sill said mysteriously, "that's probably the reason."

It didn't take a pint of good sense either to tell that hoof print was too damn new to have been there before Barney had rolled out his bed. We had been around cows too long not to be able to tell a new print from an old one. Even in dry weather you can read the way the dust holds, the way it changes in the sun and wind.

Barney kept his eyes fixed on that print, and we could tell he was sort of measuring again the space between the hoof print and the place where his old denim-covered quilt had been. You couldn't have run a skinny wildcat through that place, not without a little pushing on one side or the other. Finally Barney shook his head and mumbled "Goddamn."

I don't know why anybody thought whatever it was would come stomping through there again the next night, but we weren't about to take any chances. Barney especially.

"Since we got all the fencing stuff on the wagon," Mont said to Barney, "you could easily put in four posts and lay four or five strands of barbed wire around your bedroll. That ought to keep him out."

Burt added, "But remember all that wire and all those barbs if you get up in a hurry to take a leak."

Barney wouldn't go to all that work. Besides, it was not according to good trail-drive rules. "All we need is a night watch," Sill said. "If the old man was here, by god he'd have us doing it anyway. Even if there ain't any Indians or wolves or ball lightning, there's the sag in a cowboy's backbone. Nothing like looking at the dark from midnight to two, three, or four in the morning to put the stiffness back in."

Sill was right about the old man, but he was wrong about our being able to follow the rules. We organized all right, with each man to sit up three hours, but somebody or maybe everybody must have dropped off because there right next to Barney's bedroll, *on the other side,* was another damn hoof print.

"By god, Sill," Mont said, "that cold wind came stomping through here again last night."

We all gathered around the print, another five-by-five with the delicate dust still crumbling along the edges.

"Feel it," Sill said. "I'll bet it still feels warm."

"Damnit, Sill," Mont said. "How can a cold wind leave a warm hoof print?"

"And smell it," Sill went on. "Get your nose right down close to it. I'll bet you can get a whiff of sulfur."

But Barney said, "I ain't going to sniff no goddamn cow track."

I said, "The old man come along and see you with your butt up and your nose down in that range dust, and he isn't going to just give you your time and a good kick in the ass. He's going to put you in a grain sack and haul you over to Pinville, where they keep the cowboys who think they're hearing godalmighty every time an owl hoots."

Sill got down and gave the track a sniff. "Sure as hell smells like sulfur to me."

"Trouble is," Mont said, "cooks have their own way of smelling. They get mixed up with a pot of burned beans and they never smell anything right again."

"Try it," Sill said. "Just give it a quick sniff."

But we all agreed with Barney. We weren't about to go that far out of our way to smell some damn cow track.

Still even if that track didn't smell like sulfur, there was something mighty strange going on around there. There wasn't going to be any problem lining up the nightwatch, because everyone of us was going to stay awake with both eyes peeled.

"Maybe you'll see him. Maybe you won't," Sill said.

"What do you mean 'maybe'?" Mont said. "If we're all setting here and that big bastard comes stomping through, we'll see him."

"That all depends," Sill said.

"Depends on what?" Burt said.

"On whether he wants you to see him or not," Sill answered.

Mont exploded. "What the hell is going on around here?"

Sill sort of smiled to himself, the way he does when he's tasting his beans. "You're a lot closer than you think."

"Goddamn it, Sill. Will you crap or get off the pot?"

"Ever hear of a demon?" Sill said.
"Sure I've heard of a demon," Mont answered. "I've heard of four or five demons. What the hell's that got to do with this track?"
"You mean that track was made by a goddamn ghost?" Burt said.
"A demon. Not a ghost," Sill smiled.
"Bullshit," Mont said.
"And I don't mean just a little old hind tit of a demon," Sill went on. "I mean the old man demon himself. That's how come the sulfur."
"Well I'll be goddamned," we said in a chorus.

Later in the day when we rode in for some dinner, we could see Sill was about to serve up something besides his left-over stew. I once saw a minister who had that look. You couldn't blame Sill for taking on so. It isn't every week that a fellow gets to be a sort of resident theologian for a cow camp.
"You mean if we *could* see him," Burt said, "he'd look like a bull?"
"Black probably," Sill answered.
"You mean Angus?" Mont said.
"Not necessarily Angus," Sill answered. "Just black."
"Goddamn it," Mont said. "If he's black he's got to be Angus."
"It don't work that way with him. It's not the breed that counts. It's just the color. Course it's true, just to make it easy, he may have possessed old man Barnes's bull."
"I hope the old man got a bill of sale."
"It don't work that way," Sill went on. "He don't move the bull out. He just moves into the bull."
"Then why ain't he over there where he's supposed to be, in Barnes's south pasture?"
"Fences don't matter to him any more than making a noise when he stomps through a cow camp."
"Supposing it is the chief old bastard himself," Mont said. "Why the hell would he want to take up in old man Barnes's bull?"
"Maybe because of all the cows that's running around this country," Barney said.

The Devil and Barney Tullus / 79

"The horny old bugger," I said.

"If it was me," Burt said, "I'd go on past the bull and take up in old man Barnes himself."

"There's another problem," Sill added. "They say once the devil himself has been at it, nobody else will do. Next year Mr. Pulley's cows are going to be waiting for the old dark stranger. That old Hereford bull is just not going to have what it takes."

We'd all just about run out of wonder.

Sill smiled to himself again. "They all say it's cold but exciting."

Barney managed to grunt a soft "goddamn."

It turned out that Mr. Pulley wasn't worried about what the cows were going to think next year. He drove out to our camp in his pickup just after noon the next day. Barney was asleep on his bedroll. The rest of us were sitting in a daze. Stay up all night looking for a cold wind to come stomping through your camp and you don't have a lot of zip come morning and even less come the warm afternoon. Pulley slipped out of the pickup. He limped right past Sill's fire and just stood staring at the general state of things.

"What the hell's going on here?" he yelled.

That woke us up some, at least got our eyes to blinking at the sunlight. Still I don't suppose we moved much.

"Mr. Pulley," Sill said, "there's something strange going on here."

"Strange is it?" the old man said. "By god I'd say so. Strangest goddamn cow camp I ever had the bad luck to walk into."

"We've got this strange thing," Sill went on, "that comes stomping through the camp at night."

"Well, by god if he's any stranger than what I can see right here in the bald daylight, he's got to be mighty goddamn strange."

"He's probably a demon of some kind," Sill added.

"Well get the son of bitch out of here," the old man yelled. "Raising good beef is hard enough without having some damn demon fooling around. Tullus," he shouted, "you get the hell onto it. I'm paying you cowboys to look alive. I'm even going to keep on hoping you'll get those fences fixed. But by god I ain't running no rest camp for a bunch of owls."

With that Mr. Pulley limped back to his truck, crawled in, slammed the door hard, and drove off.

So there we were, caught between the devil on one side and old man Pulley on the other.

We turned to Sill. Somehow he was the one that had got us in that fix.

"There's only one thing to do," Sill said. "We've got to find that demon and exorcise him."

"Exercise him!" Mont exploded. "Godalmighty. All that bastard does now is exercise. Chasing cows and stomping through cow camps at night. You'd think he'd be so pooped his balls would be dragging in the salt grass."

"It's not that kind of exercise," Sill said.

"I just hope you can make the old bugger understand," Burt said. "Because if there's any other kind of exercise for a bull, this cowboy's never heard of it."

"He doesn't really have anything to do with it," Sill said. "In fact he's likely to put up quite a fight."

"In that case count me out. I hired on as a cowboy, not a goddamn bullfighter," Burt said.

"Me too, only more so," Barney added.

"Can't be that way," Sill said. "Especially not with Barney. That old demon's showed too much interest. He wouldn't stomp on a cowboy's bed if he didn't mean to show some special interest. That means Barney's got to be in on this exorcizing. At least he's got to be on the committee."

Barney had the look of a cowboy caught in a chute.

"But first we've got to find him," Sill said. He sounded *him* as if he was speaking out of a well hole.

We talked a while, with Sill a sort of chairman. The only move we could come up with was to send the committee to take a close look at the old Angus Barnes kept fenced up in his south pasture. Sill figured he could tell from the way the old bull was acting.

"What you going to look for?" I said.

"Signs," Sill answered.

"What signs?" Mont said.

"Well, it will be a sure thing if his head is on backwards."

"Wait," Mont said. "If anybody thinks I'm going to saddle up and ride ten miles just to see if old man Barnes's bull has got his head on backwards, then count me out. I'll stay here and dig a posthole. There may not be any comfort in it, but at least I won't be looking like a horse's ass."

"That's only one sign," Sill said. "And we don't have to depend on that."

"By god I hope not," Mont said.

So we saddled up and took off, hoping old man Pulley wouldn't come back to see how we were doing. It didn't take a hell of a lot of imagination to guess what would happen if he drove back and found his whole trail crew had gone off to find out if the Barnes bull had his head on backwards. We could have made the run a lot quicker if we'd had the pickup, but as the old man might have said, by riding that far in the saddle we probably stiffened our backbones even if we didn't find a black bull with his head on backwards.

Trouble was we couldn't just ride up and look the bull over. Even after we'd jounced those ten miles, we still had to ride down the Barnes lane, right past his frame house, and on out to where the bull was fenced in. And you couldn't ride past the house without somebody seeing. Whatever the serious reasons for the committee's going there, we still had to make a social call. Otherwise, old man Barnes would come stomping out with his 12-gauge ready, yelling, where the hell do you cowboys think you're going?

Turned out the old man had headed out to Pinville to get a set of shoes for his bay mare. That left the missus in charge, as we found out when we saw his three-quarter with the pipe rack wasn't parked under the poplar trees and she came out on the front porch to see who was coming. She was some years younger than her old man, but even so she was ripe enough to have lived a time or two. Burt was right. Why would any damn demon want to stop with the bull when he could go a few rods down the lane and end up in old man Barnes himself.

"Howdy, Mrs. Barnes," Sill said. "Wilford out back?"

Of course we knew he wasn't, but still we had to play it dumb and social.

"Bay mare lost a shoe," she said. "Wilf said he didn't have one he could make fit." She smiled. "Probably had some other reasons too."

Sill jumped in. "Mr. Pulley's thinking of going to Angus," he lied. "He sent us over to have a look at Wilford's bull." Of course when you're after demons, a little lie isn't going to make a hell of a lot of difference. If the game's that big, you got to use whatever comes around the corner.

She said we were welcome to ride on down to the south pasture. Burt said he thought he would stay and visit a bit. It wouldn't take the whole group to check the head and whatever Sill had in mind to look for. But we said, no, by god Burt was on the committee and he had to go along with the rest of us.

We found Wilf's bull in the pasture, big, black, and planted solid on his stocky legs. He watched us as we rode up close to the fence, his eyes curious but not at all mean. We studied his head carefully.

"Seems straight enough to me," Burt said.

"He looks pooped," Mont said. "Sure as hell don't need no more exercise."

"Get in there and sniff his breath, Barney," I said. "If it's hot with a touch or two of sulfur, that ought to mean something."

Barney said, "What I said back there still goes. I ain't no goddamn bullfighter."

"If the devil's somewhere under that old black hide, he sure ain't acting up much," Mont said. "Maybe we got to stir him up some."

"We got to be careful about this," Sill said. "As I was saying, a barbed wire fence don't mean a damn thing to him. He can go through that like a breeze through an outhouse window."

Burt picked up a small clod and threw it. It banged and broke right smack between the bull's eyes. He blinked and shook the dust that rolled down his nose. But he didn't move one of those big feet one damn inch.

"He's pooped," Mont said again.

"If you'd been bulling all night," Sill said, "you'd be pooped too."

"I am pooped," Mont answered. "And all I been doing is watching for the bull that's doing the bulling."

"What other signs?" I said to Sill.

"For one thing," Sill answered, "talking strange tongues."

The Devil and Barney Tullus / 83

"That old bastard ain't said one goddamn word. He don't seem to have anything to say."

"They say," Sill went on, "his worshippers like to kiss him on the backside."

"Goddamn it, Sill," Mont said. "How's that sign going to help? You going to get in there and see if his rump is wet with fresh cow slobber?"

"I ain't used to all these problems," Burt said. "I move we go back and see if that nice lady will make a pot of coffee."

Sill wasn't finished, at least he hadn't made up his mind, but he had just about run out of signs to look for. So he agreed to the coffee, maybe thinking it might freshen up his thoughts about other signs.

Wilf's wife was tickled to make the coffee. A handsome woman like that must get pretty damn lonesome with nobody but Wilf around. She even brought out some little cakes she had stored away in her bread box.

"Been hearing anything strange at night?" Sill said as we sipped our coffee.

"Besides the wind, the coyotes, Wilf snoring, and the bellowing of that old bull?"

"Bellowing?" we all said in a chorus.

"Yes, bellowing," she answered. "Why, aren't bulls supposed to bellow?"

"Louder than usual?" Sill said.

"Maybe," she answered. "But I thought maybe he was just getting lonesome."

Drinking that coffee and eating those sweet cakes and talking to that handsome woman sure beat exorcising, but we had to get on with the work at hand. It was like running a fence across a rocky stretch. Only thing to do is dig the holes in the rocks and get the damn thing done.

When we had ridden out Barnes's lane, we pulled up.

"We can't be sure," Sill said. "But it looks to me like it has got to be that bull. We just can't take any chances. Next time he may not be so careful where he puts his big feet."

We waited for Sill to go on.

"We're down to the grit of the matter," he said. "It's time to take some action."

"As I said before, I'm pooped," Mont said. "Once I get down on that bed roll it's going to take more than a herd of demons to wake me up."

"No," Sill said. "We've got to act now. Things may get a whole lot worse. He may not be satisfied with just stomping on Barney." So Sill laid out the plans. "There's one thing that used to work. You heat up two horseshoes and burn 'em into the ship's mast."

"Ship's mast?" we said in a chorus.

"Godalmighty, Sill," Mont said. "You ain't even closer than a thousand miles to the ocean, let alone a ship's mast."

"The point is," Sill went on, "you have to make do with what you got."

"Goddamn it, Sill," Burt said. "We sure as hell ain't got no ship's mast."

"No," Sill answered, "but we got the horseshoes. It's like making biscuits. The recipe says flour and eggs. You got the flour even if you ain't got the eggs. Anybody around here going to say they ain't biscuits even if they ain't got the eggs?"

Somehow Sill was more convincing as a cook than as a camp theologian, but he was about all we had to count on.

"Right now we got to ride back to camp, fasten a couple of horseshoes on the end of a branding iron, and get back here tonight."

I was beginning to think for a cook Sill was sure hell in the saddle.

"How come we can't find a ship's mast closer to camp?" Mont said.

"Wouldn't have the same effect," Sill answered. "We've got to bring our power right to him."

"Goddamn, Sill," Mont said. "I ain't got enough power right now to hold steady for a long leak. If I ever get back here again tonight, I won't be able to even stand up at a tilt."

"We got to do it," Sill said.

I could see this exorcising had really got hold of him. For a cook who complained about having to hoist a dutch oven, he was a real goer once the spirit had grabbed him.

"Couldn't we just bring one horseshoe and burn it into two places?" Burt said. "That would save having to carry all that extra load."

"That's not the way it's done," Sill said. "And by god we got to do it right."

The Devil and Barney Tullus / 85

We rode into camp about the middle of the afternoon, with Mrs. Barnes's sweet cakes completely used up about five miles back. But that didn't matter because we spurred on, knowing that once Sill left his saddle he would jump right into stirring up a batch of something good. Trouble is when a cook turns into a theologian, he's too busy plotting against the devil to think about food.

"Let's find those shoes," Sill said.

"Wait," we said in a chorus.

"I'd rather die because the devil stepped on me than starve to death," Mont said.

"Me too, only more so," Barney said.

Sill could see the committee was damn near on the point of mutiny. "I'll throw together some hotcakes."

That wasn't exactly what we had in mind, but at least there would be quickness in it. While Sill mixed the sourdough, we dug around and found two shoes and wired them right over the face of Pulley's lazy P. By the time Sill had the first batch ready, we had the exorcising work all done, and Barney and Mont were sound asleep. That gave Burt and me first turn. When we had eaten all we could hold, Sill hit the old triangle with the handle of the branding iron and Barney and Mont came straight up like they'd been bitten by a six-inch centipede.

About sundown we headed back, knowing it would be as dark as the inside of that old bull when we got there. "There's two reasons for working in the dark," Sill said. "First we got to deal with the devil in his own time. And second we got to do this when old man Barnes can't see what the hell we are doing."

Because we had to sneak in, we left the Barnes road well before we could see his light. We cut across a string of low hills, dropped into a dry wash, and followed it down toward the south pasture. When we bumped into his outer fence, we jerked out the staples, held the three strands of barb down, and led the horses through. We needed to get close before we made our fire, but we also needed to keep tucked out of sight. If the old man came outside to feed his dog and saw our fire, he would come charging faster than his old bull, his 12-gauge waving in the nightlight.

"We should have made a map," Burt said, "or better still we should have put the old man's lady on the committee. She could steal his pants or hide his boots. That way we could use his road."

We found a low place about fifty yards from the pasture fence. With chunks of greasewood and some dead sagebrush we got a small fire going and shoved in the shoes. In the little circle of fire you couldn't see a damn thing in any direction. You couldn't hear anything either except our own sounds and those of our horses.

"Damn bull's probably out stomping," Burt said.

"If he is, he'll get the message when he flies back," Sill said.

"Flies back?" we said in a chorus.

"How do you think he gets across that wire?"

"Only thing that bothers me," Mont said, "is where the hell we're going to find that ship's mast."

"Just this side of the old man's shed there's a gate post," Sill said. "Maybe it ain't a ship's mast, but it's tall and big enough around to take two shoes, and you might say it's right on the devil's gateway."

"If the old bastard is in there, maybe we could just run on in and burn them shoes on his bare backside."

But Sill was too steady to fool around with that. Exorcising was a serious business. It had to be done according to the rules.

It took a lot of greasewood, but we finally got a faint glow on the shoes. Sill announced that Barney had to carry the irons because the devil had made it personal. "He'll lead off and the rest of us will follow close behind. But by god we've got to hurry, because those irons are going to cool like dog turds in a snowstorm."

Barney got a good grip, jerked out the irons, and took off on a dead run. We had barely got up our own speed when we heard a loud "goddamn" and saw the irons fly off by themselves and damn near ran over Barney sprawled in a greasewood thicket. We pulled him out, found the irons, and went back to start over again, at least the part about getting them real hot.

Next time Barney made it, but he had slowed down to save his neck. There couldn't have been much heat in those shoes when he rammed them against Barnes's tall gatepost. At least you couldn't see any smoke or smell any juniper burning. But maybe they left some kind of smudge. "Besides," Sill said, "it's the doing of it that matters. That old bastard don't have to see a deep-burned mark to know we dared to put our power on him."

The Devil and Barney Tullus / 87

Whatever power we put on that gatepost, we didn't have much left by the time we staggered back to our fire. With all that riding and all that running, two stretches of it, anybody could see we were pooped. Besides when we sat down to rest up around the coals that were still glowing, we felt kind of good and peaceful. Exorcising does give a man a good feeling. "If there was any pay in it," Mont said, "I might take it up as a steady job."

That was the last thing I remember hearing before I felt this round cold hole against my left cheek and opened my eyes to look straight up the barrel into the eyes of old man Barnes glaring down at me. When I dared move about a quarter of an inch, I could see he already had the branding irons in his other hand.

"A bunch of goddamn rustlers, is it?" he said.

"Wait," Mont said. "You got this all wrong."

"I'll wait until I get my rope and come to a good strong tree," Barnes said.

"You lost any cows, Mr. Barnes?" Burt said. "Can't be rustling unless the cows are gone."

"Haven't counted," the old man answered. "Don't need to. Got all the evidence I need." He held up the branding irons. "But one thing I will say, you ain't adding 'em to Pulley's herd, even if that old bastard would like to own every goddamn cow in this country. Unless the old bugger is claiming the horseshoe brand too." He pulled up to think. "But who the hell ever heard of a horseshoe brand? Cheapest goddamn way to make a new branding iron I ever seen."

Some of the steam was going out of him. At least he pulled the shotgun back a few more inches. Or maybe he was too busy waving those irons around to keep track of what the other hand was doing.

"All right," he said. "Suppose there ain't any cows missing. Suppose you fellows can fix that fence up better than it was when you came ramming through. Suppose I only got one rope and suppose I don't want to take the chance of breaking a limb off my new poplar trees. All right. Now which one of you sleepy-looking bastards is going to tell me the lie?"

"Want to tell him, Barney?" Sill said.

"Hell, no," Barney answered. At least we had stuck to the truth so far. And it was the truth too that Barney couldn't talk his way out of a burlap bag, telling lies or telling the truth. So we handed the bucket to Sill.

"Go ahead, Sill," Mont said.

"There ain't nothing worse than a cook turned rustler," Barnes observed.

So Sill took off, and since whatever he told would be a lie anyway, he decided to go with the truth. He went through the whole affair from the first hoof print to the burning of the shoes on the gatepost. The only thing he left out was our pleasant little visit with his wife. We all nodded at the right times to make it seem true, and once or twice he turned to Barney and said, "It happened just like that, didn't it?" and Barney answered, "Hell yes, only more so."

"And so that's exactly what happened, Mr. Barnes," Sill concluded.

"That's the biggest pile of bullshit I ever heard," Barnes said. "I got to hand it to you, Sill. A cook may not be worth much as a rustler, but he sure as hell makes a damn good liar."

The old man put the gun away, and every once in a while he would chuckle about Sill's story. Everything was getting back to normal again, except we still had ten miles to ride before breakfast.

Then old man Barnes said it. "I know you boys ain't hungry, and I know you got to get back to Pulley's cows, but by god I believe the little lady wouldn't mind fixing up some breakfast for a herd of crazy liars."

I tell you we felt mighty good as we rode up to that frame house. If the devil himself had stepped out from behind a sagebrush, it wouldn't have mattered. "Come on, you old bastard," we would have yelled. "Let's get in there and start the eating."

The Devil and Barney Tullus

THE SINGING COWBOYS

"The cowboy made no pretensions to an elaborate repertoire."
—*Prose and Poetry of the Live Stock Industry*

Summer evening is the soft-assed time of the day. We sit letting the stiffness ease out of our tailbones. Mr. Pulley still hasn't laid in that set of pretty green awnings, and he's still a long way from setting up that wooden tank for swimming naked with the whores, but we've brought in a loose cushion from a still-good Hudson and the spring seat from a left-over wagon. In the northside shade of the bunkhouse wall, we don't even have to wait for the sun to go down.

Still, when she's getting on toward dark is the best time of all. The air all around is cool. The air all around is quiet. Maybe there's a clink now and then when Sill throws the cleaned spoons into the bin. Maybe there's a snotty snort when Barney's old sorrel moves his hay with his nose. But mostly it's as still as a week-old grave. You can hold your breath and almost hear the dust settling down for the night.

Mont pulled the boot off his right foot and hung the foot in its dark grey sock over his left knee. "See that sock," he said, and we all looked. "Now if I was to peel off the other boot and put that sock out to view, you'd see a sock that ain't the same color at all. Color's completely different."

"Pink, I'll bet," Burt said.

"No," Mont said. "None of them fancy colors. Just brown. Plain old dirty brown."

"It don't seem right to me," I said. "Pulley find out those socks don't match, he's going to check up on a lot of other things around here."

But Mont was in a philosophical mood. "One of the most important things about being a cowboy," he said, "people don't even know about. They think it's wearing high boots with fancy heels and stars or clovers or some other damn thing on the side. A cowboy wears boots 'cause his feet are hid, and when his feet are hid his goddamn socks don't have to match."

Suddenly Burt seemed to be moved by all that philosophy. He got up, said, "Let me know how it all comes out," and started up the path to the little house on the hill. We studied quietly the way he was walking.

"Or take a pair of chaps," Mont went on. "A man drags a little when he walks. He says, you'd drag too if you had half a cow hide wrapped around your butt. Take Burt there. I've seen better legs on a camp cot. I've seen better walking on a hobbled mule."

When Burt shut the door, that ended that. Mont sighed a kind of period, and we all leaned back again to hear the dust settle.

I think I was almost asleep when suddenly Burt's baritone came booming through the half moon. "No, she won't go home with you, cowboy. She's in love with a rodeo man."

We weren't doing anything at the time but listening, but you could still say we were knocked right back into silence. Up to that point we didn't even know that Burt could sing, let alone come up with words that sounded like a love song.

"Barney," Mont said, "you better get on up there and see what's gone wrong. I'd go myself except I got this thing that cripples me." He pointed to his bootless foot.

But Barney was not about to get mixed up in a situation like that, even if he did have two good feet. "Don't sound to me like he's dying," he said. "Not just yet anyway."

So we waited. Finally the door swung open and Burt stepped out. Even from the bunkhouse wall, we could tell that he was smiling. Must have been to himself because there sure as hell wasn't anybody else close around. He started back down the path, and we still waited. When he got close enough to sort of sidle into sitting position, kind of fold his front legs a bit, Mont started in, direct-like as usual. "As I was saying, you can't ever tell the color of a gopher from the size of his hole and that goes

The Singing Cowboys / 91

for other varmints too, but by god, Burt, we got a right to know what the hell is going on."

Burt pretended to look innocent. "Anything wrong?" he said.

"Don't know if it's wrong," Mont answered, "but by god it's different."

"Oh, you mean the singing," Burt said.

"Singing?" we all said.

"Sure, singing," Burt said. "Ain't that what a cowboy is supposed to do?"

It turned out that Burt was way ahead of us. Turned out he'd been over checking out that old Barnes bull again and Mrs. Barnes—seems her name is Mabel—had told him about this nice young man who'd come around wanting to know what songs her old man sang. Seems he even wanted the old man to sing them while he took them down with a tape recorder. Mabel said she couldn't remember the old man ever singing any songs. Besides, even if he did know a song or two, he couldn't carry a tune as far as her kitchen stove. About then she and Burt were probably sitting close-by having coffee and some of those little cakes, so that wasn't very far to carry a tune. She did tell him, though, that she knew about some cowboys who probably did know a lot of songs. She guessed these other cowboys sang almost every night and sometimes while they worked.

So it seemed we couldn't disappoint that nice young man, or maybe it was Mabel we couldn't disappoint. Anyway it turned out we had to start singing and start singing fast. "That young man may be coming down the road right now," Burt said.

"Barney," Mont said, "you go around to the other side of the bunkhouse and see if you can see any dust moving down the road."

But Barney wouldn't budge. "I'm too goddamn tenderfooted," he said. He had already taken off both his boots.

You could say we threw ourselves into it down a long flat hill. Once he had pulled the bung from the barrel, Burt showed more eagerness than a deaf preacher at a come-outers' meeting. We still held back some. It wasn't that we wanted to prove Mabel wrong, and we sure as hell didn't have anything against that nice young man. The truth was we didn't know any songs, not at least in anything bigger than a little chunk or two. And two out of the rest of us together probably couldn't have helped old man Barnes make it to that stove.

But Burt kept working on us. "We just need a little practice," he said. "Everything a cowboy does needs practice. Singing ain't no different than riding and roping."

"Except one's got a horse you can sometimes count on," Mont said, "and the other's got a rope."

"It would help," Burt admitted, "if we had a mouth organ or a banjo or a plain old four-string guitar."

"Or a string band," I added, "with a bass drum as big around as a poker table. You could even have something pictured on the side, say a bare-nekkid woman with Pulley's Pickers painted across her butt."

"No," Burt said, "we've got to keep it small and folksy."

We dug around in the clutter of our minds. I guess you could say that a cowboy's head is a lot like a harness shed or the bed of any pickup truck. Most of the stuff isn't used much. We finally came up with a scrap or two.

"Now you've stirred up the poet in me," Mont said, "I do recall this sad little song." He coughed a time or two and then took off.

We're out with the cattle and it's starting to rain,
And my goddamn slicker's in the wagon again.
   Come a ki yi yippity, ki yi yea.
   Come a ki yi yippity yea.

Sill joined us about then. "How's the tune go?" he said.
"Well?" the rest of us said.
"Well, what?" Mont said.
"Well, what's the rest of it?" Burt said.
"Goddamn," Mont said. "That's it. That's the whole shitteree."

The Singing Cowboys / 93

"It won't do anyway," Burt said. "That nice young man ain't coming all the way out here just to hear you fellows use words like those. He don't want that kind of stuff on that machine of his."

"Maybe we could change it a bit," I said. "How about 'my goldarn slicker's in the wagon again'?"

"And some folks don't know much about slickers," Sill added. "Maybe we ought to change that to raincoat."

"Besides," Burt went on, "it's too short. We can't even get going with that much. We can't even get the feel of it."

"What do you mean *we?*" Mont said.

"I mean all of us together," Burt answered. "I'm not thinking of some poor bastard off in some corner of the pasture all by himself, singing all alone because the cows won't listen. I'm thinking of something big, a whole goddamn chorus."

Turned out he was ahead of us on that too. Turned out he had found the words, most of them at least, to "When the Work's All Done This Fall." "Now there's a song," Burt said. "Just the thing for a bunch of cowboys. It's got mother and horses and cows and her dying boy. Every time I even think those words, I get goose bumps on the balls of my feet. If I was ever to hear 'em sung by a chorus, I'd be a goner myself. You'd have to carry me away in a grain bag."

So we worked on it every night along about dark. It beat looking at Mont's socks, and probably it gave the coyotes something to listen to. Burt took over as leader since he was already running the show. He didn't know any more about songs than Sill did about devils, but the world, at least our part of it, hadn't come around to letting that matter. "Now somehow," Burt said, "we got to get together on the tune."

"Burt," Mont said, "you could go up there in that house on the hill and give us a chorus. Coming through that half moon might sort of bend it back into shape."

"No," Burt answered, "a chorus has got to be together. Can't have one man up on the hill, another man out in the horse shed, the rest of us scattered like turds in a cow pasture." So as close-in leader he took off alone, and when he hit *fall* at the end of the line he hung on for a minute to let us hear and get the note.

Trouble was, when we got it or thought we had at least a slippery grab on it, we didn't know what the hell to do with it. Still, when Burt said, "All together now," we dug in our spurs and opened up. Charlie died about four different times from the same fall, but by racing a little here and there and yanking on the bit some, we ended up pretty much in the same time of year, though Barney came damn near slopping over into winter.

"I've heard worse," Burt said. But that was easy to say. If you've worked around a branding chute as much as Burt, comparisons like that are not very hard to come by.

"If you're going to lead this outfit," Sill said, "you've got to have a stick. A tune like that has got to be chopped in the air."

"You could easily saw off the skinny end of that cedar post," Mont said. "Or maybe Sill will let you use his second-best fly swatter."

"No," Burt said, "we got to keep it plain and folksy."

"Then how about wearing a glove on that one hand?" I said. "That way we could see it better."

Once we began to get the hang of it, even without a stick to go by, we found practicing easy. After a few times, you get used to strange words coming out of your mouth in a funny way. Charlie didn't always die at the same time for all of us, but we kept getting closer, and so Burt decided we ought to add a special touch or two. "Nothing fancy," he said. "We still got to keep her plain and folksy."

The final touch came in the chorus. "Start her up," Burt said, and we gave it our best.

After the round-ups are over and after the shipping is done,
I am going right straight home, boys, ere all my money
   is gone.
I have changed my ways, boys, no more will I fall—

"Hold it right there," Burt said. "Now here's the cream on Mabel's cookie. On that last line you fellows hum and let Barney take her alone."

So we hit that chorus again, and when we had made it right up to the last line, we clamped our mouths shut and gave off a sad moaning sound while Barney opened up: "And I am going home, boys, when the work's all done this fall."

Burt was right. Anybody around with even half an ear would have cried out, "Go get that grain bag. I can't make it on my own."

Anybody could tell we were ready for that nice young man.

As it turned out, I guess you could say that we were too ready. You could say we hit prime too soon, before the market was even open. Any time of the day and almost any time of the night, Burt would sing out "Fall," holding her a minute, and the sweetest goddamn chorus you ever heard would come floating out around the cow sheds or out among the sagebrush. Burt said, "By god that nice young man better have that thing ready because we're raring to go."

So we waited. Burt even rode over to check with Mabel Barnes again, make sure the young man had not gone off to Pinville or some place else. He figured it was a good idea too to let Mabel know how right she was. He knew how good she'd feel when she heard what a singing bunch of cowboys we turned out to be.

So we waited. Every time there was a flash of dust on the road we sort of eased our ropes or lowered our saddles or let the pickup idle while we found our notes. Mostly it was just the wind. A lot of little whirlwinds jumped around that summer. Sill called them dust devils, but the rest of us still stuck to the old familiar name.

Then one afternoon one of the pokes of dust steadied down to a straight line along the road, and then the bottom got dark and chunky, and sure enough there was a car coming. Burt didn't need to sound that note. He could have made it as soft as a muffled mosquito or he could have roared like a bull with his balls caught in a bear trap. It wouldn't have made any difference. Seeing that car was like hearing that note. Our eyes and our ears had grown that close together.

When the car pulled into the yard, we were lined up ready to go. Of course the driver didn't have that tape recorder out and ready, but hell, we could afford to waste a chorus or two. What mattered at the beginning was that he hear without any waiting that he had come to the right place, that Mabel was giving him the truth about the singing cowboys.

So even before he had time to open the door, smack after he stopped the motor, we cut loose. And when Barney came in sad-like with that last line, you could see that young man was limp as a soaked saddle blanket on a dry seat. Even so, he managed somehow to crawl out and stand kind of blinking with his glove on the door handle. A sudden thought shoved out to the front of my mind: he may be nice all right, but he sure as hell ain't young. As a matter of fact there were all sorts of short grey mane sticking out from under his old brown Stetson.

"This a cow ranch or a goddamn singing school?" he said.

I guess Burt had heard so much singing he was getting a little weak in the eyes and the ears too, because he sure as hell didn't seem to be seeing all that grey hair beneath the hat. "If you want to get out the recorder, Mister," Burt said, "we'll do her again."

"About the only thing I'm going to get out," our visitor answered, "is this pair of boots and damn near everything else that grows out of them. And when these boots get out, they're going to march right up to an old man named Pulley and say, 'What the hell is going on? You send me out to look over your cows and what do I run into? A goddamn vaudeville show!'"

You could say that the scales fell off Burt's eyes right then. They didn't even hang on long enough to get ripe. He suddenly began sputtering and stuttering about all the cows we had out there waiting, but that didn't do any good. By then that nice old man was spooked bad. He got back in that car and took off. And this time he made more dust than a bin full of elephants.

You could say that if we had been doing a play instead of a song we had come to the end of act two. Much as we wanted to call the whole thing off, we knew there was a little more to come.

"All right," Burt said, "the first guy that sings *fall* or any other word that comes close to it is going to get his tonsils scorched out with a running iron and his lips stitched shut with rawhide."

But he didn't need to say that. He didn't need to get us ready this time. Any one of us could have told him how the play would go.

The Singing Cowboys / 97

When Pulley's pickup came charging down the road, throwing more dust than that nice young man and that nice old man together, we had hidden the cushion of the still-good Hudson and Mont had both feet, boots still on, as firm on the ground as a rusty anvil. Sill was in his kitchen banging away with his pots and pans. Mont was splicing a broken rope. Burt was putting a new snap on his old chaps. I was sorting horseshoe nails, and Barney was darning a pair of grey socks. There sure as hell wasn't much singing, but industry was shining all over the place.

Pulley drove up, close as usual, sat looking at all that industry, then climbed out of the cab. He didn't say a word. You had the feeling he didn't want to talk, because talking might get in the way of listening. If you've ever seen a man sort of go over the ground with his ears, you can understand what Pulley was doing. He moved around slowly, turning in funny ways, kind of poking his ears into this corner and that. But all he could hear was Sill's pans, my nails faintly clicking, and once a faint "goddamn" when Barney stabbed himself with his needle.

Finally Mr. Pulley seemed about to say something, then pulled his jaws tight, slid back into the truck, and drove off up the road, keeping the engine in second until it really roared, as if by god he was making up for all that singing he didn't hear.

That at least was one end of the play. However it came out from now on, it wasn't going to be one of those tragedies like *Hamlet* or *Love in a Homestead Shack*. You could say we almost got back to normal again. But even normal had to be a bit different ever since Burt had gone over to check on old man Barnes's bull.

Mont still had his mismatched socks and he still preached a little about what it means to be a cowboy, but other things had come in, and come to stay. At least when Mr. Pulley was away.

Maybe it was Barney who ambled up the hill.

"I've seen better legs on my mother's wooden churn," Mont said.

Then we grew still and waited. But this time we weren't listening for the dust to settle. And sure enough the singing came:

"And I am going home, boys, when the work's all done this fall."

We didn't say anything. We just kept listening, even after the last word had come busting through the half moon.

"Goddamn," we all seemed to be thinking. "There just ain't nothing in the world like a singing cowboy."

THE WESTERN EXPERIENCE

I studied the matter for a considerable time and then I said, "I figure you ought to put that bucket out about three hands."
"He'll never make it out that far," Burt said. "He'll be lucky to get two hands out."
"I was counting on a little run," I said. "I was thinking he could get up some speed along that two-by-four before he makes his turn."

We were laying there in our bunks looking at the baling wire Mont had strung across the room to hold his pretty saddle blanket.

"Of course if he hits it going full tilt, he might shoot out a bit," Burt said. "Maybe three hands ain't going to be enough."

"It pretty much comes down to motive," Sill said.

"And we can count on his motive," Mont answered. "Ain't nothing a proud mouse would rather do than piss on a poor cowboy's blanket."

We never did get that bucket fixed in the right place to catch that falling mouse. Pulley's truck came roaring down the morning road. Even without sending out a scout, we knew enough to pull on our boots and get lined up for business.

The pickup stopped and Pulley eased out. Already you could tell that something was up. When the boots came first, one at a time, instead of the old Stetson, and when he stood there a minute kind of squinting in the morning sun, you could begin to back away and take a careful look. He even closed the pickup door, and there wasn't a dog within fifteen miles.

"Morning, boys," he said.

"Morning," we all said together. We hadn't practiced singing since the last time he was out, but we hit her pretty much in one big voice. We maybe even held it just a bit, to feel how well she held together.

"I know you boys've kept that old chuckwagon in good repair," he went on. "I know you've had her in the pond to keep the wheels swelled out to hold the rims."

The truth was we hadn't thought much about the wagon since we got the devil out of old man Barnes's bull.

"Was figuring on another trail drive," Pulley announced.

"Moving some cows out to desert range?" Mont said.

"No," Mr. Pulley answered. "I wasn't thinking much about moving cows. Wasn't thinking about trailing any place particular."

A man who works around cows soon learns it don't do any good to show surprise, but even so I guess we showed a bit of wonder.

"I wasn't even thinking about the character building in it," he added. "To come down to the jerk at the end of the rope, I've rented the bunkhouse."

Turned out he really had. Turned out he'd let her go for a whole week. "I know you boys won't mind a bit," he went on. "I know you all agree ain't no home like the old chuckwagon out under the stars. Besides, they'll want to see the cowboys out on the long, long trail."

That's all he said except, "Better clean her up some. And better let her air out." Then he was gone and we were left with more unknowns than if we'd cornered four steers in an oak thicket. We didn't have the faintest idea who the *they* was, and we sure as hell didn't know where the long, long trail was trailing.

Burt said, "Maybe we can trail on over and check out that bull again." But Barney said, "Even if we did finally get him exercised, I don't ever want to see that old black bugger again."

Not the least of our unknowns was how clean was clean. You could clean that old bunkhouse a dozen ways a dozen times and still somebody could come along and rub a little harder or find another turd the mice had hid. Being clean, we might have said, don't mean opening the cracks to wind and sand and the blowing perfume of the old feed yard. It don't mean prying out the old socks we had tamped in all those cracks for all those years. We finally left it up to Sill. Cleaning a dutch oven ain't got much more to do with cleaning a bunkhouse than it does with cleaning the devils out of a bull, but sometimes you have to make do with what you've got, just as we had to settle for that gate post when we couldn't come up with a ship's mast. Sill came out of his kitchen wiping his hands across his dirty apron and looked her

The Western Experience / 101

over. "Only one thing," he said. "That old saddle blanket ought to go. It don't look right hanging there all alone. And besides you ain't got that bucket figured out." But Mont wouldn't budge. "That's the only place she's safe," he said. "Put her in the wagon or put her out on the ground and no telling what'll happen to her."

So we packed our bed rolls out to the chuckwagon and waited.

Along toward sundown we saw the first signs of our answer. A half-mile away we could tell it wasn't Pulley's pickup, especially when it broke into two chunks, with the first one looking as short and high as a rolling breadbox.

"It's one of them goddam four-wheelers," Mont said. "But that second outfit. She's got me."

About all we could tell at that range was that it was longer than a buffalo and had more windows than a schoolhouse.

We didn't have time to get up a good round of guesses before the four-wheeler eased into the yard about three miles an hour, stopped between the bunkhouse and the kitchen, and waited while the other outfit pulled up right behind it. We could see then it was a small bus and we could hear then it was full of faces.

But mainly we were still looking at the four-wheeler. The left door finally came open and a leg reached out for the ground. We followed that leg out, then we backed up and followed it out again. From where it poked out of the opening to the top of the boot heel, it was all a faded levi blue. "By god," Mont said, "I've seen some pants as stiff as leather. I've even wore some of them myself. But I never figured we'd get around to making boots out of them."

But that wasn't the main surprise. Because when that leg got hooked on to what came with it, we could tell it wasn't just any run-of-the-range leg. By god it was fastened on to a woman.

Those of us who were sitting stood up, and when she had walked a few steps to bring her so close we could read the brand on her buttons, some of us had even pulled off our hats.

"You must be the hands," she said. "I'm Dr. Assumption," she added. "Francine Assumption. But let me explain, that's Ph.D., not M.D. That means I'm a doctor of philosophy. And you probably thought I was going to perform a vasectomy on your bull."

Well, you could say we were hurrying to catch up, but you could also say that we were a hell of a long way back of that probably, at least two miles I'd say. You could even add that we guessed philosophy needed a lot of doctoring, but that we never expected to have the chief vet herself standing right there in front of us, all dolled up in her denim boots.

"Howdy, mam," we said in a chorus.

"This the whole crew?" she went on.

"Yes, mam," Burt answered.

"Where's your token black cowboy?" she said. But before we could try to get a rope on that one, she took off again. "Of course I didn't expect to see any black faces under the old sombreros. Ever read a monograph called *Racism on the Range?*" I was getting my mouth ready to say something when she loped off again. By god, she was harder to square off with than a bee-stung steer.

Several of us, especially Barney, were just getting ready to go hide in the cowshed when the other door of the four-wheeler opened and another pair of boots dropped to the ground. That was a good sight, especially since they were big, brown, and ugly as a preacher's widow. This time it was a man, a man big like the boots, with a buckle the size of a dinner plate shining just below his belly button, his grey hair topped by a genuine Stetson with a tiny blue feather, and below the well-shaped brim a round, pink, smiling face.

"Howdy, boys," he said. "I'm Professor Duncan. Simon Duncan. But you boys may call me Butch."

"Howdy, Mr. Duncan," we said in a chorus.

"You boys look great," he went on. "Nothing like the good old open air to give a man a feeling of contentment. Nothing like a prairie breeze to make the spirits soar."

"Yes, sir," we said together.

"It's here you've got to come to get the real roots of America," he added. "It's a place like this where you can see democracy starting up like a field of wild flowers. It's in men like you that you see the sturdy stem of self-reliance as firm and free as a western willow in the wind."

I was thinking it would be better to get back and shoot for that monograph, when all of the doors of that bus pushed open and all of a sudden there was the goddamnest milling around of people and suitcases and guitars and at least one mouth organ swinging on the end of a leather string. It didn't take a printed sign nailed to a fence post to tell us who the *they* turned out to be.

Turned out to be a college class come to the ranch for what they called the Western Experience. Turned out Pulley had rented the bunkhouse in the cause of higher education. What the hell made him do it we never did find out. Could be he believed in higher things. Or at least it could be that his wife did. She could have said, "J. G., your life is all tied up in little matters. Why don't you open yourself to the higher things?" And could be he believed her especially since he knew damn well a week's rent would come close to what a utility cow would go for, the market being what it was.

"We'll do some reading," Dr. Assumption explained. "We knew you wouldn't have any books here at the ranch so we brought our own small library, just a few important titles. You know, basic studies like *The Working-Class Movement in America.*"

"Yes, mam," we said in a chorus.

"But mostly we're here to talk," she went on, "and experience. You know, get the firsthand sense of the grinding monotony, the way the big alien world pushes down on a man's ego until he wants to shoot somebody so he can feel himself again."

"Yes, mam," we said.

Turned out it didn't matter we had a few books. Even Sill's Bible had most of Deuteronomy missing. He probably ran out of cigarette papers or needed to start a cooking fire in the rain. But they didn't want to know about that. Dr. Assumption knew that we didn't have any books because she knew that cowboys are too dumb to read. And Professor Duncan knew that we didn't have any books because he knew that cowboys are too smart to read books when they can spend their time reading the pages of nature.

They sure were out there to talk all right, all day long and damn near half the night. "Goddamn," Mont said. "I haven't heard this much chatter since the last roundup of the Pinville Pie-Baking and Poetry Society." Some of the talk sessions they called seminars. Mostly the difference came in what they called the talking. Sometimes we couldn't any more tell they were seminaring than we could tell five steers from five steers on a dark night.

Started out the first night with Mr. Duncan riding point. Seems he got to come first because he was nineteenth century and the doctor of philosophy was twentieth. Seems he didn't know anything about her century and she didn't know anything about his, except that she knew that what he knew was mostly wrong, and he knew that what she knew was all present and no past. After a few days or so of that, we didn't know what the hell to think. As a matter of fact, we didn't know what the hell cowboys were supposed to be. "I've heard of calves with two heads," Burt said to Barney, "but by god I've never seen a cowboy as mixed up as you're supposed to be."

When it came Mr. Duncan's turn, we got him some half-rotten posts we had pulled out of an old fence. He had some of the students pile these in a flat place south of the bunkhouse, and just before dark and just after chuck, as he called supper, he started a fire, banged on Sill's old dinner bell, and the seminar started. The students gathered in a circle, sitting on the ground, and Professor Duncan took up a spot near the fire where the firelight could flicker on his face. Must have been hot though. One good spark from those popping chunks of juniper, and he could have had a hot new hole about where those levis bent tight across his butt. "You boys," Mr. Duncan said to us, "just as well join in. We may even be talking about you and you wouldn't want us to talk behind your backs, would you?" He chuckled a bit. Even in that half-light you could tell how good he felt about himself. So we pulled in behind the circle.

"Let us start with the cowboy," Professor Duncan announced. "But starting with the cowboy we also have to start with his horse. For the cowboy and his horse were inseparable. Some said they were a centaur."

"Myth. Myth," shouted some of the students.

"Perhaps. Perhaps," said Professor Duncan. "But remember in any case that we are concerned with the cowboy's mythic dimensions as well as with his matter-of-factness."

"Please, sir," said one of the students, "will you define what you mean by mythic dimensions."

"I gave that to you in a lecture back home," Professor Duncan answered. "Where are your notes?"

"I got my notes with me, sir, but I can't read 'em in this crummy light."

"Well, look it up when you get back to the bunkhouse."

"The light's pretty crummy there too, sir, but if you want me to I'll wait till morning."

"Do that, son," the professor went on. "Do that, so that we can get on. As a matter of fact, the cowboy spent so much time in the saddle that he became bowlegged."

"Documentation. Documentation," a student called.

"Hough. Emerson," the professor replied. *"The Story of the Cowboy,* 1897."

"Exact page. Exact page," a student shouted.

"George," the professor said, "go get the book."

"What's the call number, sir?" George said.

"Never mind the call number. Just go find it." We could tell that Professor Duncan was starting to feel a little bit like an old cow horse with a horsefly on his rump.

"But, sir, you said always get the call number first." Still George got up, disappeared into the bunkhouse, and finally came back with a book.

Professor Duncan took it, opened it, shoved it into about fifteen places in the air trying to catch some light, and finally began to read. "His legs are bowed, with the curve which constant horseback riding in early youth always gives. Page 34."

"I still don't believe it," the student went on.

The professor's smile stopped, as if he had chewed down on a stink bug in his silage.

"He doesn't say how many cowboys he studied," the student went on. "He doesn't say how many legs he looked at. How do we know the sample is adequate?"

"But he was a historian," the professor answered. "He had to know what he was writing about. He even had a book published by the Yale University Press."

We could see that last was a telling blow.

"I still don't believe it," the student persisted. "It's probably all a part of the myth."

"I move we have a committee on legs," another student said, and there was a big roar of laughter around the fire. "We could go at this whole thing scientifically—anybody here who doesn't believe in science?—study a bunch of legs. All you'd have to have is a straight board to run from the crotch to the ground and a ruler to measure from the board to the knee."

"But where are we going to find enough nineteenth-century legs?" a student said. "We can't go around digging up old graveyards. All we got around here are twentieth-century legs."

About then I could suddenly feel my boots and some sort of sign went up my pants like a fast-running wood tick. Barney and Mont moved too.

"Legs are legs," somebody shouted. "In the same conditions, that's a constant."

About then, when it seemed that science was going to win out, we sort of backed away into the darkness and took up our secret quarters behind a wall of hay bales. "I'll be damned," Barney grumbled, "if I'm going to let somebody put a cold board between my warm crotch and the cold ground."

"Not even that Dr. Assumption?" Mont said.

"Especially not that Dr. Assumption," Barney answered.

"Of course it would be good to help out that other fellow," I said. "The one that had the book published."

"I wouldn't let him use that board," Sill said, "even if he wrote all of Ezekiel and damn near all of Amos."

Turned out we were safe. Turned out when morning came that things had changed. It wasn't that the committee had forgotten about legs, just that the next day belonged to the twentieth century and Dr. Assumption wasn't interested in legs, at least not in legs that weren't her own.

One seminar should have been enough for all us cowboys. We should have done what Pulley suggested in the first place. We should have loaded up the old chuckwagon and hit the trail. By going slow we could have made Mabel's in three days. With three days back, that would have come to six, and then the seminars would have all been over. But cowboys are a lot like yearling cattle. They're curious. Put up a tent out on the range, and within a couple of hours every goddamn steer within two miles will be gathered round trying to see what's going on inside.

So when Dr. Assumption opened up the seminar in the twentieth century, we were all there. And this time the backing away wasn't going to be so easy. Seems the doctor of philosophy thought gathering around camp fires was what she called a bunch of romantic crap. So she stuffed the whole herd of us into the bunkhouse. Still, there were some smells that were better than the usual run, and we were just settling down to enjoy a few of these when she opened up.

"First I want to say to the hands that when you need to fart it's all right to do so. We know you live mostly on beans, so we know you are naturally flatulent. And all of us need to smell the cowboy as he really smells."

She had us right off. We couldn't come up with any answer to that. Even if we had practiced a *yes mam* the way we had practiced that song, we couldn't have got it out. All we could do was hang in there and wonder if anybody would yell "Documentation." But all the students did was look around and smile a shitty understanding smile.

Well, that was about as high as our higher education was going to go. When we finally got a chance to make our break for what Mr. Duncan might have called our natural freedom, we were seminared right up to the throat latch. When the doctor finally slowed down her talk enough to let a fellow shove in, Mont raised his hand.

"Yes?" she said. "You have a question?"

"No, mam," Mont answered. "Just something I need to say."

"Go on," she said.

"Well, as you know, mam, cowboys don't work no ordinary eight-hour day. They slave pretty much from sunrise to sunset. Which means, mam, that these hands had better go recover their needed strength."

The doctor smiled her doctor's smile, and we slowly trailed out. And when we hit some solid ground a long, long rope away, Mont said, "By god, I feel like I been damn near stoned to death by pea-sized pieces of cow shit."

That was the end of our seminaring, except for one last bit. We were having a smoke in the shade of the cowshed when this kid turned up, looking around, hunting for some more of that Western Experience. Probably what he wanted to see was our legs.

"Howdy," he said.

"Howdy," we said.

"Great life you fellows live," he said.

"None better," Burt said. "Even if a fellow's legs do get bowed, it's a good life."

"I knew Professor Duncan was right all the time," the student said.

"Hell, yes," Mont said. "I know a fellow makes a good living just nailing coffins together especially for cowboys. Your plain

---

108 / The Western Experience

ordinary ones won't do. Too narrow where the legs fit in. Of course some undertakers take care of that problem while the carcass is still warm and bendy. Five feet of good half-inch rope wrapped several times around will usually pull the knees close enough together so the guy will fit. Even in a fairly skinny box."

"Come on," the kid said. "You're pulling my leg. After all I'm not a greenhorn."

"We don't know that, son," Burt said. "You show us your horns and Barney will show you his bare bowed legs."

Turned out to be a lot of fun. He was a good kid who knew we were putting him on. He enjoyed it so much he squatted down too. Burt offered him a smoke but he said he had his own makin's. He did too, a sack and a packet of papers, and when he had a thing rolled that looked like a dirty white coyote turd, he lit up.

"There is one thing," I said. "Never mind about those legs. What about that other matter? You got a book in there to prove that too?"

"It's not exactly a book," he answered. "It's what we call a periodical."

"Who wrote the periodical?" Burt said. "That guy been in that Yale Press too?"

"It's not who wrote the periodical," the kid explained. "It's who the periodical cites although it doesn't really cite him. It just says he told the truth about cowboys."

"What outfit did he work for?" I said.

"What do you mean, what outfit?" the kid answered.

"I mean like the Dotted Lazy Heart," I said. "Or the Flying W B."

"His name is Mel Brooks, and his outfit is something like the MGM."

"That on the hip or the shoulder?" Mont said.

"Oh, you mean a brand," the kid said. "He's not a cowboy. He's just a maker of movies."

"Oh," we said in a chorus.

"We know about those dudes," Burt said.

"You do?" the kid said.

"Hell, yes," Mont answered. "We had one of those dumb bastards around here for about a week."

Finally, but not a damn bit too soon, the Western Experience was over. They loaded up their suitcases, guitars, the mouth organ on the end of a leather string, and the small library of selected titles, and prepared to head back to civilization, as one of the students told us, not a damn bit too soon. Dr. Assumption started up the four-wheeler, Professor Duncan waved his genuine Stetson, the students gave us one last look, and off the western wagons rolled.

"By god," Mont said, "if that isn't a happy sight. I haven't felt so good since we watched the disappearing assholes of that herd of breachy steers."

So we headed for the bunkhouse to rest up while we had a peaceful smoke.

But even before we could get comfortable, Burt said, "Say, Mont, where the hell's your saddle blanket?" We all looked up at the empty wire, and Mont yelled, "By god she's gone." We scrambled around, looked under all the bunks, felt in all the dark corners. Then Mont yelled, "By god she's been stole."

"We can still head 'em off," I said. But there was no time to rope and saddle the horses. Barney ran as fast as his newly bowed legs would let him and started up the old John Deere, ugly as ever. The loader was still on out front, so Burt and Mont jumped in, dried steer or not, Sill straddled the hood, and I hooked my boots on the rear coupling bar. Barney put the dirty green monster in 4 and off we roared. You could say we headed for the pass.

Straight up the bottom of the draw you could save maybe half a mile, if you didn't mind sagebrush as big as a goddamn tree, thickets of greasewood, and on the open places quimp mounds as big as a buffalo's butt. Barney set the hand throttle all the way down, took aim for the pass right between the heads of Burt and Mont and scrunched down in the loader, and held the old Deere steady. All we had to do was hang on, duck the flying sticks, tossed up quimps and cow dust, and hope we could make it to the pass in time.

The lead four-wheeler had just eased down the last long turn around the side of the hill when Barney swung the old John

110 / The Western Experience

Deere across the road. The Western Experience pulled to a dead stop, and Dr. Assumption shoved her denim boots to the ground.

"I see you men are seeing us off in the grand style," she said. "True to the myth and all that. I'll wager Professor Duncan put you up to it."

"This here's a posse, mam," Mont said.

"And you're probably Matt Dillon," she answered.

"There's been a robbery," Mont went on.

"No doubt," she answered. "It wouldn't be the Wells Fargo office, would it?"

"No, mam," Mont said. "Just the bunkhouse. Saddle blanket missing."

"Come on, cowboy," she said. "Can't you make up something better than that?"

"No need to," Mont answered.

By then the students had piled out of the bus and were crowding around. Professor Duncan was looking serious. "Anyone know anything about a saddle blanket?" he said.

A student pushed forward. "Sure," she said. "I took it. It wasn't doing any good up there on that wire gathering dust. Besides, you know, after all you and John Wayne have done to the Indians, you don't deserve to have it."

"Just hand it over, mam," Mont said. "Never mind about John Wayne and the Indians."

The student disappeared into the bus, came back, and shoved the blanket to Mont. "There," she said. "There's your old blanket."

"Thank you, mam," Mont said. And turning to Dr. Assumption, he lifted his hat in a fancy way and said, "It's been a real pleasure to make your acquaintance, mam. I trust you'll not encounter further difficulties as you travel through life."

With that, Barney shoved the John Deere into 2, swung around the western caravan, and started up the road to home. We'd had enough brush running for one day.

Mont spread the blanket carefully on the wire, and we settled down in our bunks.

"By god, Mont," Burt said, "that was the best show I've seen since Gary Cooper quit the trail. That Mel Brooks knew anything about making good movies, he'd be right out here to sign you up."

I said, "I haven't seen so much truth since Pulley sold his old bull to that pilgrim packer."

But we had more important things to talk about.

"You know," Burt said, "I still think three hands is not enough."

"And there's other things we haven't figured in," Mont said.

"Like what?" Burt said.

"Like maybe if he wants to bad enough. Could be he'll try to find some way. Could be he'll take up sailing like a flying squirrel or walking wires with his toes. As Sill was saying, it all comes down to motive. And there ain't nothing a proud mouse would rather do than piss on a poor cowboy's blanket."

THE EXHIBITIONIST

"The public has a right to privacy."
—Anon.

Any one of us would have given the biggest rosette from his oldest hat band to have been there. Altogether we would have been willing to pass up a free renewal to the combination offer we'd somehow never got around to taking. This kid shows up one day, says he's working his way through college, says every American home needs at least a couple of periodicals. Turned out we knew something about college and not a hell of a lot about periodicals, so we listened. He said he thought he could put both the *Hereford Journal* and *Playboy* in our hands for about twenty percent off. But we didn't even have the down payment. Burt offered the calf hide we had drying on the bunkhouse wall. The kid said he sure would like to put those two fine periodicals in our hands, but he didn't think Mr. Lummer back there in Pinville was about to take that calf hide, not with the hair still on and some of the hair sort of streaked with green. The kid never did come back. It wouldn't have mattered anyway. We never did get around to building up a pot for periodicals, and that calf hide got to looking less and less like a thing worth trading.

Still, we would have given that much and more to have been there. We pieced her together pretty much, maybe even adding in a special touch or two, but however tight we had the pieces fitting, it wasn't the same as being there. History don't often come running across our ranges, so when she does, by god a man ought to have a chance to get in the way. Maybe he'll be knocked flatter than a soft cow turd in a big baking pan, but at least he'll know from the wheel tracks across his withers that he's been there.

The first piece, the one that made our ears jump straight up, was the sudden sight of Barney's sorrel, dragging his reins and packing Barney's old high-pommeled saddle, empty as a piss pot full of bullet holes. Still it wasn't the sorrel or even the empty saddle that made us guess that something damn near like a half-assed miracle had jumped the fence and was running bare nekkid down the feed yard trail. It was Barney's old blue shirt and Barney's old blue pants hanging limp as a tired rag from the horn of the saddle.

The second piece came along a few days later. It was second-hand, but we could no more throw it out because it was streaked with doubt than we could have stopped believing what the ashes told us if old Elijah's flaming buckboard had suddenly landed smack on the dry top of Pulley's bales. The word came from old Joe Tittler, who was sober as a preacher's mother and damn near as honest as the weigh scales on the back road to heaven. He sold a spring steer to Pulley one year and took off an even buck from Pulley's bid of thirty. "He ain't all meat," Tittler said. "Look up in there where his balls used to be, you'll find damn near five pounds of good hard mud. Never did figure out how the hell he got it stuck up there. Must have walked straddle a new wet ditch bank one time."

Seems Tittle was riding along this low ridge looking for his old brindle cow when this apparition caught his eye. Only it wasn't an apparition. "I should have stopped looking," Tittle said. "I should have pulled old Perk around. I should have remembered he's good at coming around with the reins though he ain't worth a shit when you want him to get going forward. Many a cow I've lost while old Perk kept turning when the goddamn cow hadn't ever thought about it. Or maybe I should have shut my eyes. The sun was too damn bright anyway. The old woman's always saying, 'Joe, why the hell don't you stop looking away off there in the bright sunlight. Your left eye's damn near as cloudy as that left thing Perk thinks he's using to see with.' But I didn't. I just kept staring. Something about a strange sight that keeps a man looking. Like that time I was passing Mabel's place when the wind was blowing. Probably that same damn cow I was hunting. In all that breeze you would have thought maybe she would have pinned a rock or an old clevis to the rear hem, but by god she just shoved the whole front part of her deep down into that clothes basket and that wind let go. Could be, she'd had a rock pinned back there, it would come all of the way over and banged her right between the ears."

Seems Tittle looked down across the flat and there was this guy trotting limpy along the hardpan. "First thing I saw he was toting a flag. Next time I saw he was bare nekkid except for his hat and his boots. Then I studied that damn flag, and it wasn't no flag. Didn't have a goddamn star any place. Didn't have any more stripes than a skunk at the bottom of a deep well on a dark night. Turned out to be a pair of men's shorts on the end of a stick. But in between that hat and those boots, that was the hard part. Even if I was beginning to get to know that flag, I was still a long way from putting the right name on that stretch of skin. And then I sort of backed up and come at it another way. Looking at that skin was about like studying a steer with the hide off. So I fixed in on the hat and then I read the brand on those boots. And then I was ready to say out loud to myself, 'By god, that's Barney Tullus.'"

The next part took some guessing. By the time Joe Tittle got the word to us, Barney had come in, unhooked his pants and shirt from the high-pommeled saddle and had no more hide showing than a schoolmarm on a cold night. When Mort said, "Barney, how come you running bare-assed through the salt grass?" Barney simply grunted. Dig a spur into a tired horse on a steep hill and you get the same clear answer. When Burt added, "Barney, what you using on the sunburn, saddle soap or axle grease?" he opened up enough to say, "Whatever suits you peeking pricks will suit this old horse fine."

So we had to do some guessing. We had to answer some basic questions and try to make whatever we figured out sort of bunch together. First question: why was he carrying that damn flag? Answer: because she was wet, because Barney had peeled down and poked his old dainties down under the scum in the cow trough to soak a bit, because when the crunch came he'd rather wave them on the end of a stick than slap them cold as a wet ice sack around his still steaming middle. Must have been hot that day. Must have been hot enough to melt the sense out of a rock wrapped in rawhide. The water in that trough looked cool and inviting, even with all that scum and cow slobber and maybe a layer or two of bunched-up wasps. Barney pulled his boots and stacked them on the ground. The pants came next, followed closeup by the shirt. He hooked both outfits to the saddle. Then while the shorts were beginning to linger softly under the cow scum, Barney must have stood for a minute bare as a parsnip in the sunshine. Bare except for his hat. We figure he never did get around to pulling his hat.

Next question: why did the sorrel decide to go off without him? Answer: because he got so badly spooked he trotted seven or eight miles before he remembered he was supposed to be standing back there by that trough acting like a clotheshorse. Question: what spooked him? Answer: some sight so startling he concluded he would get the hell out rather than take a second look at it. At this point all we could do was guess. Maybe he woke up enough for one look back and saw the dainties waving once before they sank. Maybe it wasn't the flag at all. Maybe it was the sudden shine of Barney's bare butt. Whatever his eye caught, it was enough. Faithful or not, he wasn't about to wait around for another chance at that.

This should have been the end of it. Once Barney got his clothes back on and once we figured out how he got them off, things should have started rolling along in the old wheel rut. Trouble was the times were out of joint.

About a week later we had just started an after-supper smoke when this box-like outfit comes down the road. "If that's another goddamn school bus," Mont said, "I quit. I'm taking my blanket and heading out. You boys can tell old Pulley I've had enough experience to see me through. You tell him by god I'd rather shear a herd of stinking sheep."

But it wasn't a school bus after all. Turned out to be a van. So Mont settled down and waited. Wasn't anything right then he had against a van, especially one painted a kind of Hereford red with big white letters we couldn't read until it swung through the gate and pulled up broadside. HERK HIGGINS, RODEO ENTERPRISES, INC. "By god," Mont said, "that's more like it. I'm still going to take that blanket, but this time I'm going to throw it across a bronco's bones."

But it turned out Herk wasn't looking for riders. "Hell, no," he said, "riders is two-bits a dozen. Every damn kid who can tell a bay stud from a bicycle wants to get into the chute. You got to beat 'em off with a piggin' string. No, what your successful rodeo needs today is your specialty act. Riding broncs and bulls ain't in it. Barely break even with stuff like that. But you turn a bare nekkid cowboy out of the chute and by god that crowd really comes alive. Streakin', some calls it. No, riders is out. What I'm looking for is an honest-to-god, genuine streaking cowboy. And according to what I hear over in Pinville, I've come to the right place."

Herk probably didn't know up to that last word which one of us was Barney, but all our heads kind of swung around just enough to put a rough fix on the old Stetson.

"Mr. Tullus," Herk went on, "I'm prepared to make you a real goin' offer. I'm prepared to put as many as fifty smackeroos in your pockets—that is, after you get your pants back on." Herk had to stop to laugh at his joke. "I don't mean fifty bucks a month. I don't mean fifty bucks a week. I mean fifty bucks every time you bust out of that chute. How does that offer hit you?"

We waited for Barney to answer, but Herk wasn't ready to start waiting yet. "Kind a takes your breath away, don't it? But let me refine on it some. You notice I didn't say bare nekkid this time. There was a *little* difference of meaning. That's 'cause I choose my words careful. Not like your ordinary talkers. Some guys I know just let go, like throwing handfuls of powdered cow turds in a wind storm. Now you take *bare nekkid.* You know what those words means to some people? Nudity, that's what it means. You throw even fifty cents worth of that to your honest-to-god skin-fearing everyday Baptist, and by god you better get ready to climb a wall. No, we got to keep the show clean. We got to keep her decent. You can't go the whole way, Mr. Tullus. That's why you got to wear the hat and boots."

He stopped a bit to let the rightness of all that sink in. And while he was held up on the words, he took a long pull on a pint flask he hoisted from his pocket. "Some people can just go on without wetting the old voice chords," he said. "It don't work that way with me. Tone changes somehow. Was working once on a deal—wasn't even a big one, just a middle-sized chance to make a few bucks—you know I started out talkin' bass, but before I got all the ends tied up I was squeakin' like a goddamn tenor."

"How does she look so far, Mr. Tullus?" he went on. The wetness must have seemed just right because he kept on going. "There's added advantages, practical reasons, I could call them, to go along with the spiritual side of it I've already laid bare." He paused again to enjoy his joke. "Take the hat. The hat says cowboy. Remember we're talkin' rodeo. Leave off the hat and you

The Exhibitionist / 117

wouldn't know what the hell was coming out of the chute. Might be a goddamn store clerk or a fast running dentist or maybe even an extra happy school teacher. And the boots. Ever take a long stride with a slick bare foot and hit a cow pie just right? By god a man can slide a hundred feet without even slowing down much. No, we got to take in safety too. Your well-run rodeo always has that important feature."

Herk pulled up, and it sounded like we all started breathing again. Then Burt mumbled, "Well, I'll be goddamned." Could be Barney was getting his mouth ready to say something. Could be Herk saw the movement. "Wait," he said. "Let me fill 'er out some. I said fifty bucks every time you bust out of that chute. We can call that the basic contract. That's a good solid set-up no matter how you look at it. Doubt you can beat it this side of Kansas. But it's your sidelines that really add up. That's where the special money kinda waits. It's that flag that makes the difference. Let me use a few words to set the scene. Five hundred pair of eyes is fixed on that chute. They're waitin' for that rider. Bang! out he comes, Stetson shining in the sun, boots splashing safely through the cow pies. They start to cheer. And then they see what's really special. It's the flag. There on the end of a stick is a big white pair of men's shorts. And there across that stretch of white, big and plain as a black bull on the hardpan: HERK HIGGINS, CLEAN USED CARS." He paused, "May have to cut her down some. May have to settle for HERK'S CARS. Course, anybody knows that old Herk's cars is clean."

"I'll just step into this little moving office of mine," Herk added, "and get the papers. You put your brand on this little contract, Mr. Tullus, and by god you'll be on your way."

But when Herk backed out of the ass-end of the van, Barney was gone.

"Seems like your better-than-average opportunity," Herk said. "Don't see how a man can turn her down. Any of you boys interested? Mr. Tullus has already got what us business men call visibility, but I'm sure we can take a nobody and work him up some."

"Hell, no," Mont said. And that was good enough for the rest of us.

You would have thought that answer would have knocked old Herk clear back on his haunches, but it didn't seem to bother him at all. "Could be you boys'll regret it," he said. "You know, we've all got to look out for the coming thing. Could be you boys will know it came and passed you by. But, as old Bill Hammer said when the hangman let him drop, that's life."

Once we had a missionary come out to save our souls. We gave him the same answer, and he took it with the same cheerful look. Seems some guys get so used to saying a big yes to things they don't even twitch once when somebody heaves in a no. Like that old dog Sill had once. Kept smiling even when he backed into the firebox.

Herk drove his van up the road, and we all sort of laid back and enjoyed the silence. "Old Herk's got some pretty good ideas," Burt said. "If he just wouldn't tie 'em up in all those goddamn words."

The dust barely got settled after the disappearance of Herk's van when Pulley's pickup came roaring down the road. You could tell his feelings were in high gear, because he had the old truck in slow-down second even before he passed the feed yard. The rate he was hurrying to slow down, he was going to need compound to make the last couple of rods before he reached the bunkhouse. He ground up to where the bumper damn near shoved our door, threw the door open with his gloved hand, and stomped out. It was one of those good days for dogs if they had wanted to get in at that steering column.

"All right," he started in, "let's get some crooked things straight. This here is a cow ranch. Cows is four-legged critters that eat grass and hay, and sometimes they get fat enough to make a good piece of meat. Raising cows is *our* business. Selling cows is *our* business. Cussing the goddamn market is *my* business. You got that straight?"

We smiled a sort of dumb agreement. Even those cows could have kept up with the speech so far.

"This means," he went on, "we ain't running any goddamn peep show. This means that I and my cows are not going to put up with any goddamn freaks. You can call me old-fashioned. You can say the times have passed me by. But by god when I think of a cowboy I think of a man. Anybody who wants to flaunt his bare ass to the whole goddamn world is no cowboy. He better turn in his spurs and join the cricus."

We kept smiling.

"You got that, Tullus?" Pulley said.

We kept smiling.

"All right." This last was almost softly said. Could be, did the old man good to come out and cuss us around. Let the lid loose a bit. Better than shooting at an unseen target like the BLM.

"Keep those cows in good shape," he added. Then he climbed slowly back into the pickup and drove up the road.

We listened to the silence again and then Mont said, "This cow ranch may not be a peep show, but it sure as hell is getting to be a good place for giving speeches. Maybe we ought to give up on that wooden tub and have the old man put in a pulpit."

This certainly should have been the end of it, even if the run of things couldn't hold up on that other stopping place. But when the times are out of joint, by god they're really out of joint. Only thing to do is sit back and ride her out.

This time history had a witness, though I was some way off and I sure would rather not believe I saw what happened. You could say we were doing exactly what the old man said to do. You could say we had our minds on cows. You could say if we had been watching out for anything else Barney wouldn't have walked into that trap.

One morning I said to Barney, "You and me don't need the old man to tell us to get those big steers out of that cottonwood wash."

"We sure as hell don't," Barney said.

We saddled up and rode the two or three miles to where a spring ran out of a thicket of maples and poked along down a little valley. We called it a wash though the water flowed most of the year, seeping a couple of meadows green and keeping a long jungle of cottonwoods and willows more than half alive. And back from the bottom were strands of scrub oak thick enough to scratch the hide off a steel-plated jackass. If you were a lazy steer, there wasn't a better place to spend a summer day, with enough water, lots of shade, some grass, and considerable cow company.

"Barney," I said, "I'll take the hill and you take the bottom."

If he had spoken first, it would have been the other way around.

"You got those chaps on your saddle," I said. "Besides you're shorter. The limbs won't knock you down so easy. And besides that old sorrel don't like to walk where one leg needs to be shorter than the other."

I had him. So he spurred the sorrel down into the cottonwoods, and I moved on an easy angle to where I would be above the oak and where I could see what moved ahead.

"You better get those chaps off that saddle and around your side bones," I called. But he didn't stop, and I couldn't hear what he was saying, though it didn't take much more than a spoonful of brains to make a damn good guess.

So I rode along, enjoying the view, letting my horse pick his own easy way. I even tried one soft chorus of that song we all knew so well. Poking along a half mile or more, we had come to where I could look down on what we called the upper meadow, a patch of green as big as the floor of a barn or two. I was thinking it was kinda pretty. I was thinking it would be a good place for a picnic or a pageant when suddenly, even way up on that hill, I could hear a chorus of squealing. And before I could even catch on to the tune, this guy in a Stetson hat shot out of the cottonwoods above the meadow. He was limpy as hell with all those holes the cows had made and those boot heels not made for running. And right behind him, as close as a pack of coyotes on the tail of a crippled calf, scrambled a herd of screaming women. He made it to the next bunch of cottonwoods just barely two or three jumps ahead, and then the whole shitteree disappeared into the woodworks. I couldn't see a hair and the yells kept getting louder. Then for a minute or two the excitement seemed stuck in one place. I was just beginning to think the race was over, when it picked up again and rushed toward the lower meadow. I and my horse were watching and kinda cheering in our hearts when old Barney shot out again, still limpy in those boots, but this time as bare as a pine pole with the bark off. By god, they had picked him clean. But somehow he must have grabbed back his boots and yanked them on on the run.

Now I have to fill out history again with some guesses. I could have poked around down there like a two-bit detective with a fancy paper from a home-study school. I could have asked every question in the teaching book. But it wouldn't have changed things a bit. It wouldn't have put Barney's shirt back on, let alone his pants and whatever else he was using to hide his sirloins. And besides, there could have been some danger in it. Even if that pant-pulling posse turned out to be a high-cultured outfit like the Pie Baking and Poetry Society, I wasn't about to take any chances by going down into the cottonwoods to find out what the hell they were singing.

So I'm guessing when I say those ladies were down there in that bunch of cottonwoods hard at it having a picnic. Barney's watching for cows, cussing the limbs that keep grabbing at the Stetson. He's on foot now, pulling the sorrel behind him, cussing the sorrel too because the sorrel thinks he has sense enough to wonder why the hell they don't get out where the going is easier. The sorrel probably has his ears up. He can hear that picnic even if old Barney can't. Suddenly Barney breaks through the last line of trees, fighting his way with his hat pulled down, even out into the clear, damn near, you could say, right into the thick of society. It is the jerk at the end of the reins that stops him. That sorrel knows, even if Barney don't, when he's gone far enough.

"It's the streaker!" someone yells. And there is a general cackle of excitement.

And then there must have come a terrible and saddening disappointment. Here was the streaker, but he wasn't any more streaking than he was blowing the trumpet of Gabriel. Suppose a time had come when you had begun to wake up to each plain old ordinary morning thinking, maybe something different will happen today. The church will catch on fire, or Cary Grant will stop at the drive-in for a sandwich.

So they felt cheated. They couldn't wait any longer. Some of them had been about ready to give up and go back to watching the sun go down. So they jumped in. You could say they took things into their own hands.

From here on matters get down to something pretty damn near close to the facts. At least let's say my figuring has the feel of truth in it. After Barney lopes limpy across the second meadow, he's had it. He couldn't have made it to the next meadow if a grizzly

122 / *The Exhibitionist*

bear had joined in the chase. But so have the ladies. They're winded as a herd of heifers at the top of a hill, and besides some of them are starting to blush. Barney's safe, except that all he's got between him and the daylight is a pair of high-heeled boots.

But this time Barney still has a couple of things on his side. The sorrel for one. The sorrel probably took a long second look at the picnic and thought to himself, by god save me from that, I guess I'll go back to being a pack mule. So he waited in the cottonwoods. He probably seemed glad to see old Barney stumble up beside him, even with all that bareness showing. Could be he said to himself, times is sure as hell changing. Time was, you could tell a cowboy from a movie star, but by god not any more. Life sure as hell has shot round a corner.

The other thing Barney had on his side was his own mulishness. He was too stubborn to stop and put those chaps on, even when the brush got so tight he couldn't stop to take a leak without aiming around a tree. Those chaps were still tied to the back of the saddle, riding there as useless as the hair on a wagon tongue. So when he got back to the sorrel, he had that much in the way of apparel. You could say he would now have the best-covered legs in a half-dozen sections, and the barest butt.

But there was still another thing that could come to his rescue. And it was the good sense of the sorrel that again made it likely. Between the hair blanket and the saddle, Barney used an old cotton cover, folded to a two-and-a-half-by-five. It was faded and dirty and about as fancy as a grey sock, but it was softer than leather. A man in trouble could loosen the cinches, pull it from beneath the saddle, fold it in a new way, shove it down under and inside the chaps belt, and come up with something damn near like a breechcloth. I didn't see Barney do this, but I was there in front of the bunkhouse when he rode in, bare as a melon from the waist up, breeches and cloth from the waist down. He slipped down from the saddle and limped into the bunkhouse, the breechcloth swinging out behind him. And all the time he was as silent as a horned toad in a snowstorm.

When the bunkhouse door banged shut, we sort of breathed together. Mont looked at the door, then back at the panting sorrel. "Well, I'll be goddamned," he said.

That should have been the end of it. You could tell from the way Barney shut that door that he was about ready to roll himself in a long rawhide and crawl into a deep dark hole. But the next day we barely got into our evening smoke when the dust started rolling down the ranch road. We were just getting ready to stiffen ourselves some when the dust eased back and that old red van rolled into view.

We waited while Herk stopped the motor and stepped out. You could read ENTERPRISE all over him.

"You boys are in luck again," he started in.

"You need some riders?" Mont said.

"Hell, no," Herk said. "Riders is still out."

"You need another genuine bare-assed streaker?" Burt said.

"Hell, no," Herk said. "They're out too. Didn't last long at all. Coulda predicted it was a passing thing. Knew enough to keep my contracts down on that one."

Again we waited.

"No, I'm looking for a different talent this time," Herk went on. "What the entertainment market can use right now is your genuine good old-fashioned Indian. Nekkidness is out. They won't pay three bits to see any more of that. It's the leggins that's in, the leggins and the breech cloth. By god, you get a man done up in those things and you've got a winner."

Mont said, "I'll be goddamned."

"Of course, that ain't all of it," Herk rushed on. "That's only your base contract. The real money's in the fringes. What you might call your fringe benefit." He laughed to himself. "I should say in the breechcloth. I figure we ought to get a least a dozen or so letters on the ass-end of that breechcloth. Can't you just see the sweep of it? The chute swings open. Here comes this genuine good old-fashioned Indian, a war dancing around the cow pies. And there on his tail cloth, a-swinging in the summer sun: HERK'S USED CARS. By God, don't it just give you a thrill up and down the heart strings!"

124 / *The Exhibitionist*

THE EVALUATION

When the late summer turned dry and the prospects for good winter range looked dim, we were ordered to cut the winter herd down to the brood cows, a few big calves to keep things lively, and a couple of old bulls that had earned the right to stay out of the dog-food factory. It began to look like a good quiet autumn. There were some fences to fix, the pasture pond to clean out, but mostly we intended to spend our days taking in the low warm sun on the south front porch or drinking coffee around Sill's old Monarch stove.

But then there came a disturbing factor. His name was Ef. Probably there was more to it, maybe Efferdent or Efficiency or even Effervescence. We never did know. He arrived at the ranch one morning toting a clipboard, said he had been sent out by Mr. Pulley, said he was to make a study of the whole goddamn operation, especially the personnel, which was us, the cowboys. Even with that clipboard and the pencil he kept poking out in the air, we could tell Ef was still mostly cowboy. Even if the saddle sweat had dried on his britches, he had that crazy look that comes from watching too many cows. He had that scrunched up, scrawny look of having sucked in too much cow dust and cheap Bull Durham. The difference was the clipboard, that and the new vision it represented. Seems he had earned that clipboard by graduating from the Flat Mountain Home Study College of Management.

"It's the whole new thing," he announced. "Time was when you could put a cow and bull together and trail the outcome off to market. Time was when you could tell a good cowboy by the thumbs he had left. But now there's management. Now there's a new way of measuring things. Time will come"—he flapped the clipboard even higher—"when the whole shebang, cows, cowboys, everything, right down to the last golden grain of cow shit, will be run by a goddamn computer."

So Mr. Ef jumped right into business. Even before we had time to take in the grandeur of that last prophecy, he had his pencil ready with the hammer back. "First there's creativity. Anybody knows," he said, "there's got to be creativity. A cowboy may tie a good knot. A cowboy may keep a saddle from slipping on a steep hill. But unless he's creative, he's not in there. I can't give him points. I can't even let this goddamn pencil get close to the paper. Then there's evaluation. A lot of points come out of that—data, we call 'em before we add 'em up."

We could already see that we might have to choose between the fence and the pond, and some of that coffee was going to have a long cold wait.

"And then there's service," he added. "We sure as hell got to take that into account."

"Service?" Mont said. "God, Barney's going to be mighty weak in that department. He ain't even had an erection lately, not since his sorrel spooked at a beer can and bruised Barney's pizzle on the saddle horn. Barney says it's those goddamn chaps. He's been working on a rawhide codpiece ever since."

"Then she pretty much comes down to evaluations," Burt said. "He sure as hell ain't created much, and even if we don't take any points off for service—just give him a zero—he's still got to come out of that evaluation looking like a winner, or Mr. Pulley's going to move him back to oven hand or toilet guard. I can hear old Pulley saying it now, 'By god, Tullus, there was a time when I would have paid you thirty bucks a month and all the beef and beans you needed. You didn't earn it then, and by god I ain't seen no proof that you can earn it now.'"

So we got down to work on the evaluations. What Mr. Ef said was that we had to have some way of measuring the whole picture as he liked to call it. This meant that we couldn't just settle for what Mr. Pulley said we were worth, although Mr. Pulley would decide what we were paid whatever the evaluations said we were worth. We couldn't just throw in what the outfit thought about each cowboy. That allowed too much room for what Mr. Ef called disturbing factors, and a whole saddlebag full of things that didn't have a hell of a lot to do with cow work. A guy might lose points because his socks smelled like a bucket of rotten potatoes when he pulled off his boots at night. A guy might lose points because he snored not just when he slept on his back but when he stretched out on both sides and his belly too. A guy might lose points because he didn't keep his beans to himself, especially if he slept on the top bunk and rattled the bed boards a bit. He might even lose points in cow work if his rope was an extra four feet long, not because he could throw a loop that far, but because even that much rope would help the coil look good as it hung on the side of his saddle. All of us had our ways of being a little dudey. And all of us knew that even if we could fool each other by agreement and Mr. Ef by the same agreement, we couldn't fool Mr. Pulley. We could hear him shouting to Mr. Ef, "Hold the horses. You haven't taken any points off for all those goddamn spurs that keep scratching up my chuckhouse floor."

Mr. Ef said we had to have a judgment from another point of view. Who's most concerned with how the cowboy does his job? We would have thought that question pointed straight at Mr. Pulley, but we knew now that evaluations were a brand new game. We knew his question wasn't moving in that direction any more than it was moving toward the bunkhouse committee on songs and sanitation. Who knows the cowboys best? Who knows when a brand has been burned too deep? Who knows the pain when her baby boy has had his balls cut off with a knife that needed at least five more strokes on the old whetstone?

Sill spoke aloud for the rest of us, "By god he means the cows theirselves."

"There's the answer," Mr. Ef beamed. "We got to let the cows evaluate the cowboys. I ask you again, does anybody know the cowboys better?"

He had us. We had to agree with that.

So we set about the evaluation. Mr. Ef said he wanted our help and cooperation. "You boys know the situation," he went on. "What we got to do is to set up a way of measuring, a way that will give us some data." We were already learning that that was just about his favorite word.

"If we had some way of measuring push and shove," Sill opened up, "we could bend Barney over a couple of bales of hay, tie a red neckerchief across his butt, and bring in that old brindle cow who thinks life is just one long happy bull fight."

Sill's idea seemed to have some hair on it. The rest of us took our turns in suggesting the finer points.

"Wouldn't be hard," Mont said, "to step off the yards the bales slide each time."

"Yards slid times times she makes a run at her target. That," said Burt, "would give us a number. We ought to be able to do something with that."

But Mr. Ef held up his pencil. "Wait," he said. "That would give us data all right, but it would be what we call negative data. If that old cow knocked Barney nine yards in three tries, that would give Barney an average score of three. But if she knocked Mont four yards in three runs, that would give Mont a point three, three, three, and you can follow those threes forever, right up to and including the time when your pencil ain't nothing but a speck of lead. Just an unending string of threes disappearing in the distance like an old cow trail."

We could tell Ef had been knocked gently in the head by the poetry of numbers. When he hit those threes, his eyes shone like he had a bad case of the rabbit fever.

"Where was I?" Ef said.

"You were just disappearing," Sill said, "on an old cow trail."

"Wait. I got it," Ef said. "We had some data, but it was negative data. We could even say it measured the dislike factor. We've got to back up and try another hill. We've got to get some positive data. We've got to let those cows show how much they care."

So we figured out another scheme. It was as simple as this: put the cowboy in the middle of the branding corral. He could be squatting on a bale of hay, but the hay would not be the main component, as Ef called the element that made the cows feel good and come in close. The hay would simply be a seat. We could even set a saddle on it. Ef admitted the hay itself could be a disturbing factor, but when we considered what might happen if we borrowed one of the chairs from Sill's kitchen, we went along with the hay. We weren't about to create a real disturbance.

The cowboy would hold a pie plate full of salt in his lap. Or if Sill decided to ride a tight herd on his plates, we could even get by with a board, as long as it was big enough to hold a couple of fistsful of rock salt. But even before Mr. Ef had a chance to give his evaluation of this evaluation scheme, we saw disturbing factors showing through like hungry calves along a rusty fence.

"Salt," said Burt, "is an unpredictable cow taste. I've known cows to lay around a salt ground without paying any more attention to a block of salt than they would pay to a pile of books, even if those books made up a complete set of reports from the Department of Agriculture for the years 1874 to 1903. And I've known cows to climb a yellow pine just to lick the poisoned salt in a porcupine box. We can't depend on their coming into this scheme with an even taste."

"Chopped grain's the way to go," Mont said. "Only thing more dependable would be a bucket of beet pulp coated over with about two inches of good molasses. Or maybe a couple of gallons of whiskey mash."

We had the chopped grain, and we didn't have the beet pulp, let alone the whiskey mash.

"That finalizes it," Ef said. "That sure as hell ought to give us enough data."

With Mr. Ef riding point, we set up the evaluation. He ran around the branding corral, waving a clipboard in one hand and a pencil in the other, and we pretended to follow directions. We put Barney on a milking stool about a turd's toss from the chute gate. "That stool's got the ring of rightness about it," Ef said. "No disturbing factors in an old milk stool."

"Suppose," Mont said, "suppose she thinks it *is* a milking stool. Suppose she ain't in the mood to have old Barney squeeze her tits."

But the rightness of that stool was ringing too loud. Ef didn't seem to hear. He had that clipboard waving in the air and that rabbit fever in his eyes, and we knew that if he didn't damn soon get something to put down on it he was going to wet his pants, or maybe just fly off across the pasture like a one-winged turkey buzzard.

We put a bucket of chopped barley on Barney's lap or the next best thing to a lap. You couldn't say that Barney was bowlegged, but you could say that his thighs were just about as parallel as the shanks of a sawhorse. His knees hadn't touched since that time he got both feet caught in a posthole. When the bucket was firm, we let the first cow out of the chute.

"Quiet," yelled Ef. "We got to wait. We got to let her size up Barney in her own cow way."

We sat on the top fence pole and waited, and Ef waited too,

ready to jump down into the dust and dung with his clipboard. The old Hereford cow worked her way out beyond the chute a bit, each step heavy in hoof, her sharp hip bones poking up with each shift of weight. She must have sniffed the barley even through her scarred and snotty nostrils. If she could have shut her tired old eyes, she might have made it, but maybe seven feet away she stopped and studied Barney.

It was too much, the look on Barney's face, at least what we could see of it beneath the droopy Stetson and the back end of that old cow. It was what Sill might have called a juxtaposition. It was a position all right, whichever way you looked at it, and we let loose with a snicker that would have done a girls' school proud. The old cow ambled around to see what the hell was going on, and then she began backing toward Barney. When she finally pulled up, she could have knocked off Barney's Stetson with one stiff swing of her tail.

Ef jumped in, yelling, "Measure! Measure!"

Mont said, "Which end you going to measure?"

But that rightness was still ringing for Ef. If he heard Mont's question, it didn't give him cause to pause. While the old cow sidled off to one side and watched, he stamped around looking at tracks and measuring, measuring. I don't think I ever saw a clipboard cowboy so happy in his work. But finally he reined himself in, smiled over at us, and announced what he called the formula: "We're going to subtract the rear-end distance from the front-end distance and take the square root of the difference."

"Well, I'll be goddamned," Mont said. "I never would have guessed it could be so simple."

So we shoved the other cows in one at a time. One of them even moved up close enough to sniff the barley. She put her nose over the edge of the bucket. Barney did something. Maybe he started humming "Home on the Range" in his own raspy way. Anyway the old cow snorted, blowing a big puff of barley dust like a bib on Barney's shirt. Then she backed away, almost bumping Ef, who was so busy measuring he could have backed himself into a sewing circle.

We kept the cows coming, and Ef kept scratching on that clipboard. Finally all we had left was that old brindle cow. We could tell when we shoved her through the chute that she was chomping to get in there and do some evaluating. She trotted in, her head high, smelling for excitement, her tail at the ready. She swung off to the side, eyeing Barney, not even fixing on the bucket. In fact she made one complete swing around the center of attraction, keeping one old white eye turned like a lens to her target. Then when she had the whole thing measured, she put her head down and hit that milk stool going about fifty miles an hour. The bucket soared, chopped barley rising like a plume in the bright summer air. Barney soared too in a lesser orbit, and then he bounced once in the fresh cow shit and came to rest against the far bottom pole.

In the meantime Ef had jumped in and was trying to figure out how to measure all that sidling around. He should have stayed up on that top pole. Trying to measure where that old brindle cow was moving was like tracking a sun-struck hog with two short legs on the same blind side. But he kept after the measuring, and when the old cow had sniffed Barney a couple of times while he played dead, she looked up and took in Ef wth her mean old eyes. We could even tell what she was thinking. It was as if she had stopped in a meditative mood and said to herself, "By god I think I'll just meander over and evaluate the evaluator."

It was the blowing that gave her away. By the time she got up full speed she was sounding like Pulley's old steam tractor. Ef heard her just in time, turned, saw the oncoming rush of doom, and hit for the fence in something between a foot race and a stove explosion. He scrambled up that pine ladder like a squirrel with its tail on fire, banging the clipboard on every goddamn pole. Afterward when we remembered the sound of it, it had the pleasant musical rhythm of a stick rubbed along the old picket fence.

That was the end of the data gathering. The cows went back to eating and chewing their cuds, and we went back to waiting as long as we could before we started in to fix the winter fences. Mr. Ef went off some place where there was a wide table and a new pencil and worked on his report. We knew that when Ef was done, when he had his data all squared and rooted, he would give the word to Mr. Pulley. And we knew that Mr. Pulley would try hard to figure out what the hell it all meant and that when he had it figured out, or when he reached the end of his rope and said out loud to himself, "By god, I should have quite the cow business when I was still young enough to take up dancing in a vaudeville show," we would hear about it.

So we waited. And then one morning before we even had time to plan our coffee break, Mr. Pulley's pickup came roaring down the hill. As usual he could have got there faster if he had shifted into first gear, but as usual he got there with more determination by coming full speed in second. When he turned her off, she dieseled a bit, and that gave us a chance to evaluate his mood. When he was really fired up, he could talk over a small Cat or a middle-sized John Deere with the muffler off. But when he was waiting for his anger to decide just how fierce it needed to be, he sometimes let the pickup finish talking.

When the pickup finished, he still didn't cut loose, and we could tell he was undecided. "Mr. Ef must have turned in some good recommendations," I said. "He sure worked hard at all that measuring."

"He's a real artist with a clipboard," Mont added.

But all this pleasant talk wasn't deciding anything. "He didn't recommend a goddamn thing," Pulley finally said. "It was his job to evaluate. It is my job to recommend. That's how it's divided in what these guys call the state of the art, the state of the art of range management. Goddamn, if I had known that the cow business was going to become an art and that some goddamn pinhead was going to tell the state of it, I would have stayed a cowboy like you dumb bastards, or better still I would have cut off my boots at the ankles and joined a freak show."

Knowing he was now underway, we waited.

"The evaluations show: chopped barley 6, Tullus 1. Now it don't take any more power of mind than you can find in a good grass-fed yearling steer to know if there's a recommendation coming out of that evaluation, it comes down to this: fire all you cowboys, and hire on about a dozen good bags of chopped barley."

We waited, and we must have been smiling while we waited.

"And by god, that's exactly what I'm going to do."

He didn't. He went out to the yard and stood a long time with his elbows on the top pole of the branding corral. When he finally came back to the pickup, he put his hand on the side of the bed as if leaning a bit. Then he turned toward us. "Forget it," he

132 / The Evaluation

said. "Forget the recommendation. Those bags of barley probably wouldn't even know how to make a bad fence worse."

With that he drove off, and we all got back to smiling. As a matter of fact we had never really stopped smiling. Mr. Pulley couldn't read those cow minds any better than we could, but still he must have known what they were thinking. He could just look at their faces and see that if they had to choose between a bag of barley and a bunch of cowboys, they'd take the cowboys every time. He could tell they were sorry the evaluation was all over. He could tell they hadn't had so much fun in a long time, probably not since that Monday afternoon about two years ago when Lon came tearing in wilder than a steer with the fantods, looking back so much he should have got on the other way, with his butt against the pommel, his old horse sweating like a three-blanket bedbug and dragging three pairs of Mrs. Minute's best black bloomers still pinned on the end of her busted clothesline.

So we felt at peace with ourselves. We felt secure. We even began thinking about maybe thinking about how to fix that fence.

We haven't heard anything new about Ef. But he's probably somewhere off down the river, past where they're making that stretch of salt grass into a four-hole golf course. He's probably still doing his best to lift up the state of the art of the cow business. We can see him now. He strides across the cow dust. His eyes shine with the poetry of numbers. The pencil points. The clipboard waves. And Mr. Ef etches himself heroically against the fading western sky.

COWBOY CULTURE

It was a pleasant November evening. Sill's kitchen was warm from the old black Monarch. The air was still tasty with the aroma of fried liver and onions. Sill had cleared the plates and the feeding tools. He had wiped the oilcloth to its familiar greasy shine. The coffee cups hung back, as they always did, waiting for what we would soon be calling *café après la fève*. Other than that it felt like the beginning of a lazy couple of hours before the bunkhouse beckoned. Sill would bring out a fifth of Old Horse, and we would all slowly forget the bite of his bitter coffee.

In the first deal, I looked at a pair of aces and felt even better. I knew the ace of diamonds had been missing for at least two years and that a mouse had eaten the whole upper right hand corner out of our only joker. So I figured I held a strong hand and was on my way to pulling in my first good pot. But just as we were getting ready for the showdown, Mont shoved his way through the door with a big box of supplies from town and a small piece of news which would come to have what you might call scholarly interest. "Sill," Mont said, "Pulley cut your coffee order down about half. Said you guys are drinking too much of the stuff. Said it's probably keeping you up nights. Said too that the price has doubled in just the last month." I was waiting for him to get through with his talk about coffee so I could come down with those two aces. "Something else Pulley said," Mont added. "Seems another professor is on his way out here. Seems this professor is interested in what he calls cowboy culture."

"Funny thing," Burt said. "I thought most professors were extinct like the eohippus. I thought the last one left this country when they changed that house in Pinville to an art museum. I hear he didn't play the piano worth a good goddamn. Seems he had only one tune and didn't seem to know what the hell to do with it. I hear Bertha Bottom, who ran the place, didn't care much though. She said the fellows soon got tired of hearing that stove-up tune and hurried on upstairs with her girls. I hear those girls were pretty ugly, so I guess every extra little incentive helped."

"Seems this professor doesn't even play the piano," Mont added. "Seems he heads out from some college or university. That probably accounts for the fact that he's into culture. Probably heard about us from that Duncan fellow."

We never did finish that poker game. Once we got to thinking about the professor and trying to guess what he was up to, we let the cards get cold and finally dropped them while we had another double shot of demitasse. Ten years after, I can still remember the convincing look of those two aces and wonder what great things I might have done with them.

The truth is we weren't much into culture. The truth is it had never occurred to us that raising cows had much to do with enjoying the finer things. About the only place we even heard mention of culture was in the *Pinville Post,* and to get to the culture you had to go down through a whole lot of other stuff. You had to read that Ben Burland had been up to City Hosptital to have some bleeding hemorrhoids removed, that the cutting job had been a big success, and that a good time was had by all. You had to read that Ernest and Favlina Goodson's oldest boy, Stooky, had married a girl over in the next county, that they made a handsome couple even though she stood a whole head taller, and that a good time was had by all. You had to read that Clem Signer had been laid to rest on October 16, that the pall bearers were all fellow members of the Pinville Pork Growers' Association, and that a good time was had by all. Finally you got down to the culture. You read that the Pinville Culture and Crocheting Club had met on September the 24th, that Bessy Mooten sang a medley of favorite love songs accompanied on the piano by her oldest daughter, Turna, that Hattie Simple passed out copies of her new recipe for elderberry butter, and that a good time was had by all.

So now, whether we wanted to or not, we were about to get right into the middle of the culture business. Our whole easy way of life was about to be elevated. But even before that professor pulled in and set up camp, we knew we had some culturing of our own to do.

First we had to listen for Mr. Pulley's pickup. We knew from experience that if any culturing was to go on at his place, he would arrive in advance, riding point in that old truck in his usual manner. This time we didn't have to listen long. Even before Sill had refilled our breakfast tea cups, we heard the pickup come over the hill and roar down the road in second gear. If Mr. Pulley ever shifted into high, you knew from the sound of the engine that his coming was what you might call casual, maybe just a getting away for a couple of hours while his wife fed her garden club their tea and madeleines. By the time we had pulled our legs from under Sill's table, we heard the truck stop, the cab door open, and Pulley's left boot crunch the gravel. He stood watching as we straggled through Sill's screen door and lined up waiting.

"My old eyes tell me," he started in, "that that damn professor hasn't pulled in yet. Unless these eyes have lingered too damn long on all the cows that turned out to be clumps of sagebrush, as I stand here on this happy morning and look from left to right, I don't see a single goddamn living professor." He slowed down then and backed up some. He seemed to need to tell us how he got mixed up with this professor and his culture business. "I got this damn letter," he said, "asking could he come out here and spend a week. I said to myself, hell no. We've got enough trouble sorting out the winter steers." We could guess too that he was still remembering old Ef and his flying clipboard. He went on. "But before I could wire back a loud no, the missus jumped into the game. 'What does he want?' Phyllis asks, and I make the big mistake of telling her the truth. He wants to go out to the ranch and study culture, I answer. And just as soon as I hit that word *culture,* I could tell I was caught like a bull with three feet in the quicksand. P. P. took the bit running." He sometimes liked to call Mrs. Pulley that for short. It reminded him of the big double P brand he sometimes put on his cows in her honor. 'J. G.,' she says, 'if that man can find any culture out at that cow pen of yours, you let him find it.' That's when I wired the professor, 'Come, at your own risk.' Signed J. G. Pulley, President, Pulley Beef Production Company. I almost added, 'and chief damn fool,' but I decided I didn't need to tell him that in the wire. He could find it out when he got here."

All that telling had made Mr. Pulley sag a bit. "By god," he said, "I must be getting old. I don't remember words wearing me down so. You better have something strong in that pot of yours, Sill, or you boys may have to ride into town and tell old Phyllis that her man of fifty years has gone on to the great green pasture."

We trailed back into Sill's kitchen, and Sill poured Mr. Pulley a cup of what Mr. Pulley sometimes called Arbuckle. "But hell," he usually added, "this stuff isn't like the real old brew. You could clean your teeth with a sip of that. You could shine the copper rivets on your oldest pants." Even so, the cup revived him. He leaned back, and we could tell that he wasn't finished. "One more thing: that professor is coming out here to find some culture, and by god I'm determined to see that he finds it. I want a high-class magazine laid out somewhere where he can see it. I want a picture hanging on that wall." He hooked his thumb in the direction of the wall across from Sill's old stove. "I want all you boys to put yourselves through a change of socks, even if you did go all the way into a clean pair in October. And finally, I don't want to hear a goddamn word of profanity around here."

He pulled himself up from his chair, stomped his right boot a couple of times on the floor, then slapped his thigh with his gloved hand. "Damn leg is trying to die on me," he said. "Comes of not walking enough. Comes of sitting too goddamned long in too many hard old saddles." He limped out, and we heard the pickup drive away.

Before the afternoon was over he was back, bringing the latest issue of *The Hereford Journal* to lay on our coffee table and a framed painting of a wolf howling on a snow-covered hill. So with Mr. Pulley's help we soon had the place fixed up. Now all we had to do was get ourselves cultured up a bit, and then we could stand around and wait for that professor.

Getting ourselves fixed up wasn't as hard as a person might think. We didn't go to many weddings, and we didn't go to many burials, but we did have to be ready for all sorts of disasters, natural or otherwise. Every one of us carried at least one piece of dress-up clothing in his war bag. I had a pair of striped pants I had won in a free-moving poker game. Burt had a set of English riding trousers he had inherited from his late Uncle Clifford. The shanks didn't quite reach down into the tops of his eleven-inch boots, but except for a couple of inches of bare hairy skin, he took on a classy sort of look. Even Barney had a black coat that would have looked smilingly good on almost any undertaker. So when we had fixed ourselves up for the reception, we strolled out onto Sill's porch and waited. Mont looked us over and spoke a fitting note. "By god, if we just had a body in a long box, we could put on a damn good funeral."

The first sign of the approaching professor was a plume of dust moving down the hill. We could tell it wasn't Pulley coming back with another picture borrowed from his wife's pink wall. The main thing about Pulley's coming was the way the old truck gathered speed, coming so fast the dust had a hell of a time trying to keep up with it. This time when the slow dust got closer we could make out a pair of horses and then we could see a real dusty cowboy sitting stiff as a rawhide corset on the seat of Henry Turner's old buckboard. Only it turned out not to be a cowboy. It turned out to be the professor himself. When he climbed down and we could see him a little better through his layer of dust, we began to get the right idea, and when he reached back and pulled out a lawyer's bag big enough to hold a hundred and fifty mortgages, we had a clincher. "Greetings," we said in a chorus. "Howdy," he answered.

The Stetson seemed a size too big, but he had it tipped back enough so that we could see most of his face, the eyes squinting a bit in the afternoon sun, the dark trimmed beard salted gray with road dust. In spite of the dust, the neckerchief had a bright new redness. I said to myself, somebody should have told him to put that thing up over his face, especially when he was riding drag behind that bone yard he had rented from old man Turner. From there down he was all denim until you hit the thirteen-inch shafts of his high-heeled boots. I heard Mont whisper to Barney, "Circle around some and see if he's wearing spurs." "I'm Courtney Covington," our visitor announced. "Professor of Rhetoric and Range Management, Flatlands College of Mines and Moral Sciences. My friends usually call me Covey. I hope you boys will do the same."

We trailed inside then, and Sill fixed up another round of demitasse. The professor seemed a nice sort of fellow. He smiled all round, and we all relaxed into an easy savoir faire. "Professor," Burt opened. "Remember. Call me Covey," the professor smiled in interruption. "Mr. Covey," Burt tried again. "Just Covey. Just plain old Covey," the professor added. "I was wondering, Covey," Burt pushed on. "I was wondering how you happened to get into the culture business."

138 / *Cowboy Culture*

"Well, it's a very short story," the professor answered. "If I was to put it in the form of a bibliography, it would be like a corral with only two cows in it." We decided to wait on that one, in the meantime taking another sip of demitasse. "I saw this article," the professor went on. "I saw this article called 'Reading on the Range: The Literary Habits of the American Cowboy,' by some unknown professor named Walker. I suppose that started some unconscious cerebration." Again we just held down tight with the cards we had and waited. "And then one day I came upon a book—mind you a whole book—entitled *Cowboy Culture*. From that point on, as you boys would say, I just followed my subject up the long, long trail."

Even so, he was a nice sort of fellow. He seemed to be a bit dainty with our beef and beans. He seemed to have trouble getting his boots off at night. He would strain and grunt in a polite sort of way. I heard Mont say outloud to himself, "That professor must have the highest goddamn insteps in the whole county." He sometimes talked in his sleep, reciting some weird stuff about a face that launched a thousand ships. He asked more questions than a seven-dollar lawyer. Even so, he was a nice sort of fellow.

One morning he announced he was ready to take a close look at our library. "That Walker fellow was right," he said. "You can't really know a people until you know the books they live with." We all looked at Sill. If anybody knew that we had a library, he would know. "We keep it hidden away a bit," Sill answered with the same steadiness he uses when his sourdough has gone as flat as the pies of a scouring calf. "Partly to save space," he added. "But mostly for protection." He went to a corner of the kitchen, tossed aside Barney's old chaps, and dragged out a wooden box a little bigger than a bushel basket. In faded black letters, the side of the box said UNDERWOOD TYPEWRITER COMPANY. "That means," the professor was quick to remark, "that at one time you had a typewriter here at the ranch." But the box might as well have read *corsets and sidesaddles* for all the typewriters we had ever seen around our place.

The professor got out his satchel. Sill cleared the table of its demitasse and brushed the top layer of mouse turds off the library, and then the professor went to work, looking carefully at each item in the box and writing some words on his little white cards. We still had some steers that needed moving, but we stayed to watch the professor. We figured Mr. Pulley wouldn't mind if we lingered there in the kitchen and learned a little more about the culture business. The professor worked his way right down to the bottom of the box, and then he gathered up his white cards as if he was going to shuffle them. "Here, then," he announced, "we have a catalogue of the library. It will need some critical reexamination and some alphabetizing, but essentially it's all here." He held up his deck as if it included at least six aces.

"How do we come out?" Mont said. "I mean, how do we stack up when you put our library out there in the culture pen?" You could tell the professor was just waiting to read us what he had put down on his set of cards. So he went through it one card at a time, reminding us again before he started that the whole thing still needed some stretching out from A to Z.

> Mohler, John R., *Blackleg, Its Nature, Cause and Prevention,* Washington, 1918, Bulletin 1355.
> *Weaving Rag Rugs,* Washington, 1926, Department of Agriculture, Bulletin 303.
> *Playboy,* three issues, centerfolds missing.
> Fixer, J. P., *How to Give a Live Look to a Dead Bobcat: A Taxidermist's Manual,* Denver, 1913.
> Hare, R. F., *Experiments on the Digestibility of Prickly Pear by Cattle,* Washington, 1908, Bulletin 106.
> Poe, Edgar A., *Tales,* 1882.
> Burnside, Minnie F., *Dutch Oven Desserts for the Two-Child Family,* Pinville Culture Club, 1923.
> *The Passionate Pioneer,* by the author of *Zardoc, Warrior Stud,* San Diego, 1967, front cover missing.
> Chapin, Robert M., *The Analysis of Coal-Tar Creosote and Cresylic Acid Sheep Dip,* Washington, 1908, Bulletin 107.
> *Penthouse,* two issues, some illustrations missing.
> *Clio's Cowboys: Studies in the Historiography of the Cattle Trade,* Lincoln, 1981, bound in cowhide with the hair on, pages uncut.

When the professor had finished, he tucked the cards into a neat pile and smiled his knowing smile all around. I thought to myself, by god, he's not going to win a hell of a lot of poker games with that hand.

After five or six days of sharing our beans and demitasse, the professor said he had to be moving on. Said he had to get back to his temple of learning. Said he had to get back and reflect on what his data was telling him. The truth is we hated to have him leave, even if he still took too long getting his long-shafted boots pulled off, even if he still asked too damn many questions, even if we still didn't know how somebody's face could launch a thousand ships. You could say we were getting to enjoy the culture business. When we reflected on chasing Pulley's steers through all the flying gold and mud of autumn, you could say we held back some in favor of the finer things. But he said no matter how much he enjoyed our beef and beans, he had to go. He had to get started up that long, long trail. So we decided we would send him off with a genuine wingding and culture event.

The affair turned out to be a big success. Somebody—probably Mrs. Pulley—told the *Pinville Post* about it, so just as the festivities were about ready to break into the open, Belinda Bearing, the *Post*'s own society reporter, tied up out front and stayed through the entire operation, smiling a lot, especially at the professor, who smiled a cultured smile right back, and sometimes writing little notes on a pink pad she carried tucked into her bosom.

The ink was barely dry on the next week's *Post* when Pulley's pickup came roaring down the ranch hill. "What's he coming to announce this time?" Burt said. "By god I hope he's not planning a visit by one of those women liberators." Turned out he was just bringing the *Post*. Turned out he was pleased with how our culture event went off. "I'm proud of you boys," he said. "I'm real proud." So we trailed inside, and Sill got the old demitasse boiling, and when we all had our cups filled, Pulley handed the *Post* to me. "Read her out loud," he said. "Let's all hear how she sounds."

So I read:

One of the truly gala social affairs of the season was held last week at the J. G. Pulley Ranch and Feed Yard. The occasion was a fond farewell to Professor Courtney Covington, who was leaving to return to his learned labors at the Flatlands State College of Mines and Moral Sciences. Mr. Silliman Sanders was in charge of the buffet, which featured tender bits of beef simmered in a sauce of delicate but unknown origin. Mr. Burton Sullivan performed a graceful soft-shoe dance, accompanying himself on the harmonica. Mr. J. G. Pulley gave a moving recitation of "Socker Sets the Hen." Between entertainments Mr. Montgomery Masterson was seen chatting with Mr. Bernard M. Tullus. The high point of the gala evening came when Professor Covington himself took the stage to sing all fifty verses of "The Chisholm Trail," adding two of his own composition. Professor Covington does not have a trained voice, but his melody was true and his diction beyond the criticism of even the most studied listener.

I paused then, as if I had come to the end of the social column. But the fellows knew there was more still to come, one more final note before you could tell for sure that the culture report was finished.

"You could go on reading it," Burt said. "But you don't need to. We all know how it comes out."

"I know you do," I answered. "I was just sitting here waiting to hear you say it."

"So all together," Sill said. "Let's sing it out for the old professor."

They did: "And a real good time was had by all!"

And being pleased with the happy sound of our chorus, we sang it out again: "And a real good time was had by all."

THE BLUE SADDLE BLANKET
THE NOVELIST AND THE *NOUVEAU WESTERN*

My friend's troubles began when he received the latest issue of *Le revue bovin* from Paris, Idaho. The journal, decorated with delicate circles of blue hoof prints, contained a lengthy review of my friend's novel *Barney Tullus and la belle sauvage*. "Barney Tullus," wrote the journal's chief critic, "is a tired old-fashioned novel, a conventional literary cliché, wholly lacking in freshness and originality. Its author naively assumes that character is important. Its author naively assumes that story is central. Its author naively assumes that a novel justifies itself to the degree that it faithfully images objective reality. As Robbe-Grillet, point man for the French avant-garde, might say of this work, 'Quelle la cruche de shit!'"

My friend's troubles continued when he read on a back page of the *Gooding County Gazette* that a fellow named Claude Simon had won the Nobel Prize in literature. My friend was startled, to say the least, because he knew that Claude Simon runs the Toyota dealership over in Glenn's Ferry, and he remembered that old Claude has a hard time even putting words in the blank spaces of a simple bill of sale. However, reading further in the *Gazette*, he realized that the prize-winning fellow does not sell Toyotas. He is a Frenchman who writes what the *Gazette* calls new novels. So my friend tried out the name with a French sound, sensing at once that it had class. "By god," he said to me, "if old Claude over in Glenn's Ferry ever fixes up his name that way, he'll sell a lot more Toyotas."

But my friend's troubles were not yet over. It was that word *new* that had him tangled in a short rope. In his puzzlement he reflected on his first novel, *The Rise and Fall of Barney Tullus*. Even though it had been written on a 1939 Underwood standard, with some of the types as weak as lukewarm branding irons, the paper was as virginal as a pair of bridal sheets, and the words had never before been strung together in the same rhythmic pattern of style and the same central structure of a rise and a fall. My friend's critical logic was as rigorous as it was simple: if *The Rise and Fall* was a novel that had never been written before, it must have been a new novel. Nevertheless, my friend suspected that he had not yet got down to the special newness of *new*.

If he had not been driven by a fierce sense of literary mission, all of this would not have mattered. If the critics found his novels old-fashioned, it perhaps didn't matter, as long as there were some old-fashioned readers to read them. But my friend is what I would call a cosmopolitan westerner. He needs to know what the hell is going on in the big literary world. If he writes westerns, he wants those westerns to show that he isn't stuck somewhere back on the trail, waiting for the pony express to bring him another rejection from the editors of *The Overland Monthly*. He doesn't want some snobbish eastern critic in an unbuttoned paisley shirt to say to him, "Oh, you write westerns. Thank god some writers maintain the traditions. Where would American literature be without Cooper and the rest of you fellows." That word *new* had him stirred up; it was pushing him out into strange literary frontiers. If there was a critter called the new novel that he could get the conformation of, then by god he would write one. Perhaps that critic in *Le revue bovin* would even want to call it a *nouveau western*.

The very next day he drove his pickup down to the public library and looked over the Simons in the card catalogue. He found Neil and Paul, but not a sign of Claude. He tried the new *Columbia Encyclopedia*, finding another Simon, Herbert, a sure-enough big prize winner, but in economics, not literature. The pretty librarian seemed eager to help. "I'm looking for some novels by a French novelist," he said to her, "a fellow named Claude Simon. In translation of course," he quickly added. She smiled an eager response. "I have to admit that I've never heard of him," she said. My friend sensed there was more to follow; there was a *but* hanging ready in the quiet air. "But if we search thoroughly in our reference resources, I'm sure we can find something, at least some titles, maybe a full-length bibliography." Knowing the thoroughness of librarians, my friend glanced at the sunlight in the south window, wondering as he sighed softly if she would finish the search in time for lunch. But when she opened a big Hereford-red volume of *Books in Print,* she pounced in graceful delight. "Here. See here." Her long red fingernails traced the column of riches. "We can borrow one of these novels from another library," she said. "Some big university library. Which novel do you want?" My friend read the column of titles, pausing briefly in frustration over those in French. "It doesn't matter," he finally answered. "As long as it's new." The librarian smiled her puzzlement. "But, sir, most library books are used. That's why they are in libraries." My friend couldn't explain what he couldn't explain, so he went on glaring at the titles. "Let's try this one called *Conducting Bodies,*" he said without much enthusiasm. "I sure as hell don't know what the title means, but it sure as hell sounds more interesting than this one called *Triptych.* And if it turns out that the bodies are just large piles of copper and iron, I sure as hell won't be long reading it." He paused suddenly, aware that he was in a library talking to a librarian. "Please excuse me, ma'am." "You mad at that novelist or something?" she answered.

I didn't see my friend for several weeks, but when I happened to run into him at the Downhill Bar and Grill, I could tell at once that he was deeply into something. Even three or four shots of tarantula juice on the rocks couldn't make a man's eyes that unsteady. I guessed he was into that new novel. "You want to tell me about it?" I said. "Or shall I just sit here wondering?"

"Almost two hundred pages," he answered. "All of it in one paragraph. Longest goddamn paragraph I ever got into. And I don't know for sure that I'll ever get out of it."

"What about those conducting bodies?" I asked.

"Can't tell you a thing," he answered. "I've just read the first hundred pages."

"When you find out," I said, "let me know. And when you get a clear line onto the newness of it, let me know that too."

"God, it's new all right," he answered. But that was as much as he would say. My friend doesn't like to come to final critical meanings until the whole matter has gone through the chute, even when he's struggled more than halfway through the longest goddamn paragraph he ever got into.

Again I didn't see my friend for several weeks. He passed me a few times in his pickup, but he was driving with a fierce straightforwardness, as if he was still looking for the end of that paragraph. Yet I suspected that he had already made it through and was now past discovery and into creativeness. Maybe he still didn't know for sure about those bodies, but I had a hunch that he was already onto the newness. My friend is a proud and stubborn writer. If the new novel is the novel to be written, he'll write it. And you could be almost certain that he'd do up the whole damn thing in one long paragraph.

My curiosity about the new novel was just beginning to fade into memory when I heard my friend's pickup pull up near the tying post where I keep my Honda. I had lately been reading a couple of novels that seemed pleasantly old-fashioned. They were new, at least in the facts that they were published in 1986, but one was compared with the novels of Dickens and the other with the novels of Tolstoy. I expected shortly to find a new western that reminded the reviewer of *Lin McLean* and *The Virginian*. However, I already guessed that when I found it, I would see that it had not been written by the author of the Tullus saga.

My friend opened my door without knocking, and skipping all formalities shoved a hefty manuscript into my unwaiting hands. I glanced at the title, *The Blue Saddle Blanket*, and then I spoke the words aloud. He apparently heard a question after *Blanket* which I had not intended. "I considered some other titles," he said, "although in the new novel the title doesn't make a hell of a lot of difference. I thought of *The Gold Mine Just Past Dreaming*. I thought of *The Eye of Utah*. I considered *Project for a Revolution in Dove Creek, Colorado*. But I kept coming back to *The Blue Saddle Blanket*. Somehow seemed more western. Even the *nouveau western* needs a western touch or two."

"But why *The Blue Saddle Blanket?*" I asked.

"You'll get onto it when you've read it," he answered. "It's like those conducting bodies."

That didn't help much, but I decided to go along in trust. "I suppose that's the color of Barney's blanket," I said.

"Barney?" he said, with a distinct tone of sadness in his voice. "Old Barney's not in it. No place for him. The structure can't use him. Not a goddamn cowboy in the whole paragraph."

"But how can you have a saddle blanket without a cowboy?" I persisted.

"You'll see," he answered. "Maybe there is somebody you

might call a cowboy sitting in the saddle on top of the blanket, but he's not important. It's the blanket that matters."

You can understand that I was underwhelmed with interest. Loyalty to a friend and sharing with him of the high purpose of western literature meant that I was about to get into a thick manuscript typed on a 1939 Underwood and all about a saddle blanket. And in one paragraph to boot.

After my friend closed my door and I heard the coughing start of the pickup, I glanced at the first page of *The Blue Saddle Blanket*. There was an epigraph. "You try to put a brand on reality and the son of a bitch just goes up in stink and smoke." Then as I began reading, I quickly had to admit that the author of *Barney Tullus* had indeed rushed into advanced modernism with the supreme confidence of an old steer shoving his way through a scrub oak thicket.

The world is structured in a pattern of intersecting lines. The vertical is marked against a pale yellow sky by an upward-pointing finger. The horizontal of the flat watching hat brim cuts across the bare torso made golden on the left shoulder by the late long sun. The eyes beneath the hat brim seem fixed upon the mustard-colored roll held up by the horizontal quiver and the darkly purple pommel. Above the roll half a belly button looks out, it too goldened by the sun. The two horses stand in a frozen moment of waiting: the bay with his tail slightly lifted, his ears up, his eyes shiny, his four white feet planted; the blue pony reined back by a taut cord, his yellow forelock tossing, his lower jaw pulled down and open, his front feet weightless above the brushed in strokes of brown and gold. The bay horse is watching the blue pony, and the blue pony is watching where we cannot see. It is a linear movement which thrusts diagonally across our vision, the cattle marching, their horns white and yellowed by the dust and sun, their hooves rumbling soundlessly somewhere in a memory of cattle heard before, a day not yet forgotten when we watched a distant plume of whitened air grow thick with frantic eyes and lolling tongues. Midway between the horses an entire cow is white and yellow, and we can measure time by the progress of light between the bay and the blue. We can also measure it against the mauve and yellow and blue-grey

The Blue Saddle Blanket / 147

background where it loses its sharpness of canyon and hill and washes vaguely away in the distant light. But when we turn to watch the long line of cars along the yellow-lined freeway, we are caught for a moment in motion. Yet when we look back, we see that the cattle have not moved: they have stopped time. They are as if painted in still life. The white and yellow cow still centers our vision. But our watching cannot ever seem to stir them into action. Yet we notice that one cow has turned back to watch the blue and the bay that we are watching.

I paused ready to turn the page of manuscript. I sighed faintly, irrationally eager to see an indentation. Already there was no doubt in my mind. My friend had indeed written a new novel, a *nouveau western*. And already, as I steadied myself before plunging on into the pile of pages, I could begin to hear the critics stirring, their word processors beginning to sing their faint busy song. I could see papers on the program of the Western Literature Association: "Patterns of Style and Symbol in the Nouveau Western," "Mythic Structures in *The Blue Saddle Blanket,*" maybe a whole section devoted to this new kind of literary pioneering. And already I could see a proposal for a dissertation. The title had an appealing length and elegance: *Suspended Indentation: The Demise of the Small Paragraph in Western American Literature.* In academic reflex I smiled my approval.

THE BUNKHOUSE MURDERS

Five old cowboys sleeping in the sun. Fate rode by, and then there was one.

Sometimes big things happen when a little thing is enough to make a dead man shudder. That's the way it was that warm and dry October.
Work at the ranch had slowed to a standstill. Pulley had sold the steers and a sizable bunch of cull cows. The breeding stock had been moved down the river where the scrubby winter grass would keep them from getting fat and lazy. Once or twice a week we drove down to take a look. But the fences were good. The feed was enough to keep the old girls happy. There wasn't much to do but walk through the herd, stepping now and then on a pie for old time's sake and to keep our boots seasoned, and then head on back to Sill's kitchen to wait for supper. When we came down the hill, we could see what remained in the corrals, two old cows with some sort of hip problem and one old bull who had damn near lost his reasons for being, on a barbed wire fence he had tried to jump. You could say the old boy deserved his humiliation. At his time of life he didn't need to prove anything to himself or that young heifer on the other side of the wire. So mostly we sat around the kitchen or out on the porch when the sun was good. Sill complained about our being so close at hand. Said we got in the way of his planning and preparing. But we all knew that Sill did damn little planning, even counting the time it took him to calculate how many beans to throw in the pot. And as for preparing, that didn't fool us either. Sill had heard that old pot rumble and belch and sizzle for so many years he knew its magic better than he knew the sweet sound of his mother's voice. He admitted that he usually listened to it with an off ear. "She whispers to me how the stuff is doing," he once said. No, the real

The Bunkhouse Murders / 149

reason Sill complained was that he wanted more time to spend with the girlie magazine he kept hidden down the side of the woodbox. Even so, we were beginning to get on each other's nerves. There may not be much excitement in taking care of a herd of cows, but at least there's the comfort of active habits, of what old Ef would have called a structured day. At least there's the genuine need to do something, to walk out to the feed yard and see some different faces, hear some good cow sounds, smell air that's tangy with the aroma of sun-warmed cow shit and straw. But after we had been down to the corrals and back, we still had to crowd into Sill's kitchen and look at each other.

"It's too bad there isn't a bank or a train somebody could rob," Mont said.

"What about the First Pinville Land and Lending?" Burt said.

"I'm not forgetting," Mont answered. "I just figured that nobody would bother with the First Pinville. Be like sticking up the minister's wife while she's still counting the Canadian quarters in the collection plate."

"An earthquake would be good," Burt said. "But you can't count on earthquakes. Sometimes they just rattle the hell out of things, knock a few bottles of good whiskey off the shelves, scare the ladies who just happen to be looking at the china they've never had a chance to use, but otherwise leave things pretty much as they've always been."

"Maybe what we need is a good juicy murder." We all turned to Barney.

"I hope you don't mean one of those with a lot of blood on it," Sill said. "Everybody knows that seeing too much blood throws a cook off balance."

"Could be just one of them poisonings," Burt said. "Just a few drops of something sweet slipped into a cup of coffee when only God is watching."

About then we decided we had drunk enough coffee, even though our cups were still mostly full.

"I think I better walk down and check on that bull," Mont said. "He may be getting ready to try that fence again."

We all got up and followed him. You could tell from the grin on Sill's face that he suddenly knew he had a good pry on the situation. Saving coffee would save him the trouble of making it. But saving coffee would damn near bring the rest of us to a complete standstill. We once saw an old Tom Mix movie. The cowboys were running for their horses, running so fast their legs blurred together, and those cowboys sort of twitched across the landscape. Then something happened. Everything slowed down till it was barely moving. Could be that dumb operator in the Pinville Filmorama thought the machine was running away with itself. He must have put on the brakes or whatever there was to put on, and the first thing we knew old Tom was trying to get in the saddle and he couldn't get his right leg up over the cantle. It was a sad situation. But that's just the way we were going to be without coffee.

Turned out we had a right to worry about the coffee, at least about the cook that made it. Turned out there was a lot of blood on it, enough blood to keep a hard-hearted cook tipped slantwise for God only knows how long.

A couple of days later, Burt came back from town wearing a sort of sucked-in mysterious grin and carrying a burlap bag with a head-sized lump in it. The grin seemed to say that he had taken the long way home with a tea time stopover to check on old man Barnes's bull, but when we asked about the sack the grin got more so. Even if he had a honey bucket full of Mabel's cookies, he didn't need to look so sure and sappy.

"Burt," Mont said, "what the hell you got in that bag?"

"Maybe it's a gallon of good French wine," he answered, still grinning. "And maybe it's my new chamber pot with flowers painted all around the rim."

"And maybe it's a head," Barney threw in.

"I've heard about carrying a head around in a hat box," I said, "but I don't recall anybody dragging a head around in a grain sack."

"Cut it off yourself?" Barney said. "Or did you get Pod Beaner to slice it off with that big knife of his that looks like a goddamn sword?"

But Burt just kept on grinning, and when he could tell we were getting tired of looking at his smirky face, he headed off toward the bunkhouse.

Barney called after him. "Don't hide that goddamn head under my bunk."

That evening when we sat on Sill's porch for one last smoke, the head came up again. Burt's face had smoothed out some, but he still had the look of a kid with a toad in his pocket.

"I been thinking some more about that head," Mont said. "I been wondering who must have worn it before Pod Beaner whacked it off."

"A head ain't worth a hell of a lot to have around," I said. "I'd rather have a statue of a cow or maybe an old boot that's been stuffed with good cement."

But all our talk couldn't draw Burt out. He seemed to want to keep that head all to himself.

About the usual time of early night we moved to hit the sack, but when we got inside the bunkhouse we did an extra bit of peering around, looking for full or empty sacks, even for a head that might be hanging from a roof beam like some damn begonia. Things seemed pretty much as usual, same smell of old socks, unaired bedrolls, tracked-in mud and cow shit. You could say the place had a homey feel in spite of all our talk about heads and Barney's words about a juicy murder. The snoring began pretty much on schedule.

I woke up next morning with my nose wide open. The air was alive with a strange smell, not heavy like the trail of a skunk or pungently rich like the bottom floor of an overfilled outhouse, but still sickmaking in its allover faintness. Without even looking around I yelled, "Where the hell is that stink coming from?"

My yell must have bounced Barney awake and out on the floor. "Godalmighty," he croaked. "Old Burt's been murdered. Old Burt's been chopped to pieces."

We stood in our longhandles and looked at Burt's bunk. It was the bloodiest mess I ever hope to see. Blood on the quilts, blood on the pillow, blood even dripping down the chaps Burt had hung on the side of the headboard. But with all that blood, there wasn't any body.

"Poor Burt," Mont said. "Whoever it was who committed this dastardly deed must have ground Burt up and squeezed the sausage. Even when he had been drinking red port for a week, he didn't have that much juice in him. At least that's what I thought. Could be I was wrong. Could be he had some stored away where we couldn't see it."

"But where the hell is Burt?" Sill said. "At least there ought to be some bones."

"It must have been the guy who owned that head that came and got him," Barney said. "Funny thing is that he didn't just take Burt's head. He chopped up the whole damn carcass."

"Poor old Burt," I said. "He was a good guy, even if he did snore in a funny way. You just got used to the even hum of it and then it skipped a beat and jerked around like a wounded bumblebee."

Barney restored the proper moral tone. "He had the goddamnedest snore I ever hope to hear, but that doesn't seem quite enough reason for splattering him around like a loose hog in a meat mill."

"Wait," Mont said. "We're jumping to conclusions. We've seen the blood. We've seen it all over Burt's sougans and chaps. But until we find the carcass or the sidemeat that spilled it, we can't be certain it was Burt. As far as I know Burt's blood was just the same as any other blood. Nobody here can say for sure that all this red stuff came leaking out of the late Burt Sullivan."

He was right. Before we started planning the funeral we had to find the body. We poked into every corner of the bunkhouse and came up with nothing but a pair of Burt's old boots and a long-lost saddle bag. Then we searched the saddle shed, the shadows back inside where the tractor waited, and the loose hay where the bales had broken. We even thought of the outside. "Barney," Mont said, "go take a look. We can't leave a single stone unturned."

We found nothing, not a scrap of clothing, let alone a bone or something we could recognize as a piece of old Burt's meat.

"It's a mystery," Sill said. "It's a genuine mystery."

"It's a genuine murder mystery," Mont added. "And that calls for a genuine detective." He turned to Barney. "Barney, you get the hell into Pinville and give the word to Turly. It's urgent. You make that old sorrel think he's running the pony express."

Barney saddled up and headed out, and then we had some

waiting to do. We gathered again in Sill's kitchen. After all that blood the coffee looked harmless and tasted good. And finally we heard a sputter at the top of the hill and knew our waiting was over.

"That'll be Turly," Mont said. We trailed out onto the porch to watch the approach of Deputy Turly Sinker, Chief Investigator of the Pinville P.D., Homicide Division. Of course, that is what Turly called himself on a sign he had tacked up in what he liked to call his office. The truth was he was the only deputy in the whole county, the only investigator in the whole damn state, and as for the homicide division he could have called it the Department for Eradicating Hotel Bedbugs with just as much truth.

The announcing sputter came from Turly's cycle. Somewhere he had found himself an old Harley-Davidson complete with a sidecar. It was that that sputtered as it started down the long ranch hill.

If you had ever met Turly, you remembered how he looked. And if you knew anything about him, you knew why he looked that way. In some parts of the country you can't tell the sheriff from the rustlers. Same damn boots. Same damn hat. Same damn gun with the same damn bone handle. You could say Turly was an individualist. If you thought about it, you could hear him saying, "Cowboys are not sheriffs, and sheriffs are not cowboys. When you enforce the law, you don't look the same as when you break the law." So when you waited for Turly Sinker, you didn't wait for another damn cowboy with a high pair of boots and a fancy Stetson hat and only a two-bit star telling you he was coming to investigate the bloody murder of the late Burt Sullivan.

The cycle sputtered on down the hill, and finally we could see the chief investigator's hat and the shoulders behind it as Turly rode scrunched down behind the handle bars. Somewhere Turly had found a campaign hat of doughboy vintage. Maybe he found it in the sidecar when he bought the Harley. Wherever he picked it up, he couldn't be choosy about size. When he pulled it down to keep it tight while he faced the push of the wind, it bent his ears a bit. If you kept your eyes on Turly and not on the Harley, you saw the line of the hat cut across Turly's head just above the eyebrows and beneath that line the curious bulge of Turly's ears, like two dirty pearls pasted alongside the middle of his close-clipped head. You could also see his eyes still squinting to see the road beyond the Harley bars. Then as he pulled along in front, he threw out his right leg as if he was riding a two-wheeler and needed the braking balance. You could see the leather legging was still polished a golden brown, even after all the dust from Pinville and miles between.

The cycle stopped, gave its last sputter, and Turly pulled off the other leg. We could see that whatever the wind and dust, the hat had not budged an inch on Turly's head. Tight and straight as the law itself. "Deputy Sinker here," he said. "Hear you've got a bit of a mess."

Mont stepped forward with his hand out. "Glad to see you, Turly. Glad to have the law in charge."

"Pot's on," Sill said. "Want a cup to jerk the old brain into sharper focus?"

"Thanks," Turly said, "but we better get right onto the case." You could guess it was that part about jerking the old brain into focus that made him turn down the coffee.

Mont led the way and we all marched out to the bunkhouse. But before he joined us, Turly reached into the sidecar and pulled out a small notebook, the kind that folds back from the top. We supposed he had a pen or pencil poked away inside the heavy blue shirt he was wearing. There were pockets all over the front of it. "You see something," he said. "You remember seeing it. It's just as clear in your mind as the look of the fried egg you had for breakfast, but unless you wrote it down you can't be sure. Things start crowding in. First thing you know you start thinking you saw a big hoof print in the mud, when what you saw was nothing but a mark where somebody's pot had rested."

We went in the bunkhouse and lined up a polite distance away from Burt's bunk. Turly took a quick look and then backed up a step. "Trust nobody's touched a thing," he said. "Trust every bit of blood and bedding is just as you found her."

We assured him that everything was just as we found her. "We figured if Burt was underneath that bloody quilt, there would be a lump of some sort."

"There's a basic problem," Turly said. "We think we got a murder on our hands, but we can't have a murder for sure until we have a body. It's called the corpus delicti."

We could get the corpus part of it because it sounded enough like *corpse,* but the delicti pulled us up some. "What's that supposed to mean?" Barney said.

"It just means the dead body," Turly answered. "It just means the body's dead."

"Then why in the hell don't you just say so?" Mont said. "It don't seem to help much to say old Burt is delicti."

Turly stopped studying the bunk to look at us. His blue eyes, still watery from the ride on the Harley, had the shine of saintly rightness. "There's a right way to name things," he said. "and there's a wrong way. If you were into the science of investigation, you would know that. I wouldn't have to explain a goddamn thing."

We could tell that old Turly was really into the science of investigation. At least we could tell that he had found his role in life. It was as if he had sometime looked around and taken stock and said to himself, "The world don't need another cowboy." He could thus forget the fact that he probably looked like a stove-up preacher every time he got on a horse and that whenever he uncoiled a rope he somehow ended up on both ends of it at the same time, holding the dally part with one hand while the loop settled softly around his own head and shoulders. That's when he found the Harley waiting for its man of destiny. That's when he pulled the campaign hat down square upon his head.

"I'll continue with my close examination," Turly said. "You boys can wait outside." We started to leave. "But don't go away. I'll need to ask some questions. I'll need to get some alibis."

Outside we added some afterthoughts to what we had been thinking. "Strikes me," Mont said, "that Chief Investigator Turly Sinker has been reading too many goddamn books."

"And that's funny," Sill added. "I didn't even know that old Turly could read."

"Anyway," Mont went on, "he's got the twist of the investigating business. He's learned enough to know that if there's a corpus delicti hiding in the bushes, there must be somebody else who pulled the trigger."

"Or carved away with a butcher knife," Sill added.

"Or chopped away with a woodpile ax," Barney added.

Turly, who had just backed out of the bunkhouse, heard these pleasant possibilities. "That's a fair enough deduction," he said. And we all wondered where the hell old Turly had come up with the word *deduction*. "It's those goddamn books." Mont said. "There was a time when Turly wouldn't have known a deduction from a dried rhododendron."

"And we all sure as hell know what one of them little buggers looks like," Barney said.

Turly still had his notebook open. His pencil was still gripped in his tight fist. You could tell Turly meant business by the way he squeezed that pencil.

"Suppose we get right into the interrogations," he said. The pencil pointed upward poked the air around him. "We don't know where we are, we don't even know where to start until we've made our way through the interrogations."

"The pot's still on," Sill said. "We may as well ease our way into those interrogations with a cup of demitasse. It might even help one of us remember how he sliced the meat off poor old Burt."

Turly stopped poking the air. "No," he said, "we can't pretend this is just a tea party. We can't pretend this is another meeting of the Pinville Garden Club. Murder has been done. And that fact changes how we go about our business."

We were all ready for a cup of Sill's best brew, but we had to go along with the chief investigator. We had sent him the word that things were out of joint. We had placed ourselves in the hands of the law. And now we had to wait while Turly got things straightened out again.

"We'll start out right where we are," Turly said. "Let's just say you four boys are the prime suspects. That is, unless you want to include that old bull with the cut-up balls. And even then you'd have to prove that the old fellow knows how to use a knife or an ax or maybe the blade of a scythe. Being an old bull, he might choose that as his weapon." Turly grinned for the first time. "Just surrounding the facts with the aura of possibility."

I thought to myself, Mont's right. It's all those goddamned books.

"You boys make yourselves comfortable on the steps leading up to the crime," Turly said. "And I'll just stand back a bit and open the game with some questions."

We sat down and waited.

"Mr. Silliman Sanders," he said to Sill, "that your full name?"

"I did have an initial somewhere in there," Sill answered, "but I doubt it has much to do with murder."

"Never can tell," Turly answered. "Once heard about a suspect named Carlton C. Chidester. Turned out his middle name was Chumley. Turned out that made him a fourth or fifth cousin of Jack the Ripper."

"F. for Frederick," Sill said. "F. Silliman Sanders."

"I once saw a bank robber named Frederick," Mont said. "He was on his way to a hanging. Good-looking fellow, except for one eye that wouldn't open when he smiled. Didn't matter much though. He didn't seem to do much smiling."

Even Turly could see that at the speed the interrogation was moving, he wouldn't get through the first round of suspects until late July. He poked the pencil upward like a preacher reaching for a rope of glory. "Suppose I make some rules," he said. "Suppose I asked the questions. That's my job as the chief investigator. And suppose the suspects, one at a time, answer those questions. That way we'll get some evidence. That way we'll get some answers."

And that way, I thought, he'll get something he can write in that waiting notebook.

"Where were you, Mr. F. Silliman Sanders, on the night of October 15?" Turly plunged in.

"Was that last night or the night before?" Sill answered. "If it was the night before, I was in Pinville until damn near midnight, mostly at the Pinville Pin and Pickup Club. The pin is for bowling and the pickup is for getting a lift in life from one of Harvey's half-dead beers. I don't know why in the hell Harvey can't keep that stuff on ice. It would live a whole lot longer. But I did notice this dame at one of the lanes. Every time she leaned over to let the ball go, she showed us about six inches of white thigh, with only a couple of black straps to keep it modest. I'll admit I've seen better even in Pinville, which I trust you'll agree, Mr. Chief Investigator, isn't exactly your ordinary Mount Parnassy or whatever that Frenchy place is called."

"The fifteenth was last night," Turly was obviously trying to get back on the trail.

"That does make a difference, doesn't it?" Sill said.

"And the difference?" Turly asked.

"Well, mostly I was sleeping that night," Sill said.

"Mostly?" Turly said. He sort of pounced on the word.

"Yes, mostly," Sill answered. "I think it was twice I got up to take a leak. Probably a combination of my own good coffee and that watery beer Burt hauled back from Pinville. Could be my pipes are getting clogged a bit. Could be my tank is starting to shrink. Stands to reason a man breathes all this desert air he's going to dry up some of his parts a bit. Ever notice that a stock pond gets a little smaller each year the rains don't fill it to the top?"

"Hear or see anything strange when you left your bunk?"

"It seemed to me that Barney was snoring in a little different way. The air sort of snuffed in jerks and then popped out all at once, like a small explosion. Reminded me some of a .22 short fired under a pillow."

"Are you sure it wasn't a .22 short fired under a pillow?"

"Of course you can't be absolutely sure about a thing like that. It's the pillow that throws you off. Pillows always seem to have a strange effect on things. And the strangeness seems to depend on what's inside the pillow. Take your ordinary white chicken feathers. They give one effect. It's quite different from what you get with the down of a large goose. And even then there are interesting variations."

So far Turly hadn't heard a thing he could put down in his notebook. "But it could have been a gun shot?" he said.

"It could have been," Sill answered. "Or it could have been a late night fart. I can't swear which end of the bunk it came from. It could have been a shot under Barney's pillow. It could have gone through the thin part of the cloth. It could have gone on to hit the board across the back of Barney's bed and then slid around wild-like till it reached old Burt and made the blood to flow."

"And then there would be a hole in the pillow," Mont said. "A little hole, not bigger than a pencil. Now if it was a .44 or maybe a shotgun, there would be a hole you could put your finger through or even several fingers. It would depend—"

The Bunkhouse Murders / 159

"Wait," Turly said. "Just wait. We've got to take this investigation one step at a time."

"Or you could say," Sill said, "one pillow at a time."

Turly hesitated. You could tell he needed to ask his questions so he could write something down in his notebook. But he could tell we were waiting now while he inspected that pillow.

Still carrying the open notebook, he turned and charged into the bunkhouse. We waited, trying as hard as we could to be sober and duly respectful of the law. Finally he appeared at the door, the campaign hat still square across his unsmiling face.

"No hole," he said. "Not even the hole a good hat pin could make."

"I'm not surprised," Mont said. "It's been at least three years since Barney kept a hat pin. I don't even remember what he did with it."

"That means," Sill said, "that Barney couldn't have done it. He didn't have a weapon. He didn't have a gun to make a hole in the pillow. He didn't even have a hat pin to stab old Burt."

"Wait," said Turly. "Just wait. It's my job to figure out the meanings."

"We've been waiting," Mont said. "We've been waiting to hear you read the name of the murderer out of that goddamn notebook."

But old Turly had done about all the investigating he could stand for one day. "I've just started," he said. "I've just started with Mr. Sullivan. And I've got all you other suspects to interrogate. But for now I'm closing the book. I'm heading back to Pinville."

"We could put you up," Sill said. "Save you all that ride. Save you wearing out your Harley. Plenty of room now in the bunkhouse. Wouldn't take long to wipe some of that blood out of Burt's bunk."

"I've heard that murderers like to return to the scene of their crime," Mont said. "In which case you'd be right there waiting to put the law on him."

Turly was getting a little green around the jowls. Then he stiffened some. "I need to get back and make my report. I need to get back to see what my facts are telling me."

"Let us know how she all comes out," Sill said.

"Oh, I'll be back," Turly said. "I'll be back first thing in the morning. I'll be hot on the trail again. In the meantime keep an eye out for anybody carrying a knife or an ax—"

"Or a hat pin," Mont added. "If we run onto a hat pin with blood still drying on its sides, we'll tie it up for easy finding."

Turly squinted in a determined way. "And don't let me find all my suspects run off to other lands and places. I ain't got time for all that fancy travel." With that he stomped on the Harley. It began sputtering, and finally it coughed up enough power to roll away on its own three wheels. Turly held his head down and didn't look back.

"That old Turly's a regular Mister Doopin," Sill said.

II

While we waited for Chief Investigator Turly Sinker to return to the scene of the crime, we had some matters of our own to take care of. First there was the business of a funeral for Burt. We all knew that old Burt was not much on funerals, especially his own, but we knew that it wouldn't look right to just slide by his passing. Chief Investigator Sinker might be blind to a hundred things that fell right in his way, but he would notice if we didn't stir around to do Burt the proper honors. And of course what would come out of that noticing would be the conclusion that criminals don't put on much of a funeral show for their victims. The truth was that we were ready for a good funeral. We had the right outfits waiting in our war bags. We had a stored-up sense of sadness. We even had a sort of notion about the words that ought to weigh solemnly on the air. You could say that we needed a funeral just to keep our spirits firm. As old Burt himself used to say, a man needs to slip in a cow pie at least once a year so he won't start thinking that life is nothing but a bed of roses.

The trouble was that to hold a funeral we needed a body to be sad about. We could nail together a box of about the right size, and we could even put Burt's name on it, but it would not be the real thing unless Burt was inside starting his long journey back to dust and ashes. Sill suggested we could have a memorial instead. Said he had heard of a case where the deceased had slipped onto the feeder belt of an old steam-powered threshing machine. He had gone into the machine before they could get it stopped. They considered holding a funeral over the thresher itself, using the big ugly contraption as a sort of coffin. But then they began thinking that if they ran it a few more minutes something might come out alive, maybe the man himself pretty much in his entirety. So they started her up again and let her run for about five minutes. But nothing came out that was especially unusual. The wheat they were threshing was a red winter wheat, and Sill said he supposed they could have said the wheat coming into the bags was a little redder than usual. But you couldn't be sure. It may have been just the way the afternoon sun hit that part of the thresher. So they gave up having a genuine funeral and had a memorial instead. They all stood around a bag of wheat with their hats off, and the old man who had charge of the steam tractor said a few words about the way life is filled with moments of sorrow which we must accept along with the pleasures of a good meal, a good wife, and the knowledge that the winds of fortune don't always blow against the way we are going. He concluded by expressing the hope that Mr. Coolidge would be duly reelected.

We agreed that a memorial was clearly the way to go. We could gather in the bunkhouse. Sill could read a passage from "The Cowboy's Farewell," and then together we could hum a chorus of "Little Joe the Wrangler." It wouldn't exactly be high church, but it would do for Burt, especially since we didn't have a single remain to weep over. It would maybe clear some of the dust along the trail, keep his horse from stumbling on the long ride to the great pasture in the sky.

But first we had to figure out a way to spend the night. Even if we took the trouble to wipe out some of Burt's blood, his bunk would come out as something less than a cozy corner. Nobody seemed eager to stretch out in the bunks nearby. "Nothing in there that can harm a fellow," Mont said.

"It's not what's in there that bothers me," Sill said. "It's what's not in there."

"It's like a goddamned hole that's haunted," Barney added.

"We've got to sleep somewhere," Mont went on. "Unless we go down and share the straw with that old almost-deballed bull."

"What we can do," Sill said, "is board her up. Not actually

board her up, because we haven't got the boards, not unless we want to spend some time taking the nails out of some old ones. I mean we can close her off by nailing Burt's saddle blanket across the open side of his bunk, that old blanket he always had to fold an extra time to keep it from flapping down around the old mare's belly. I remember once when that blanket slipped clear down and almost rubbed her old dried tits. She didn't like it a bit. She just stood there trying to bring her right rear hoof up close. She couldn't even come within a decent fanning distance."

We got some fencing staples and a hammer. The blanket was already in the bunkhouse, a little dusty with range dirt and dried sweat, but she unfolded all right and fit over the opening as if Burt had that need in the back of his mind.

"We could do a little cleaning up first," Sill said. "Scrape a little here and there. But this blanket will save the trouble."

"Besides," Mont added, "it may turn out that Chief Investigator Sinker hasn't yet finished his close look at the scene of the crime."

"He may find out, when he opens that notebook, that he don't even know what color the ticking is. He can probably guess that old Burt's blood was pretty much red as usual, but that ticking is going to give him pause."

It turned out that we didn't need to worry about the pause that ticking would give old Turly. Turned out that there was a lot more than ticking to investigate. Turned out the crime had doubled or maybe more than doubled, if you counted the long hole a knife had made in Burt's old blanket.

We rolled out after a long night. Even with that blanket nailed over the opening, it was not easy to settle down to some sound sleeping. We rolled out—all of us but Sill. In Sill's bunk, all over the blue-striped ticking was another reckless scattering of blood. And no matter how open-eyed we looked, there wasn't even the littlest sign of Sill himself, not even a bone of the hand that had so lovingly tended our coffee pot. And when we happened to look up at Burt's bunk, the blanket we had nailed so tight was slashed damn near in two from top to bottom.

Overnight the situation had changed. All the planning we had done was scattered to the side of the road. It was like a good load of baled hay when one of the front wagon wheels comes off.

First of all we couldn't hold the memorial service for Burt because we didn't have anybody to say a few lines from "The Cowboy's Farewell." We could have turned that sad duty over to Barney, except that he didn't know "The Cowboy's Farewell." Unless he had been keeping his literary talents under a grain sack, we supposed he knew only one poem and that began "A Bunch of the Boys Were Whooping It Up." We had to admit that the poem had a certain musical charm to it, but it lacked the sound of sadness. We had to have sadness, even if we had to resort to Mont's imitation of a love-sick coyote with his hind leg caught in a trap while his bitch girlfriend trots on over the hill.

But now things were getting out of control. We couldn't easily have one memorial serivce, and now we needed to have two. Things were all out of balance. To have a good funeral you have to have a bunch of mourners. It isn't a matter of certain numbers, but at least you have to be able to count the bowed heads on no fewer than two hands, and you have to count on at least six to carry the box. A memorial service may not need the six to carry the box, but it ought to be clear at a glance that the memorializers outnumber the memorialees. Putting it another way, those on the outside of the boxes ought to outnumber by a few head those on the inside of the boxes.

So the impending formalities were our first problem. Even before we began looking for the corpus delicti, or the delicate corpse, as we decided to call it. Turly said it was Latin, but old Turly didn't know any more about Latin than he knew about lanolin. But since we couldn't get on with planning the formalities, we decided to work on the immediate practicalities, to wit, locating the carcass of one Silliman Sanders. When the chief investigator sputtered down the hill, we could be ready with our report, namely that we had searched the hereabouts and found no sign of the late and now lamented Sanders. We could tell Turly that for all we had found out, Sill was somewhere up there heating up the great coffee pot in the sky. We looked around, checking the outhouse, the darkness behind the old John Deere, even the crevices where the bales had slipped. But Sill had vanished. Except for the blood, he had disappeared without leaving enough meat and bones to make even a weak cannibal stew.

We were waiting on the late Silliman Sanders' porch when we heard the sputtering of Turly's Harley. Mont had brewed up a pot of demitasse, a little bitter with the grounds floating to the top

164 / The Bunkhouse Murders

like straw on a feed yard pond, but it could be we judged the brew unfairly out of respect and memory of the cook we had honored, even when the stuff he poured looked like mud from a stomped-in spring.

Turly pulled up pawing the air with his right leg. Mont said out loud before the sputtering stopped, "If I was that sidecar, I'd say, goddamnit, Turly, if you can't trust me to keep this outfit upright, then leave me off somewhere so the turkeys will have a place to nest in. There's nothing as humiliating to a sidecar as to just go along for the run of it, as if somewhere down the road there might be a German general who needs a quick ride to the front."

Turly turned off the Harley, and when he had got both legs together and his hat squared off, he turned to his row of suspects.

"All right, men," he said. "Let's get on with the interrogation. Let's pick up where we left off."

"Chief," Mont said, "you forgot to open your notebook. Personally I hope some of the things I'm about to reveal are worth putting down in that notebook."

Turly lost his stiffness a bit. His investigator's engine sputtered like that old Harley. You could tell he didn't like to forget anything, especially the notebook where the evidence gathered. It was like telling a dancer his shoe was untied. At the same time his bent ears under that campaign hat must have twitched a twitch or two when he heard the word *reveal*. There he was about to hear revelations and he didn't have a thing to put them down in. You could say he looked a little bit like Moses waiting for God to start lining up the commandments and suddenly realizing that he had left the tablets somewhere back in the kitchen or wherever he kept them.

Turly could have said, "All right, you guys, shut your eyes for about half a minute while I reconnoiter." He didn't, probably because he didn't know a damn thing about reconnoitering. If he had said it, he would have had to stand in a twitchy way another minute while he figured out what he had to do if he went reconnoitering. We didn't shut our eyes, so we saw Turly let go and almost dive out of sight into that sidecar. When he came up he had the notebook, and when he had the notebook he had something solid to hang onto. "All right, men," he said again. "Let's get on with the interrogation." Then he realized he was one suspect short.

"Where's Sanders?" he said. "I didn't finish with Sanders."

It seemed like a good time to tell him. "He must have been murdered," Mont answered. "At least he didn't show up to make the morning coffee. And you could say there's a hell of a lot of blood in the place where he usually does his sleeping."

That shook up Turly some. He squinted quickly into the morning air. He gripped his pencil as if he was planning to scratch a word on a stony tablet.

"There ain't any body," Barney said. "Same as yesterday, only now there are two of them."

About then you could tell old Turly was about ready to get back on his Harley, sputter back into Pinville, and tell whoever would listen, "I quit. I turn in this cheap-looking badge. I'd even turn in my gun if I had one. I'm giving up the detective business. I'm going into something sensible and rewarding, like painting the stripes on buggy wheels."

But old Turly held firm. You could tell he was suddenly jerked into a sense of duty by a hard pull, as if his brown suspenders had become too short. "Let's have a look at the scene of the crime," he said. "Let's see what the evidence is trying to tell us."

We marched into the bunkhouse, and even before we had a chance to see the splash and splatter of Sanders' blood, he saw the two-foot slash in Burt's old blanket. "Godalmighty," he said. "Somebody around here is carrying a real wicked knife."

"Could be a sickle," Mont said. "You know one of those curvy things the Communists carry. They can be sharp enough. I remember once I was cutting the thick weeds out of a corner where two slab fences came together. I was whacking away. I wasn't even looking close-up at the weeds. First thing I knew I had sliced both ears off a big jackass rabbit. He shot past me and took off across the pasture. God, he was a funny sight."

"Or it could be a scythe," Barney added. "I remember a time I was cutting some ditch-bank rye and suddenly felt the swing slow down a bit. I could guess I had cut up something, but I couldn't tell what until I—"

"Wait," Turly said. "Just wait."

"Don't you want to know what Barney cut up?" Mont said.

"No," Turly answered. "No. That don't matter. We got to get on with the cutting here. Here and now."

"One question," Mont said. "Did the knife, sickle, or scythe—it couldn't have been a hat pin, could it—cut up Sill before it cut up Burt's old blanket?"

"Goddamnit," Turly said. "I'm supposed to ask the questions."

"If there's blood on the blanket," Barney said, "that means old Sill came first."

"And answer the questions," Turly yelled.

"Unless he or she wiped the knife, sickle, or scythe—no it couldn't have been a hat pin—on his or her pants—of course she was probably wearing a skirt—before he or she sliced the blanket."

"It's natural to wipe the blade regular," Barney added. "I remember an old fellow who was especially good at cutting calves. He always said, 'You fellows run the iron. I'll just hone up this old stabber and pop the oysters.' I think he had always wanted to be a doctor, one of those cutting doctors. As a matter of fact, I believe his mother's brother's cousin was one of them cutting doctors. Anyway he always wiped his blade on his pants just where the cloth was tight around the thigh. By quitting time he had enough blood on that thigh to make a scab big enough to top off a medium-sized blood pudding. Turned out too his mother was Swedish and had a reputation for cooking up a damn good pudding."

"Wait," Turly yelled again. "Just wait."

"We're just trying to help solve the murders," Mont said.

"We can't call it murder," Turly yelled, "until we find some bodies."

"You mean until we have some corpuses delicti?" Barney said.

"That's what I mean," Turly said. "Blood don't necessarily mean murder."

"Then what the hell does it mean?" Mont said.

"Goddamnit," Turly said. "That's what I'm trying to find out."

"Could be, Barney," Mont said, "The witnesses talk too much. It could be that the chief investigator will have an easier time of it when all us witnesses have been sliced up and sent riding up that great long trail into the sky."

Turly seemed jerked up a bit by the possibility. "We can't let that happen. There's laws against murdering witnesses."

"But does the guy who's doing all the slicing know about those laws? You notice I said *the guy*," Mont went on, "but I don't for certain know that's the right way to name him. Still could be one of what we still like to call the fairer sex. I remember a big girl I knew one time in Hooterton. She could scrape a scalded hog faster than any man this side of Denver. And when that hog was clean and hairless, she could chop him up in no time at all. She used the biggest goddamn butcher knife I ever saw, throwing the roasts and sidemeat out every which way. Turned out she got her love of cutting from her mother. That old lady could take a fistful of live chicken legs in one hand and with a few swings of the ax scatter heads and blood all over the goddamn woodpile. She only used one hand on the ax handle."

"I knew an old lady like that," Barney broke in. "Seems she had only three fingers on the chicken hand—"

"Wait," Turly yelled. "Wait. Wait."

We waited. But by then old Turly seemed to have forgotten what we were waiting for.

"See what you wrote down last in the notebook," Mont said.

He took a quick fierce look. We knew he wouldn't find anything. We knew he hadn't yet got around to writing any evidence.

"You were just about ready to see if there's blood on the blanket," Mont said.

If there had been anything else he could think of that he had been about ready to check on, Turly would have been glad to have it. But the complexities of the crimes had him surrounded. He was backed all of the way into a corner. Even with that campaign hat square as a board across his forehead, even with a little of the morning sun getting in to give a shine to his badge, he reminded us of a movie cowboy whose horse and girl have both been stolen. It seemed clear that we would have to give him some help.

"While you're looking for that blood," Barney said, "you can easily check on something else."

"Something else?" Turly answered. "Something else?"

I was about to suggest that maybe he had better get on the Harley and run into Pinville to pick up a bigger notebook. With all the elses that kept coming up, he was going to need a lot of writing space.

"It seems to me," Barney said, "that when you're investigating that blanket up close, you can maybe figure out whether the hole was cut from the outside or from the inside."

---

168 / The Bunkhouse Murders

"The inside?" Turly said. "The inside of the bunk? The inside of Sullivan's bunk?"

"Don't think it would be hard to do," Mont said. "You can probably tell from the way the wool ends are bent. If they're bent out, it stands to reason the blade was used on the inside."

"But who could have been in there?" Turly was still trying to get squared off again.

"We of course don't know," Mont said. "That's what you chief investigators are supposed to find out."

"Could have been Burt's ghost," Barney added. "I don't figure Burt's ghost would like being shut in there."

You could tell old Turly wasn't much into detecting ghosts.

"But whatever it was in there," Turly said, "it had to have a knife to cut that hole. Unless he hid a knife in there before he became a disappearing corpse, I don't see how there could have been a knife to cut that hole."

"That's the trouble with all you investigators," Mont said. "You have to be so goddamned reasonable. You have to expect that the remains when you find them will have five toes on every foot. You have to expect that the thumb will be on the inside of every hand."

Turly blinked twice in the morning light. He still held the notebook open. The pencil was waiting at ready.

"I knew a man once," Mont went on, "who had seven toes on his right foot. I saw these toes once when I said to him, 'Wilford, I always wondered why the boot on one foot is wider than the boot on the other foot.' He pulled off the boot, peeled down his sock, and sure enough there was a row of toes like the short side of a goddamned accordion. Those toes explained a lot about old Wilford. Whenever he chased a calf in the branding pen, he ran in a sort of circle. I realized it was that extra weight in the boot that tipped him out of balance. If he had been barefooted, he would have tipped the other direction. I once saw a cougar with just one extra claw on his jumping foot, and that goddamned cougar was a springer. I imagine sometimes he got such a grip on things that he sailed right over the top of whatever it was he was meaning to use for meat."

"Wait," Turly said. "Wait. We don't even know that the hole was cut from the inside."

The Bunkhouse Murders / 169

"But it could have been," Barney said. "It could have been. I figure if I was a ghost nailed up behind that blanket, I would be feeling around for something to cut a hole. You ever been close up to one of Burt's old blankets? That bay horse of his has a special kind of sweat. Some people like the smell of horse sweat. I knew this old puncher once who rode a sorrel horse with one black leg. I remember that horse because except for that black leg he looked a bit like that old sorrel of mine. Of course he must have smelled better. He was the best cutter I ever saw working a herd. If you had in mind to take out the steers, that old sorrel was soon onto it. I guess he could smell the difference. Wasn't much chance to pick out the tits or the scar where the balls might have been. Yes, I guess he could smell the difference. When he worked a mixed herd, he was a regular goddamn bloodhound. Which probably accounts for the fact that no matter how much he sweat on the blanket he left a certain comforting sweetness there. At least that old puncher always said so. He never spent a night on the roundup without using that rolled-up blanket as a pillow."

"Wait," Turly said again.

"We have been waiting," Mont said. "We've been waiting the whole damn morning. And so far the chief investigator hasn't found a single goddamn corpus."

"So far," Turly answered, "it's one of your stranger cases."

I could have added, and the strangest thing about it is the chief investigator himself. But I didn't say that. In a matter like this you had to go with the law, and you had to go with what the law looked like, how it wore its hat, how it filled its notebook so that it could ride its Harley away into the sunset.

"If you will permit a suggestion, Mr. Chief Investigator," Mont said, "let's use some of that logic you were talking about. Let's do some reasoning."

You could see some surprise in Turly's face. You could guess that he supposed he had been the very embodiment of logic and reason. After all, isn't that what an investigator is? Turly probably didn't know a syllogism from a swivel chair, but his thinking likely went like this: all investigators are logical. Turly Sinker is an investigator. Therefore, Turly Sinker is logical. You could see surprise, but you could also see pleasure. After all, or at long last, we were coming around to his style of detecting.

"Yes?" he said.

"Well," Mont answered. "I would go about it this way. I would say to myself, now if you were a corpse, especially one of those delicti kind, where would you hide yourself?"

"I think that puts us on the right track," Barney added. "It stands to reason that you can't get anywhere without first taking into account the reasoning of the corpse himself or, in this case, the corpses themselves. It stands to reason that one corpse will be happy in one place. Another corpse will be happy in another place. Take being stuffed down between some bales of hay. Hay dust has different effects on different fellows. I knew a cowboy once who would sneeze at least three times if you ever said the word *alfalfa* out loud. It didn't make any difference how soft you said it. Did you ever see the nose of a badger when it's ploughed up a bed of red ants? This cowboy's nose was just like that."

You could tell that we had lost old Turly again. You could tell that he was having trouble making our logic his logic. Probably there was nothing in those books he read that touched on how a badger looks when he's in trouble.

"I figure I'll just go out and look around," Turly said. "Check out some places where corpuses may be hidden."

"That's a real good idea," Barney said. "Just remember when you're poking through those bales of hay that you may be one of those fellows who just can't be comfortable around a sniff of hay dust."

"Don't worry about that," Turly said heroically. "I've spent my time smelling cows and cowboys."

"Course there's another thing to think about," Mont said.

"And what's that?" asked Turly.

"You may uncover the corpus just about the time he gets ready to sneeze."

"I don't believe I ever saw a sneezing corpus," Barney added. "Not up close at least."

Turly had had enough advice. He strode off toward the cow pond. There were cattails growing thick along one side. Turly probably figured in those cattails would be a good place to dump a body.

"Watch out for the quicksand," Mont called.

"And look out for the moccasins," Barney added. We all knew that nobody had ever seen a moccasin in this country, let alone around that pond, but we all figured it would be a good thing to

The Bunkhouse Murders / 171

warn Turly anyway. Bloody crimes had been done, and Turly was the man to solve them. Maybe he wasn't much as a detective, but he was all we had. We had to go with Turly.

We all sat down on the bunkhouse steps and watched him detecting. When he got down to it, his head bent forward. Even though he was walking, he looked like he was riding that Harley.

"That old Turly," Mont said, "is sure as hell a real old Mister Doopin."

III

While Turly was searching, we had a chance to ponder the formalities again. It seemed clear to even the most patient of cowboys that we had better damn soon get started up the funeral trail, or things were going to get completely out of hand. Having a funeral without a body was hard enough. Having a funeral without two bodies was twice as hard. Already we were beginning to see the problem of having a funeral without three bodies or maybe even four. And if we swung over to the memorial style, we still had our problems. The raw truth was that we were getting mighty short of sad-faced talent. You had to have sad-faced talent or you could easily end up with a coming-in party instead of a going-out party. We could all remember when old Jim Bassel started up the final trail. His friends wanted to give a him a good send-off, so they hired the preacher from over to Brancher. Trouble is they didn't make clear to the preacher whether Jim was dying or marrying. And after the long dusty ride from Brancher to Pinville, he stopped off at the Pickup Club and soaked up seven or eight of Harvey's late draft beers. By the time he got to that old warehouse where they sometimes put on funerals, he was ready for celebrating, even if he had been told it was to be a burying speech and not a firing-up for the happy nuptials.

"Remember when they sent old Bassel on his way?" I said.

"God yes," Mont said. "That old preacher stood there by the coffin, and when he made a powerful point about love and understanding in the home he brought his fist down hard on the coffin lid and old Jim must have thought he was on the inside of a goddamn bass drum. When that preacher really warmed up, he shoved his big hand into the sky and we waited while we held our breath, until the fingers curled together and down she came. I remember a part about riding life's trail hand in hand together. 'That's what matters. That's what makes the glue that binds forever. In that is the hobble that's stronger than rawhide and softer than silk. In that is the mystery of the two become one.' Each time he came to the word *that* he banged down on the lid. I figured if the sermon had gone on much longer, old Jim would have risen up out of the box, yelling, 'By god, I don't mind being buried, but I sure as hell hate being pounded to death along the way.'"

"It was a good preach," I added. "Maybe it didn't have a full dose of sadness in it, but except for the pounding I think old Jim must have enjoyed it."

"Maybe that old preacher is still banging away over in Brancher," Barney said. "Maybe we could get him to ride over in Turly's sidecar and give us a real service, one of those two for price of one jobs."

"We could try," Mont answered. "But I figure he's probably long gone. I figure the good people of Brancher finally said to him, 'Preacher, you are a good man, and you have a powerful sense of sin and salvation in your heart. But the truth is we've run out of boards. Unless we start making pulpits out of cedar posts and shed iron, we aren't going to have a preacher's place to stand in.'"

"Besides," I said, "there's the problem of the boxes. Up to now we need two. But if they're both empty, they're going to have a hollow sound. And he's going to have to decide which one to pound with his fist. Unless of course he's what they call ambidextrous."

"I knew one of those guys once," Barney said. "He could swing a rope with his left hand, or he could swing it with his right. He had that trouble too. While he was deciding which hand to use, the calf sometimes got out of range or got mixed up with the cows again. I remember once he threw his rope anyway and came up with a sad-faced old cow that could have been the calf's grandmother. I still remember the look of pity in that old cow's eyes."

"On the other hand," Mont said, "two boxes might be better than one. One could be bigger with a deeper sound. Or we could fill one part way up with rocks. Sort of like a box duet. This band came through Pinville once. The drummer had more goddamn drums than a second-hand drum shop. It took that guy most of an hour to set them all up. They had to be close around so he could hit a little one or a big one or both at once. I suppose it depended on the music, but once they got started I swear to hell he didn't pay any attention to the other guys, just pounded away crazy-like with both hands while he stomped his feet and grinned like a cat with the summer colic."

We got about that far along on the memorial plans when Turly showed up with his notebook still open and the piercing look still fixed in his eyes. The shine was pretty well gone from his leggings. A half-dried crust of mud, cow shit, and alkali dust reached clear to his knees. I thought at once that even if he was an investigator and not a cowboy the boots would come in handy. The thing about boots is that they don't expect much shining. Of course there are exceptions to this rule, too. I rememer seeing a dude in Pinville who kept looking down at his toes. At first I wondered if he was trying to make sure that he had his boots on the right feet. But when I looked closer I could see the shine on those pointed toes. I figured he was trying to see his own reflection there, maybe wondering if he had his hat tipped at just the right angle. He was a handsome son of a bitch, so I didn't judge him harshly. But the thing about leggings is that they demand shining. No point in wearing leggings unless they catch a bit of sunlight every time you walk across the street.

"I see, Chief Investigator," Mont said, "that you didn't go the whole way down in the quicksand."

"And from the fact that you ain't limping too bad," Barney added, "I'd say you made your way through that nest of moccasins. Probably tried biting through those leggings and found the taste a little gamy."

"And I don't see you've got your tie rope on anything bloody, killer or killee."

"Made a circle around the whole goddamn place," Turly said. He was still panting a bit from all that walking. "Looking for tracks," he added. "I figure if the murderer ain't still here, if he ain't hiding out in some place like the attic of the cowshed or the basement of the outhouse, then he must have fled the scene of the crime. And then he'd have to leave tracks—unless he's a goddamn vampire."

"Too bad we can't have a look at Burt's neck," Barney said.

"Burt's neck?" Turly said.

"See if there are any teeth marks," Barney answered. "I've heard that's the way the vampires get their blood."

But you could tell that even if he had been the one to bring them up, old Turly wasn't into vampires. "I'm convinced," he said, "that this murderer doesn't fly around with wings like a bat."

"Something in that notebook tell you that?" Mont said.

"No," Turly answered. "Just stands to reason."

"I agree," Mont said. "A vampire wouldn't have wasted all that blood. Wasting blood runs against their basic habits. Now a weasel's different. Seems like he enjoys just throwing it around. I heard about a chicken coop once. Somehow the weasel got in. When the farmer opened the door, the blood ran out like a small river with feathers floating like cute little ships. That weasel had slaughtered every goddamn hen."

That wasn't the reason Turly was standing to. He needed to keep his doubts about vampires in general, not just about unreasonable vampires.

"Then there's got to be a track," Barney said. "There's got to be a murderer's track."

"That's right," Turly answered. "There's got to be a murderer's track. Unless—"

"Let's hold the *unless,*" Mont said, "until we get used to the track. You say you didn't see the murderer's track, but maybe that's because you were just looking for a certain kind of track."

You could tell Mont shouldn't have said that. Turly's lips sucked in as if he had bitten a raw chinch bug. It was almost like telling the minister that he didn't know the cloven hoof of the Devil himself.

"You could say," Mont went on, "that a murderer leaves a special kind of track, maybe a drop of blood on every other bush. Or if he's dragging the carcass of Burt or Sill, maybe he's making a shallow furrow, fertilized from here to there with bits of blood and brains. But this kind of track would be your obvious track, and maybe this murderer is not your obvious type. Still I figure the murderer does leave his track. A bunch of murderers don't

The Bunkhouse Murders / 175

tramp the ground down in the same way as a troop of Boy Scouts or the ladies of the Pinville Gin Rummy and Jogging Society. Say an ax has been the bloody weapon. Now if the murderer carries that ax away in his left hand, his left boot print is going to be a bit deeper, not much, but enough so that a good tracker can see the difference. I once knew a fellow like that. As a matter of fact he was a second cousin of the guy with seven toes on his right foot. If he ever had a chance to see an outlaw's boot tracks, he could tell whether he was left-handed or right-handed, the gun in the holster making the difference in the look of the track. I believe that fellow was shot by a one-armed bank robber. Seems the robber had lost his left arm to a bear trap somebody had set in the vault. But he never switched sides for his holster. Habit I guess was what kept him going on the old way."

"I heard about a man," Barney said, "who escaped from a whorehouse wearing a pair of high-heeled slippers. Seems he was bare-nekkid otherwise."

"Wait," said Turly. "We ain't into banks and whorehouses."

We waited.

"Remember," Turly went on, "there's still that *unless* you made me save."

"Unless what?" Barney said.

"Unless the murderer didn't leave," Turly answered. "Unless it's what we call an inside job. Unless he's waiting here until the whole thing blows over."

"That don't leave a hell of a lot of suspects," Mont said.

"I look around," Turly said, "and I come up with right around three."

I looked at Mont and Mont looked at Barney and Barney looked at me.

"But we already proved that Barney couldn't have done it," Mont grinned. "He can't even remember the last time he had his hat pin."

Turly tried to grin back, but you could tell he was still biting down on that chinch bug. "We got to get back to the interrogation. We got to get back to taking a careful look at the whole situation. We got to find out about motives and alibis. We got to gather all of the facts of the case."

"But before we do all that," Mont said, "we got to get some

chuck. I figure death by starvation is a kind of murder. Starving an officer of the law is one your more serious crimes. I remember a sheriff who got his boot caught in an old posthole, and before he got his foot out of that boot, he went for three whole days without so much as a good veal cutlet. Of course in a way it was his own fault. He wore his boots way too small, usually a lizard skin with extra pointy toes. Still, on principle I'd favor a judgment against that hole, maybe around three years and a fifty-dollar fine."

So we adjourned to our cookless kitchen. Turly took off his campaign hat and set it carefully on the woodbox. There was no reason for him to bare his head. There wasn't a lady within ten miles, and some of the women just beyond that line wouldn't have cared whether Turly wore his hat or tied his hair up in rusty rollers. In her pink-walled living room, Mrs. Pulley would have expected a man's hat to come off—even J. G. knew that much about the geography of etiquette—but out at the old man's ranch and feed yard the same rules did not apply. As far as any of us could remember, J. G. had never pulled his Stetson while he sipped a cup of Sill's best brew. So for a time the tightly drawn skin of Turly's bald head kept our minds away from the bloody events of the past couple of days. Here was a little mystery that called for investigation. You might say that for a couple of minutes we stopped to investigate the investigator.

It was a big bald head, or at least it seemed big, though probably it didn't run to much more than a seven. Heads are that way. When they suddenly spring at you in all their skin and bone, they seem to exaggerate themselves. Like another important part of the body. I remember riding along a ridge once and looking down in some brush just as Jenny Merkle had finished taking a leak. She hadn't had time to pull up her bloomers, and I thought, that's the biggest shine of a woman's moon these hills will ever see. But the next time I saw Jenny in Pinville, I made a point of getting behind her while she walked toward the Pinville Merc. I didn't see anything out of the ordinary, and I thought, a dress sure does make an unhappy difference.

It could be of course with all that investigating that Turly's brain was pushing out against that campaign hat. There was a red ring where the hat had pushed down, and maybe it was deeper and redder than usual. You couldn't help thinking that

The Bunkhouse Murders / 177

Turly had a tough problem to think about and that maybe his mind needed some room to push out into. It could be of course that Turly's thinking didn't have anything to do with it. It could be that Turly was the kind of man who always dropped his hat at the threshold of the door. Could be his mother had said to him a number of times when he was around five or six, "Turly, dear, when you come inside my house, you take off your hat or your mother will lay this poker sweetly across your bottom." The more you studied Turly as he sat there with his blue eyes blinking and his bald dome drying in the warm noon sun, the more you were convinced that whatever his other social weaknesses, he was a hat dropper, even when that hat was a campaign hat and somehow squared old Turly off against the lawless world. It didn't take much imagination to see him pulling the hat when he walked into Pinville's best house and said, "Madam, the law expects you all to behave like ladies and gentlemen." Sill used to tell about a famous French writer who never took his hat off, even in the final service. You knew somehow that Turly was not that kind of cad. But of course you knew too that Turly wouldn't be there in the first place.

We were four hungry men, without the slightest imitation of anybody you could call a cook. We looked at the old black pot on Sill's stove, hoping somehow that it would start sizzling or bubbling all by itself. After all, it had been cooking beans in the same sort of way for as long as any of us cared to remember. We had the feel of desperation.

"We can all starve to death just staring at the pot," Mont said. "Poke around in that grub box, Barney, and see if there's anything that even looks like food. If it's still alive, we'll kill it."

He shouldn't have said that about killing. The last thing we wanted to see on our plates was something that had recently had blood on it.

Barney poked around in Sill's big grub box, calling out the names of the things he knew and skipping over the mysteries. "A sack of pinto beans as raw and hard as petrified mouse turds. A sack of Arbuckle. The beans don't seem to want to move much, but if we roast them and grind them, I figure they'll lie still for the boiling." Finally he turned up a two-quart can of stewed tomatoes. "Not exactly what you can call food," he said, "but maybe the red juice will add some to a man's blood supply. If we can just figure out some way to get this goddamn lid off."

"We can use the ax as a last resort," Mont said. "But it always splashes the stuff around some. Maybe we can find a knife, one without any blood on it. One thing we can't use. That's a hat pin."

You could tell from the look on Turly's face that he was getting less hungry by the minute. Barney found an old hunting knife in Sill's tool box. The tip had been broken off, and the leather on the handle was beginning to peel, but Barney kept stabbing until finally he could pry up pieces of the top like cuts of a small pie. He found some bowls that looked clean if you didn't look too close.

When the tomatoes were poured into the four bowls, it seemed a passing meal, although you could guess that Turly expected something a bit meatier. "Now we've lived this long and found some food," Mont said, "I figure we ought to say a word of grace. No telling when and if we'll ever eat again. Since you got the text right there in your praying hand, Barney, suppose you do the honors."

Barney held the empty can out above the waiting table and cut loose. "Of tomatoes. This can contains thirty-two ounces of number one red ripers seasoned with a dash of pepper and an unknown amount of salt."

"Amen," Mont said, and then I added an echo. Turly seemed moved. I decided right then that Turly was a regular church-going man. That helped to explain why he took his hat off.

We dived into the tomatoes and held up on the talk. Even the investigator was too busy eating to get on with official business. But when we all stopped to catch our breath and feel the juices sliding pleasantly into the deep hole inside, Mont opened with a bit of reflection.

"It seems to me," he said, "that all this chopping and hacking is the wrong way to go. It lacks style. Anybody who knows the first thing about the art of murder knows there are better ways. Quiet ways. Subtle ways. Take this bowl of red ripers, for instance. Have you ever considered that a grain of rat poison no bigger than a mouse turd dropped into this bowl would do the trick? The victim probably wouldn't even be able to taste it. He might even speak with appreciation on his face and say, 'Sill, I want to compliment you on your new seasoning. It adds a special zip which I haven't tasted since that calf got loose and made the mistake of putting his left front hoof right square in the middle of the dutch oven.'"

The rest of us went back to eating, but Turly put his spoon down and pushed his bowl back a bit.

"Funny," Mont said. "I would have thought that all that investigating would make a man hungry enough to eat a nice fresh slice of coyote bait."

"Must be the old ulcer," Turly said. "Always did have to go easy on tomatoes."

"Beans is what you need," Barney said. "I knew a man once had the biggest and meanest goddamn ulcer ever grew inside a cowboy gut. I saw him bite into a tomato, and before he even had time to spit out the pits he was doubled up like a fistful of baling wire. We sat him down in a corner of the bunkhouse and fed him nothing but beans for about seven days. Straightened him out like a well-used ax handle. Bunkhouse never did smell the same. Finally had to burn the damn thing down."

Turly watched with unsmiling eyes.

Mont watched Turly and said, "Sounds like a pile of bull shit to me."

"But the main thing," Barney said, "is the way it took care of that ulcer."

Barney poked around some more and found a fistful of roasted Arbuckle beans. The grinder was a big old hand-cranked outfit bolted to the wall of the kitchen. Its flywheel was large enough to fit a tractor. When Barney got it moving at full speed it shook the whole kitchen. But it sure as hell ground those beans. You could have thrown in a handful of gravel, and it would have come out looking for all the world like nutmeg.

A quick fire in Sill's old Monarch got the pot boiling. With that new-ground Arbuckle we soon had a tasty brew. If it lacked the finer aroma of Sill's after-beans demitasse, it got the old blood stirring. You could feel the drag easing out of your hocks and the sharper thoughts start jumping around in your mind.

Turly drank his coffee, sort of straining it with his teeth.

"No reason to worry about coffee," Mont said. "Between the unground bean and the poured cup, there's not a hell of a lot of distance. Not much chance to drop in that grain of rat poison.

Besides, cowboy coffee is a brew you can trust. Putting poison in the Arbuckle would be sort of like pissing on the flag."

Turly didn't seem sure about that last part, but he went on sipping. Finally he took a deep breath, put the cup down with a lawful thump, and said, "Now we can get back to the investigation."

"I'm sure glad you're in charge, Mr. Sinker," Mont said. "I wouldn't know where the hell we are. I'm lost in a thicket. I don't know whether we're still onto vampires or the tracks murderers make or where an old cowboy might hide a bloody hat pin."

"Speaking of hat pins," Barney said, "I remember a time when Sill lost the lid to the dutch oven. We were camped on a small hill just past Pinville Creek. A little before supper time Sill started roaring around, yelling how the hell could he cook anything when the goddamn lid was missing. He said any number of strange things were waiting to jump into that pot. Turned out the lid was not really missing. Turned out it had rolled like a wheel down the hill and ended up in the waters of Pinville Creek. Didn't take a diver to find it. Water was just deep enough to cover a flat-bellied catfish."

"We had reached the conclusion," Turly said, "that either the murderer is still here or he has made some tracks when he fled the scene."

There was something commendably dogged about old Turly.

"Blood is the key to those tracks," Mont said. "What you need, Mr. Investigator, is a good bloodhound, maybe a whole pack of bloodhounds. They could sniff out the trail in no time. You can't fool a good bloodhound."

"They don't even need any blood," Barney added. "I remember a time when all this bloodhound had to go on was a pair of dirty socks. Didn't bother the bloodhound a bit. He wrinkled up his nose a time or two and headed out straight through the greasewoods. Call Bixon was sheriff then, and he damn near scratched himself to death jumping through those greasewoods. Turned out when they caught the fellow he hadn't done it."

"Done what?" Mont said.

"Stole that stray calf from the Watson herd. The calf turned up in Mrs. Watson's sweet corn patch. The corn that was left wasn't worth a good goddamn, but that calf got a good head start. As I remember he weighed in with an extra hundred pounds in the fall sale."

"I didn't find no blood," Turly said. What he meant was that he didn't need no damn bloodhound to tell him where the murderer's trail went.

"Maybe he wiped his boots carefully on some old saddle blanket," Mont said. "Did you look around for an old saddle blanket with blood on it?"

"I didn't find no blood," Turly repeated.

"Which means he could have had those bloody boots in the stirrups of a saddle. Horse tracks wouldn't show any blood, would they?" Mont went on. "A horse wouldn't be in on the murder. I doubt you could get most horses to hold still while you loaded on the delicti."

"I knew a horse like that once," Barney added. "He had a long neck and one funny eye. If you ever tried to throw a side of fresh meat up over the ass-end of the saddle, that horse would bend that long neck around like a fence staple and stare at the meat with that funny eye. About when you thought you had fooled him, he would let a snort of air at both ends, bend his neck between his legs, and shove his rump straight into the air. No telling where and when the fresh meat would come down. But he came to a bad end."

Turly waited. Whatever official question he was getting ready to ask, he couldn't resist finding out about this other bad end. Bad ends were sort of his business.

"I think I know this story," Mont said. "But if the chief investigator has no objections, I wouldn't mind hearing it again."

"No objections," Turly said. He said it with a kind of open roundness, and you couldn't help thinking that maybe old Turly had a future in the courtroom. Of course he would have to turn in that notebook for a briefcase and give up the Harley for a Buick or a Packard still in good condition.

"Ben Burling got squashed in a branding chute," Barney went on. "The boys couldn't think of anything to do but throw him across the ass-end of a saddle and haul him back to Pinville. That horse had different ideas. About the time Ben settled down to a good mashed-in slump, that horse bent his neck around and saw up close what he was supposed to be carrying. It was too much. He broke loose, threw Ben about forty feet straight up into the air, and hit out for anywhere else. When Ben came down, he bounced a couple of times, but there wasn't much bounce left in him. That squashing had pretty well taken that out of him. The horse hit the corral fence like his tail was on fire. But he must have had that neck still turned to see where Ben was going to light. Anyway he didn't count the top poles he hooked his hind legs into. Both legs snapped like rotten pine poles just below the hocks. That long neck was still turned when we shot him."

"Probaby buried the bodies," Mont said.

"I don't think so," Barney said. "I don't know what happened to the remains of Ben Burling, but I doubt they buried that long-necked horse. For one thing the ground was too goddamned hard."

"I was thinking about the subjects of Mr. Sinker's investigation," Mont said.

"I doubt there was any burying there either," Barney said. "If there is anything a cowboy hates more than a shovel, it's got to be weak coffee and a broken cinch strap."

"That's assuming a cowboy was in on the killing," Mont said.

"Where would you stash those delicti, Barney," Mont said, "if you had a bloody hand in the matter?"

Barney looked at his hands, but even before he looked Turly was looking.

"I figure I might try the baled hay after all," Barney answered. We knew that Turly had already investigated the stack of baled hay. "I don't mean some crack where some dumb cowboy was too lazy to pull the bales in tight. If you stop to think about it a hay bale is about the same size as a short man's coffin. I figure you could move a few bales, pull one out, fill the hole with delicti—you might have to double it up some—and then put the moved bales back where they were in the first place. It would be damn near as much work as digging that hole in the feed yard and maybe you're not fond of hay dust, even if the corpse himself don't seem to mind, but I figure it would take a close-eyed investigator to get onto it."

Turly had already put on his hat, pulling it down so that his ears poked out like gobs of unbaked dough.

"What about that bale that comes out extra?" Mont said. "It

would still be kind of green, as unbleached as a cowboy's upper ankle."

"You got to find a hungry cow to eat it," Barney answered. "Leave it out on the stack and somebody is going to start thinking, how come that bale is trying so damned hard to be different? Must be money or jewels or bodies hidden in that stack."

"So I figure an investigator has got a number of things to look out for. First he's got to find an unbleached bale of hay and if the hay is missing, he's got to find a cow with green leaves still stuck to her lower lip. Then he's got to find the hole the damn bale had made. And then I just hope the corpus doesn't start to sneeze."

"I'm obliged for the food and coffee," Turly said. "Now I'd better get out there and do some more looking around."

We went to Sill's porch and watched Turly angle off toward the feed yard. We knew he was heading for the stack of bales, but we knew too that he would want to get there by his own direction, inspired by what he needed to think was his own suspicion.

"By god," Mont said, "I hope old Turly soon finds something to put down in that notebook. There ain't many things sadder than a detective with an empty notebook."

IV

Late in the afternoon the investigator came into view across what we sometimes called our greasewood garden. We had stayed pretty close to Sill's porch, mainly to watch whatever there was of life drift by. A couple of clouds floated off toward the Cricket Mountains, and closer by a pair of dragonflies rested for a few minutes on the top wire of the fence. The porch made a comfortable sitting place. The floor was no harder than Sill's best Coolidge the First chairs, and while you leaned back against the frame wall, you could shove your boots out and let your legs get straight again.

When Turly trudged up, he didn't need to tell us he'd been checking on the hay bales again. Three or four alfalfa leaves still sparkled in the tops of his leggings. Anybody who's ever lived much with a hay field knows that the leaves develop a close attachment. I've known a hay leaf to show up in a man's hatband two whole years after he gave up feeding cows and went riding range fence.

We waited to hear the results of the investigator's latest investigations.

"No bodies," Turly announced.

"Too bad," Mont said, meaning it's too bad you can't write in that notebook: body, dead, a little dusty with hay leaves.

"Another good place," Barney said, "would be a big woodpile. Those juniper logs are pretty crooked, and when they're thrown together, they leave a lot of open places down under. You can't tell what might be down in those places. I saw a skunk come out of a woodpile once."

But Turly was not looking for a woodpile to crawl through. He had had about all the body-hunting he could take for one day.

"There's something sort of mysterious about this whole business," Mont announced.

"Maybe what you need, Mr. Investigator," Barney said, "is one of those round glasses that make little things big."

"What I need," Turly answered, "is a little more cooperation from certain suspects."

"I'll bet when you find those suspects they'll be willing to cooperate," Mont said.

Turly's eyes squinched in so they looked like marbles. "What I need," he said, "is a little less shit and a little more showing."

"It won't take a minute to show you the woodpile," Barney said. "There are other places too."

"I'm done looking at hay bales," Turley said. "I'm about ready to start looking at the faces of guilty cowboys."

I looked at Mont. He looked at Barney. And Barney looked at me. Then we all looked at Turly.

"And that's exactly what I intend to do when I start my investigations tomorrow morning. In the meantime," Turly went on, "I want you boys to stay put. I don't want no sneaking off. Anybody leaves here in the night will be followed like a wounded buck. By god I'll track him to the water's edge."

Old Turly was really getting worked up. It was all that frustration coming out. It was all that empty notebook weighing on his mind.

"With all due respect," Mont said, "I'd like to make a suggestion."

"I've already heard about seven hundred too many suggestions," Turly answered.

"Then one more won't matter," Mont said.

Turly was starting to twitch his right leg. You could tell he couldn't wait much longer to stomp on his Harley.

"If the murders seem to be what you experts call an inside job, you don't have many suspects. I look around me, and if I am even half as good at counting suspects as I am cows, I'd say we've got about three left. That's not a bad number, but what if one or two or even three of these would disappear, you wouldn't have a hell of a lot to go on, would you, Mr. Investigator? What I'm suggesting is that you roll that Harley out there into that shed where it can hunker down right next to all those good old saddles. We can find you a bed roll, and I'm sure there must be another can of tomatoes in Sill's old box. This way you'll be right at the scene of the crime, if there is a crime. You may even be able to see the ax fall. In which case you'll be able to clamp the cuffs on him even before he has a chance to wash the blood off his hands. In which case you can even proceed to the hanging. We've got lots of good ropes around here, and I figure that cross-bar on the gate ought to support a fair to middling killer."

Turly was clearly shocked at the possibility of lynching. He rubbed his hand across his badge. "You all know as well as I do," he said, "that I ain't no judge."

But Mont wasn't finished, whatever Turly's scruples about the law. "I remember a hanging that was complicated by the fact that we couldn't find a decent place to tie the rope. This guy weighed well over two hundred. He rode a small bay with a back as swayed as a four-man hammock. That's why we got him. All we had to work with was an old yellow pine with a ladder of dead limbs. We hung that son of a bitch about eight times before we finally got a hitch to hold him. Broke off every goddamn limb on one side of the tree."

"I saw a case a lot like that," Barney said, but before he could get started on his story, Turly interrupted. "Wait," he said. "Wait. We're not in the hanging business."

"And there's another way to look at it," Mont went on. Turly still had a lot more waiting to do. "There's the matter of protection. I have the feeling that the murders have not yet come to their bloody conclusion. Could be that somebody or some thing is planning to wipe out the whole bunch of us, one at a time of course. Which means that maybe tonight the next one will go, cut down by an ax or stabbed by a rusty hat pin. Personally I'm not ready. Personally I've had other plans for a time and place for shedding off this mortal coil. I kind of like that little home in Pinville, where they've got a climbing rose growing right up along the door and where Mrs. Beem is running the show. She's a little plump in some parts, but I've always figured if the time comes for my final back rub she's the one to do it."

"I have the feeling that something more is going to happen," Barney said. "I don't mean anything as superstitious as counting to three after you've got through with two. What gives me the evil sign is a strange tickle in my left ear."

"I know that kind of tickle," Mont said. "Never did have it myself, but I knew this cowboy who started scratching his left ear one night, long about supper time. Somebody said it's an omen of evil things to come. He didn't pay any attention to the omen, said it was all a pile of superstitious shit, but the next morning his cinch broke and he fell smack against a pile of rocks. If his hat had not been on tight, his brains would have spurted out like boiled-over gravy. He was deader than a year-old glass of beer. You'll be interested, Mr. Investigator, in the fact that we did some investigating. He hit that rock with the right side of his head, so the left ear was preserved from the damages of death and destruction. We examined it closely. But all we found was a black fly bite."

"I know another case just about like that one," Barney said.

"Stop," Turly said. "I figure you guys will be safe. If it's an outsider who's sneaking in to do the cutting and chopping, then he knows by now that the law is here, that the law is on his trail. If it's an insider, we'll find out by a kind of elimination. If I ride in tomorrow and only Barney's left, I'll know it's Barney who's been running a blood lust. He knows I know that, and so I don't think he's going to carry on the act. The same goes for you other guys. You might say I've got you boys in a deductive squeeze. You may feel a little pinched, but there's some comfort in it just the same."

So while we started looking forward to spending the night in a deductive squeeze, old Turly stomped his Harley into action and chugged up the ranch road hill. It was about time. That right leg had been cocked for so long it was beginning to twitch.

We watched old Turly drag his dust across the final roll of hill and then we settled back into our deductive squeeze. Turly still didn't have anything in that notebook, but he seemed to have the right ideas. You have to admit there was real country class in that deductive squeeze.

"Old Turly sure don't look like much," Mont said. "And he sure don't put much down in the notebook. He may not know a dagger from a dingus, but he sure comes up with some good ideas."

"As you said before, Mont," I added, "he's got the conformation of a real old Mister Doopin."

Turly was right about some things. When the Harley sputtered down the ranch hill next morning, we had no more cutting and chopping to report. As far as we could tell, in the whole section, between the south fence and the north fence, between the west fence and the east fence, there wasn't a drop of new spilt blood. The only problem was that Mont had disappeared.

Even before the investigator had let the engine idle and shoved his right leg out to catch the ground, he was looking around and counting. We stood together on Sill's long porch, and the empty spaces slowly filled with dust.

The Harley died, and Turly kept on counting.

"Where's Mont?" he said.

"He's gone," Barney answered.

"What do you mean he's gone?" Turly said.

"I mean he's gone," Barney answered. "I mean he's not here."

"Where's he gone?"

"We don't know," Barney said. "But we hope he's happy where he is."

"You mean he's dead?" Turly said.

"We don't even know that. We just know he's gone."

"We've got to get onto this," Turly said. He stomped both feet to shake some of the dust from his leggings. Then he dug in the sidecar and pulled out the notebook. It was dusty too, so he banged it smartly on a still-dusty legging. He turned to me with the most flinty way he had of looking. "Suppose you fill in the background. Suppose you tell me what the hell has been going on. And suppose you leave out all the shit."

"Turns out some of the facts may be just that," I said. But I decided to let my puzzle stay itchy, so while Turly blinked a couple of times and let the tight skin of his forehead wrinkle just above his eyebrows, I pushed on.

I told the investigator that just about dark, the three of us hauled our bed rolls from the bunkhouse and settled down to the comfort of Sill's front porch. "These boards are about as soft as a goddamn rock," Barney said, "but at least we won't have to put up with the smell of old blood and the bumping of new ghosts. Besides," he added as a happy afterthought, "we'll be right close when the morning coffee's made. We may even be lassoed out of dreamland by the goodness floating out that old screen door. Course that would depend on Sill's ghost putting on the pot."

"Never heard of a ghost making coffee," Mont said, "but I did hear a ghost that made a fair pot of beans. Course we didn't see the ghost, and the beans seemed to chew and taste as solid as the gristle of an old steer. You couldn't see even half-way through them. You could hold one of them up to the firelight with your fork, and you couldn't see a goddamn thing except the backside of a plain old country bean. The ghost that cooked those beans sure as hell didn't spiritualize them any."

"Then how did you know they were ghost beans?" Barney said.

"It was the strangeness of the circumstances," Mont answered. "We were on roundup. The outfit was small and the country was big. Too big. Only God could have found all those stray cattle, and I doubt that He would have bothered with some of them, unless He needed a few of them just for their hides. Pulley even had the cook in the saddle. That was before Sill although he resembled Sill in some ways. Had the same way of chewing his tongue while he stirred the mix he had in the pot. We came back to camp late and hungry, hungrier than a pack of coyotes crossing hardpan. It was going to be a miracle if we found enough canned tomatoes to hang our belt buckles on. But there it was, the biggest miracle ever whomped up in a roundup kitchen, a dutch oven fat as a small tub simmering with beans and chunks of beef. We all turned to the cook, and he just sat in the saddle

The Bunkhouse Murders / 189

looking. 'I would have swore to hell,' I said, 'that you were out there the whole day chasing Pulley's goddamn steers. Now it turns out that every time we all got lost in the scrub oaks, you raced back to camp and stirred the beans. It's a funny thing,' I went on, 'but I don't remember your horse having any extra sweat on him.' Cook said he would swear on the latest Department of Agriculture Yearbook that he didn't have a thing to do with it. 'Those aren't my beans,' he said. So then I figured that some Indian lady must have stopped by and filled the pot, but cook didn't like that explanation either. Said there would likely be a feather or a bead or moccasin track around. "Too bad you weren't there, Turly," I said. "Hunting for that track would have been just your kind of thing."

Turly was not about to hunt for any moccasin tracks. Seems we had been investigating for almost half an hour and Turly still didn't have the dust rubbed off the end of his investigator's pencil. "I said the background," he groaned. "I didn't ask for every goddamn bean the cook has cooked."

"It's hard to know ahead of time what's background and what isn't. Besides," I went on, "you can't always tell what little fact may have an important bearing on the case."

"Goddamnit," Turly yelled. "I'm the one who's supposed to say that."

So I got on with the background, telling Turly that we had some trouble deciding in what order we would throw down along Sill's front porch. We all knew that the weak spots were the outsides and that the safest place was the middle. "We got to settle this matter fairly," I said. "We got to leave it up to chance. You know that lady they call the Queen of Fortune. Maybe she can't see much behind that white neckerchief, but at least she don't slip her thumb onto the scales and she don't decide a man's right because he's so damn good-looking. "I'll think of a number," I said to Mont and Barney, "and each of you boys take a guess. The closest one gets the middle." So Mont said *seven* and Barney said *eleven,* and I said that they were both wrong because the number was three. That gave me the middle. And then Mont and Barney had to decide who got the east side and who got the west. I'll think of a number," Mont said to Barney, "and if you guess right you get to choose." Barney said *four,* and Mont said wrong,

---

190 / The Bunkhouse Murders

that the number was *one*. Mont picked the west side, maybe because the east side was closer to the bunkhouse. We finally stretched out on our bedrolls, and I was just beginning to think that if another big question didn't come up, we might be lucky enough to get a couple of hours sleep before the investigator came chugging down the hill.

Our luck ran out even before it had a chance to get out of the chute. Mont raised himself into sitting position, saying he needed to take a stroll up on the hill, this hill being the outhouse hill. He didn't even need to pull on his boots. "Just want to be ready," he would have said, "in case there's any running in the game." We all knew of course that a man in a good thick pair of socks could make better time getting safely out ahead of any breed of killer, even if the path was sprinkled thick with rocks and thistle burs.

I stopped talking and waited for Turly. He seemed to be chewing on something.

"Well," Turly said.

"That's it," I answered. "That's the background."

"That's all?" Turly said.

"That's all," I answered. "That's the last we saw of Mont. He didn't come back from the outhouse."

"Did you go look for him?" Turly asked.

"No, we just waited," I answered. "He may be in there yet. If he's still alive, he must be taking a mighty long crap. If he's dead, we may have to change the name of the story."

"No," Turly said. "We're not changing anything. I didn't come all the way out to this place to solve an outhouse murder."

"I heard about one of those once," Barney said. "This cowboy—I think his name was Emil Perkins, but most people called him String—was working alone at a line camp. Had himself a real good place, a shack with a window to the south and only three places in the roof that leaked. Even had his own outhouse, a one holer with a real board floor. In fact, that outhouse was about the best I ever saw, excepting a brick one some lady had thrown up a little west of Pinville. Made of yellow pine slabs, nailed together with iron spikes as long as a wildcat's pizzle. Inside that outhouse a fellow could have stood off Sitting Bull. Have always thought it was too bad General Custer didn't have one just like it to fall back into. Turned out though that its strength was String's undoing."

"What do you mean?" Turly said.

Barney welcomed the chance to tell his meaning. "When they found him, he was dead inside that outhouse. Seems the thing had fallen over on its door. String couldn't get out. He was boxed in by all those heavy slabs. You could tell by the look of his boot heels that he had tried his best to kick an opening. But the only opening was the hole, which looked out now like a set-back window, but you couldn't get much more than a head through that. He must have worn himself to a whisper beating against those goddamn slabs. Finally he must have said to himself, 'Ah shit,' and died."

"But how do you know it was murder?" Turly asked.

Barney again seemed glad to explain. "Only two ways that outhouse could have fallen on its face like that. The wind could have blown it over, or somebody could have pushed it. Now it would have taken a mighty powerful wind, and that wind would have had to be blowing to the west. Now I've heard of a couple of outhouses being blown about by the wind. Once over near Harson a whirlwind lifted one up by the roots and put it down right-side-up in the next county. Old man Killy rode the whole way, and after it landed he stepped out without a scratch. Even had his belt buckled. But that must have been one of your lighter models, thin boards with strips of rawhide to cut the wind a bit. String's slab house was another story."

Turly sighed and pushed his investigator's pencil over his right ear just under the rim of his campaign hat. "But does the story have an ending?" he said.

"That depends," answered Barney, "on what you call an ending."

"String died, didn't he?" Turly sad.

"String died," Barney answered. "But we still don't know who pulled the outhouse over."

"Pulled it over?" Turly said.

"Yes, pulled it over," Barney said. "I figure no man alone could have pushed it over, probably no two men. Would have been like shoving against the Rock of Ages. No, I figure at least two men on horseback rode up when String was busy, nailed or wired the door shut, then tied their lariats on the ends of the pole that made the roof beam. Then with good hitches on their saddle horns they took off down that outhouse hill. You can topple a good sized bull that way. Course the saddles would have to be double-rigged. Did I ever tell you about the time this cowboy was working over a single-cinched saddle?"

"Wait," Turly said. "Just wait. I better go check that outhouse." Turly took off up the outhouse trail.

"Watch out for black widows," Barney called. "When you get back I'll tell you about Sack Turpin. He had a painful experience with one of them bitey widows."

But Turly didn't even look back. He had a real determined stride. Funny I'd never noticed he was a litle bowlegged. Probably came from riding that Harley so much.

We sat down on the porch to wait.

"Seems kind of peaceful," I said to Barney. "Seems kind of peaceful knowing the law is on the trail. That Turly's a real bloodhound. He won't leave a single cow turd left unturned."

V

After a couple of hours Turly came back down the hill, and we opened our faces to hear his report. But he wasn't in the mood to do any reporting. Mostly he scowled under that campaign hat. Barney was all ready to tell him about Sack Turpin and that bitey widow, but Turly seemed to have heavy matters on his mind. Maybe they were suspicions.

I suggested that we go inside and open another can of tomatoes, but the investigator wasn't about to fall into that. You couldn't tell whether it was the fear of poisoned tomatoes or the fear of Barney's story that held him back. Turned out he had a couple of slabs of bread and butter and a big can of sardines hidden away in a sack in the bottom of the sidecar. He cranked off the lid to the sardines and set the whole oily mess like a center piece on the floor of the porch. "Help yourselves," he said. But if there was anything I liked less than sardines, I couldn't think of what it might be, and I knew Barney would rather bite down on a chunk of well-cooked steer gristle than shut his teeth on a fish that had gone mushy while waiting so long. "Thanks," we both said. Then Barney picked up by asking the investigator if he'd ever heard what Bart Goomer found inside a sardine can when he opened it on a dark night. I pulled Barney in at the snubbing post. I figured the law deserved to eat his lunch in peace. Besides if Turly didn't eat those sardines, the can would have to wait there on the porch until a stray cat came by and that might take a week. I figured the carrion beetles, whatever they could do with the carcass of a dead rabbit, would have a hell of a time making off with that sardine can.

Barney and I slipped inside, found another can of red ripers, and enjoyed our dinner, especially knowing we weren't partaking of the investigator's fish. When we came back out on the porch, Turly was gone again, although the Harley still waited in dusty sleepiness.

"He could at least have said where he was going," Barney said.

"I think he wants to do a little slinking," I said. "Probably wants to try a little of the private eye. Read about it in some mystery book."

"Probably knows what he is doing," Barney said. "But it could be he'll miss our help." Barney was silent a minute. Then he added, "And it could be we'll miss giving it."

Turly showed up an hour or so later, this time appearing like a late afternoon shadow from around the bunkhouse. As he came up sidewise along the porch, we could see he still wore his most determined look.

"Must have the case about wrapped up, investigator," I said, trying to give a happy note to the afternoon.

"Mr. Sinker's probably got his cuffs right down inside that sidecar," Barney added. "Or maybe he don't want to bother with the cuffs. Just go straight out and get the rope. I got a good hemp forty-footer still tied to my saddle."

But the investigator was not amused. He glared back, and I thought for a minute that Barney shouldn't have put his whole idea into Mr. Sinker's head. There wasn't a hell of a lot to string up around there except me and Barney.

It seemed a good time to suggest again that the investigator stay the night at the ranch. He was already getting pretty low on suspects. Maybe if he rolled out with us on Sill's front porch, he could keep the number up to two. Of course there was another way of looking at it. If the number got down to one, he could conclude without any more investigating that the survivor had to be the culprit.

"No," Turly said. "I wouldn't be comfortable in a strange bed. I need all the sleep I can get. I got to be able to see all the facts clearly."

He had a point, and we respected the needs of the law.

"If it's a matter of safety," Turly went on, "I can take care of that in a number of ways. We can turn this porch into a pretty good fort. We can lug two or three bales of hay up here and make a damn good rampart. Even got a small American flag in the Harley. We can poke the stick in a bale, and there she'll fly. Never heard of a gun, except maybe that cannon they keep over by the Pinville courthouse, that could shoot through a bale of hay. You fellows can get behind those bales and be as safe as a pair of gophers in an oak whiskey barrel. The only danger would come if the Indians shoot flaming arrows up on Sill's dry roof. That's one way. The other is what we call protective custody. This means I lock you fellows up for your own protection. It could work this way. You haul your bed rolls inside Sill's kitchen, find a rusty bucket in case you need to take a piss, and then I lock the door from the outside. It don't take much looking to see that the door doesn't have a lock, so what I do is this: I get a couple of two-by-fours and nail them across the door so it can't be opened, that is, until I get back with a middle-sized wrecking bar."

That was the longest speech we had ever heard the investigator make. We were impressed with the way he had thought things out.

"Of course," he went on, "there is the chance that we don't need to protect from outside attackers. There is the chance that when we throw up a set of protective custody we are protecting the son of a bitch we're trying to be protected from."

That was pretty strong language when it seemed to be aimed at Barney and me.

"But if one of you boys is the skunk in the bushes, it figures

The Bunkhouse Murders / 195

you won't want to make your final stink while you are nailed up inside Sill's kitchen."

Turly sure had the logic going. Maybe it was all those sardines he had stuffed down for dinner.

Even so, Barney and I decided to take our chances in the open. We weren't much on sleeping next to bales of hay, even if one did fly the flag of our native country, and we weren't about to be nailed inside Sill's old kitchen. That would be like String Perkins, only in a different kind of box.

So Turly stomped the Harley into action, and we again watched his dust follow him over the hill. We were sorry to see him go. I think we both had looked forward to some good stories while rolled in our sougans on Sill's front porch.

Now there were just two of us, it was easy deciding who would take the east and who would take the west. I asked Barney how many teeth Milt Siller had missing from his upper plate. Barney guessed three. The right answer was two. So I picked the west.

We lay for awhile. Then Barney sighed a sigh you could have almost called a groan. "Goddamn," he said. "Seems like the old world is sort of disappearing away. All the good old cowboys is disappearing one by one. Ain't enough left to hold a decent funeral."

"You're right, Barney," I said. "You're so goddamn right."

Along about midnight Barney reached up and yelled, "I ain't going to stay around and be the last. I'm getting out. I'm leaving."

Turned out he didn't even need to pull on his boots. Had them ready on his feet the whole time.

"Why don't you wait till morning?" I said.

"Had enough waiting," he answered. "Morning don't make it any better."

"I'd leave with you," I said, "except I don't fancy riding in the dark. And besides somebody's got to be here to say hello to Turly."

Barney shook my hand and took off in the dark. I could hear his boot pound growing fainter. Then all I could hear was my own breathing and the hoot of a barn owl way off in the distance. It was a very lonely sound, and I wished he would wait till he had more people to listen.

I finally slept. I guess I was pooped from all the investigation.

Even before the sun had got around the corner to hit the porch, I was pulled out of a strange dream by the downhill sputtering of Turly's Harley. I lay back and listened, seeing the dust without looking, guessing the puzzle beneath the campaign rim when the investigator saw I was the only one left.

When the Harley had stopped its idle coughing, I sat up and looked Turly straight in the face.

"Where the hell's that other suspect?" he said.

"He's gone," I answered. "He got crazy in the middle of the night and left."

"Left how?" Turly said.

"I haven't investigated," I answered, hitting that last word with a special seriousness, "but my guess is that he dragged his saddle out of the shed, cinched it on his old sorrel, and rode off into the night."

"Why did he do it?" Turly said.

I told him exactly what Barney had said. I even threw in a bit about the ghosts that Barney was seeing.

"I didn't see any tracks on the road," Turly said.

"Oh, he wouldn't take the road," I said. "Especially if he wasn't going to Pinville."

"Where the hell would he go?" Turly said.

"I don't know," I answered. Then I added, "I didn't ask him what he had in mind."

"Goddamn. Goddamn," Turly mumbled. "I've just about had it with these disappearing corpses. Why the hell can't they stay around where a guy can see how gray and cold they look?"

"You sure Barney's one of those delicti?"

"He ain't here, is he?" Turly answered. Then he strode off toward the saddle shed.

I lay back again and waited. After ten or fifteen minutes I could hear the investigator striding back toward the porch.

"The saddle's in the shed. I can tell it by the hair. And the sorrel hasn't finished eating the hay somebody gave him in the night."

"He must have walked," I said, "though Barney hates walking like he hates the itch."

"No tracks on the road," Turly said again. "No horse tracks. No boot tracks. I've seen those tracks around here. Heel print squashy like the boots don't fit."

"Those would be Barney's tracks all right," I answered. "But I don't think he would necessarily walk the road—unless he was headed for Pinville."

"Where else would he head?" Turly said.

"Who knows?" I answered. "He seemed to be saying, if I just walk far enough in any direction I'll be getting away from this goddamn place."

"I'd better cut a circle," Turly said, "and see what I can find."

"If you want some help," I said, "I'll be glad to give it. I can go one direction and you can go the other."

"No," Turly said. "I better do this investigating by myself. Besides, if you get out there in the greasewoods, I might lose you. You might fall in a goddamn gooney hole. I got to keep one of you crazy bastards alive even if it kills me."

He headed off to the west to find a point from which to start his circle. I was already to yell a warning about rattlesnakes, but when I got the yelling air up in my lungs, I decided, what the hell. I just wasn't in the mood to give a warning. I let the air out in a wordless sigh. Goddamn, I thought, it's getting mighty lonesome out here. If it wasn't for Turly, I would yank myself away and let this place become a full-fledged ghost ranch. Compared to this bunch of sheds and buildings, the public library in Pinville must be as exciting as Paris or Topeka.

In two or three hours Turly came trudging in from the east. He had gone full circle, crossing he supposed every out-going track, whatever the direction and destination. He was dusty from his leggings up, and his eyes had a pinched-in tired look. He had looked at too much dirt and grass and broken greasewood twigs.

"Find anything?" I said more in welcome than inquiry.

"Find anything," he smiled echoing my question. "I saw so many tracks I lost track." He smiled at what he had said. I was glad for that. He hadn't smiled much lately. "I found several thousand coyote tracks, several million rabbit tracks, so many goddamn cow tracks that I don't know a number big enough to count them."

"But did you find the prints of those squashy boots?" I said.

"I could count the boot tracks on one hand, holding my thumb in the middle, but I didn't find a single squashy boot track."

"Maybe he pulled off his boots and went barefoot," I suggested.

"Why would he do that?" Turly said. "He would still have to

leave a track. Besides, think of all the things he might step on in the dark, not to mention fresh cow pies and prickly pears. No, he can't try to sneak away like that. Ain't honest. Besides, it might suggest he's guilty and trying to evade the law."

I had sat there alone on that porch for so long that I was losing my power to think clearly. I was like a steer in a one-roomed box car. Turly's logic wrapped around me like barbed wire made of silk. I was getting so confused and weak that I was just about ready to yell, "All right. I confess. I did it. I did away with all those good old guys. Now it's over. Now we can stop investigating. Now we can stop chasing tracks across the salt grass pastures of the good old world." I was starting to suck in my breath so I could say all of this when Turly turned his now steely eyes straight at me.

"All right," he said. "Did you do it?"

"Do what?" I answered in surprise.

"Did you commit the bunkhouse murders?"

"Hell, no, Turly," I answered. "You know me better than that."

But of course he had me in the coils of his investigator's logic. "You're the only one left," he said. "You have to be the one who did it. The finger of the law points straight in your direction."

I could feel the point all right, but his sudden conclusion had knocked all the loneliness and guilt out of me. When I thought of hanging from some sad old tree, I cheered up considerably.

"You must have a lot of stuff in that notebook," I said bravely.

"That don't matter," he answered. "The barefaced evidence provides its own naked truth."

Ordinarily I like to ponder a remark like that, but there wasn't any time for that. I had to take it as it came.

"We won't have to worry about who is staying and who is going back to Pinville. We won't have to worry about who is protecting the protected and who is saving the saved. We're all going back to Pinville together. The law will accompany you, sir," he said to me. "It will see that you have a nice safe place in the Pinville Pen."

"All right," I answered. "I'll give up for now. I'll meet you at the Pinville Pen in time for supper," meaning I'd saddle my black gelding and ride into Pinville in my chosen kind of comfort.

"No," Turly said. "We can't do it that way. I've got to take you in. I've got to do it right."

Already I was getting the idea, and with the prospect of riding the whole way to Pinville in that sidecar, I was about to choose hanging on the spot.

"I've got a pair of cuffs somewhere down in that sidecar. We've got to use those. Going to jail without cuffs would be like going to a funeral without a hat."

I couldn't remember ever wearing a hat to a funeral, but I let the argument go by me. My only hope was that Turly would find some rightness in tying my rope halter to the back of the sidecar and leading me in. That way I could at least sit in the saddle and not have to scrunch down in that sidecar. But I let my hope go without saying it. Turly had to do things his way. He had to follow the law's ways as he knew them.

He dug out the cuffs, and I put out my hands. At first one of the cuffs wouldn't open, but Turly banged it a couple of times on his legging and finally it popped open like the jaws of a rusty crab.

"I hope you got a key that will open these things," I said. "I don't fancy spending the rest of my life, even the weeks before my hanging, with my hands locked together."

"Oh, we don't need to worry about that," Turly answered. "I've got a key. Matter of fact I've got two of them." He shook them like a rattle where they were ringed to his belt. "And even if the keys won't work, we can always walk down the street to the blacksmith shop. Ever notice the muscles on Ham Harkins' anvil arm? He could cut those cuffs the way most men would slice a doughnut."

The cuffs locked shut, and then I remembered that if I was going to arrive in Pinville looking like an innocent cowboy instead of a wind-blown looney, I had to pull my Stetson down, even if I bent my ears a bit. It took some doing, but I managed in a double-handed way to yank my hat down low and tight. If we didn't run into a cyclone, I'd probably arrive covered in Pinville, though I hoped I wouldn't run into any of my close friends, especially the ladies.

I climbed into the sidecar and sat with my butt too close to the ground and my knees drawn up almost under my chin. I thought, I don't know the name of the last German general to ride in this thing, but he sure as hell must have been a short son of a bitch.

Turly stomped the Harley into its coughing rhythm, and after he had tried it for its spurred-up power, we started into motion. Luckily we had a bit of downhill when we made the turn, so when we hit the road the Harley raced with the needed overconfidence. We chugged and sputtered, moving so fast I could easily count the rabbit turds between the wheel ruts. I was tempted to offer to walk to the top of the hill and wait for him there, but then I remembered again that I was the prisoner and that it was important to Turly that I act like one.

Just before we made the last little rise to the crest of the ridge, the Harley said, to hell with it. There's just too much goddamn load. She gasped a couple of times and fell silent in a cloud of faint blue smoke. "We'll have to push her over the top," Turly said. "She ain't used to all this load." I could have said, "I'm the prisoner. I'm supposed to stay confined to this comfortable paddy car." But the truth was I was glad to get out and unbend my legs. Another hour and they were going to have to hang me with my knees bent.

We got the Harley to the top, and from there the ranch road fell away steeply. "Get back in," Turly said. "We'll start her with compression."

I crawled back into the sidecar and Turly let the Harley loose. We had gone maybe fifty yards when Turly let the motor grab hold. The jerk damn near threw the investigator up and over between the Harley's ears, but he dug in his spurs and the old motor exploded into a rough new life. We went down the hill like a big steer with salt up his ass hole. Turly seemed to be getting back at something for all that stalling and pushing. I kept thinking, if the Harley don't fall apart and Turly don't run us off into a barbed wire fence, we'll be in Pinville before I can take a second breath.

When we started down the main street in Pinville, Turly slowed the Harley to a crawl. She still seemed to have power to move at a proper speed, but clearly Turly wanted to make a show of law. He looked straight ahead, and I tried to do the same, but I kept seeing people I knew gawking our way. One of them called so the whole goddamn town could hear, "Hey, Turly, when's the hanging going to be?" Another shouted, "He looks real mean, don't he?" By the time we reached the jail, I was sorry we had ever left the ranch. I wished a hundred times old Turly had nailed me in the outhouse and sunk it in the cow pond.

There were more smart cracks when we pulled up at the tying post in front of the jail. Turly seemed to stand at attention while I pulled myself out of the sidecar, trying to hide the cuffs and trying to lift myself into a proper straightness. I pondered again, no wonder the war lasted so long. It would take the general who rode in that goddamn sidecar a week to straighten out so he could see up over the trenches and spot the enemy.

We marched inside the old brick jail, Turly bringing up the rear with a special briskness. When we were stationed in official position beside a scarred oak table, he said, "I'll have to take your possessions. But don't worry about them. If you're innocent, they'll be returned in good condition. If you're hanged, I'll see that they reach your mother. You can hang your gun on that hook." He pointed to a row of empty hooks behind the table.

"I don't carry a gun," I answered. "You can see that, Mr. Sinker."

"I can see that," he said. "But I wanted you to know where you are supposed to hang it."

I emptied my pockets, and Turly carefully noted every object, using a stubby pencil on a yellowed sheet of paper. One silver dollar, three buffalo nickels, four fence staples, and an empty .22 cartridge shell.

"How many p's in *staples?*" he said.

"Two," I answered.

"All right. Time to get behind the bars." The door to the cell stood open and waiting. I walked in and Turly banged it shut. The clank of all that metal would have been enough to sound the closing of the gates of Hell. I hadn't been in many jails, but I had been in enough to know the truth of the observation the smaller the jail the bigger and heavier the door. You could easily imagine somebody saying to himself or maybe out loud, "Even if we don't have enough bricks to make the walls four-feet thick, we've got these old mine rails that will make a damn good door."

"Supper will be served shortly," Turly said as he put the list of my possessions under his paperweight. When I heard the clunk of it, I looked at it closely. It was the sawed-off primer butt of a 75-mm shell.

"How about a beer with the sandwiches?" I said.

"Against the rules," he answered. "Besides, who said anything about sandwiches?"

"Beer and sandwiches, with mustard on one side and pickles on the other," I said. "Just seems like a good idea."

"The prison system don't deal in good ideas," he answered.

So I was resigned to whatever the cook or the Fates or Turly himself delivered. But already I was beginning to not look forward to my supper.

After Turly left and closed the outer door, I knew for sure I was a genuine prisoner. If I had any talking to do, I would have to cuss at myself or yell at whoever might stop to listen in the world beyond the high, small, barred window that still let in some torn pieces of the afternoon light. There was a cot, all springs and no mattress, and one moth-chewed blanket. I had seen a hundred saddle blankets that looked as clean and home-like. There was a white enameled bucket with a dainty lid. It figured. Nobody ever supposed that a man needed a clean and decent blanket, but it followed in the rules of somewhere that if a man was going to piss in the open privacy of a prison cell, he ought to lift a pretty little lid and relieve himself into the white emptiness of an official-looking chamber pot. But that could wait until it was needed.

I shook the blanket and spread it double on the cot. With all that horny wire in the springs, at least there wasn't any hiding place for bugs. If there weren't any friendly rats or mice just waiting for the dark to come and if there weren't any sudden blizzards just waiting to blow in that window and freeze off my balls, then I could probably make it—at least till hanging time.

I lay down to stretch my legs. After all that time in Turly's Harley, they still felt as bent as a preacher's knees in praying time. I was just getting used to the stink of that old blanket when the outside door opened and Turly backed in carrying a tray that wouldn't have looked good holding the food of God's first cousin.

"Your supper," Turly said.

Without even looking I knew what the menu would be, but still I took a hard quick look, hoping. There were two slices of heavy white bread without butter. The center piece was a big oblong can of sardines unopened. To the back a tin cup held what I supposed was coffee.

"You'll find the key on the bottom of the can," Turly said. "I'll see if I can find a fork in the table drawer."

"You make the coffee yourself, Mr. Sinker?" I said.

"You might say I did," He answered. "At least I put the pot back on the stove."

"With all that investigating," I said, "a man can't be expected to do much cooking."

"That's right," he said.

"It's probably just as easy to hang a skinny man as it is to hang a fat man."

"That's right," he said again.

He left, and I studied that can of sardines a long time. It wasn't any use. I didn't get a damn bit hungry. But if I was going to keep myself from starving half to death, I was going to have to go with what the law provided. Turly Sinker was probably one of the worst cooks in Pinville, but he was the law nevertheless. I reckon I respected that fact.

VI

I finally pulled off the key, inserted the metal tab of the can, and rolled back the tin lid. The sardines lay bunched in a yellow mustard sauce. The slices of bread had dried a bit, but inside the crust the grain was thick and doughy. I ate half a slice, using it to push down the mushy fish, but when the can was as empty as full I shoved it aside. Maybe there would come a time when I was nearer dying of slow starvation. The coffee was cold, but it was wet and bitter. At least it reminded me faintly of how it is good to eat and drink.

By then the afternoon had completely gone, and the evening sounds had started. As I lay on the cot, after the first strain and rattle of the old springs, I could hear a dog bark somewhere off in the Pinville dark. And then a woman laughed somewhere down the street. I stopped all my listening just to hear her laugh again, and after what may have been minutes, the voice lifted and fell in a sort of raucous song. She's having a good time, I thought. She's having a good time with somebody. I suddenly felt trapped and lonely.

I shut my eyes and tried to fill my darkness with the sights and sounds of all the good times that now seemed to be over. I thought of the time Burt came riding in just as breakfast was over. We were all lined up on the porch when he pulled up in curious disarray. The snaps on his blue shirt were mismatched in a hurried wildness. "Will one of you good and honest friends take this faithful steed to his feeding place? After dumping the saddle of course." We didn't need to ask why he didn't ride there in the first place. "I'm not about to walk barefooted," he went on, "over all those goddamn rocks and thistles." Then we noticed he had lost his boots. "And don't any curious son of a bitch ask me where I left my boots." We didn't need to ask. We could already see them standing upright in Mabel's bedroom. Whatever Burt suddenly did, he wouldn't leave his boots sprawling. He would take a moment to fix them side by side before he got on with the business at hand. That was Burt's way. You could count on it.

I thought of the time Sill decided to cook a porcupine in the camp dutch oven. He pulled the roundup wagon into a corner of the Hannah Hills in plenty of time to open up with something special. There was an acre of well-grazed grass, a seep of a spring, and up from the spring was a grove of stunted trees including a pair of scrubby yellow pines. Even before we studied the layout carefully, we could see a dark ball in one of the trees. You couldn't tell if the porky was trying to back all of the way down to the ground and get the hell out or if he had decided to hang quiet and trust the whole show would pass him by. He would have been safe if Sill hadn't spotted him. Sill was at that point in his roundup cooking when he was bored with beef and beans. He was eager to mash a duck or fill the pot with snails. He didn't know any more about French cooking than he knew about the sewers of Paris, but somehow he had picked up the idea that cooking—even roundup cooking—was an art, what he called a culinary art, and this meant roaming considerably off the well-known track of beef and beans. "That's it," he said, seeing the porcupine. "That's the exotic touch we need." We couldn't see anything exotic in that bundle of quills, but Sill had caught his vision. "We'll have porcupine stew. Maybe throw in a couple of onions and a potato or two to soak up some of the extra fat." From that point on Sill was on his own. We had already lost the first flush of appetite. In fact we had lost the second flush. We each took a handful of the beans we wished Sill was using instead of that goddamn tree-eating rodent and settled down on the far side of the wagon to start a rousing poker game. The trouble was that winning a double handful of beans with four queens and a three is not particularly rousing. But at least it kept us from thinking about the slaughter that was going on out where our cook had been stung by a higher vision. Sill called out once while we played steadily without interest in our fortunes. "Anybody need a skin to make a nice quill coat? Put it on your wife or whatever and even the devil himself will pass her by."

Just as the sun was going down Sill banged on his big tin plate. It wasn't exactly a bell, but we knew from long experience that it meant supper was ready. Today of course it meant that the pine pig was cooked and waiting for our plates. We let Sill send his signal a few minutes longer, and then we finally strolled to his cooking fire; it was not hunger that moved us, but curiosity. Most of us had never seen a pine pig without his needles. So we sidled up close enough to take a look, letting our eyes do all the tasting. "Looks real nourishing, don't it?" Sill said. "Maybe needs a pinch or two of cumin seed." We couldn't say it didn't look nourishing, but it sure as hell didn't look like anything you'd fill your plate with. If some of us were tempted, just out of loyalty to Sill, that temptation faded when Mont said, "The strangest thing I ever heard about eating porcupines was what happened to Wilson Tuber back on the T S Ranch. He ate a couple of bowls of porky stew. Said in fact it was pretty good. Then about four years later an odd thing happened. He stopped to take a leak and when he looked closely, he found that a whole goddamn quill was working its silent way out of the end of his dinger." I don't remember what happened to Sill's stew. Mont's story seemed to have a dulling effect on the cook himself.

Remembering Mont's story caused me to think pleasantly of Mont and all the wild things he put us up to. He was a crazy bastard if there ever was one. If he got trapped in that outhouse, in a way it served him right. There was the time he bolted the end of an old derrick cable to the frame of that same outhouse. That old cable was as stiff as the stays in a schoolmarm's corset. It must have taken him a whole half day to uncoil it out through the greasewoods so he could bolt it to the ass-end of the waiting John Deere. Then he had to wait another half day until he had a rider fully situated. Turned out to be Sill, who waited until after supper before he took his magazine and strolled up the hill for a period of rest and meditation. Mont was watching. Once the door closed he hit the starter on the John Deere, and before Sill even had time to choose between a picture story on dolphins and an inside account of brothels in Juárez, he was thrown from the saddle when the outhouse jumped about ten feet out toward the eastern foothills. Sill lived, but Mont barely kept his hide. Mr. Pulley got wind of the sudden change and damn near sent Mont a-roaming. Mont said, "It's still right side up. I'll just dig another hole." But Pulley answered, "No, by god, you get that house back where you found it. Not an inch out of place." Took Mont two whole days, but he did it.

I could hear the dog barking again, but what I wanted to listen to was that woman laughing. You can't tell a hell of a lot about a dog's barking. In fact you can't tell a hell of a lot about a woman's laughing, but I guess it's the sound not the meaning that matters. The dark was getting pretty thick. I should have asked old Turly for at least a candle, though probably there were rules against candles too. Somebody might set fire to the steel cot or the walls that would turn back a cannon. I listened again, but all I could hear was some scratching outside my window. There's not much comfort in the vague sound of scratching.

Barney was the last to go. That figured. Barney always stuck it out. When things got to swirling around, he just hunkered down and let the shit fly. He survived the whirlwind measurements of Mr. Ef although the rest of us damn near died from laughing. He even survived another kind of whirlwind, the real kind that damn near blows the earth as bare as a sheepherder's campground. Pulley had the bunch of us out to hell and gone fixing fence. "You could ride back to the bunkhouse in the pickup," he said, "but that way you would miss the experience of camping on the range. And there aren't many experiences as spiritualizing as camping on the range. Bedding down where the grass has been grazed and where the smoke from the cook-fire hangs sweet in the air. Goddamn! You can't beat it this side of Kansas City." So there we were, ten miles from a good bed and the sky starting to thicken and darken. But it was the quiet that gave us the queers. The air was strung so tight you could pluck it or pound it with a metal lid. Sill had a fire going and was trying to get the oven happy on its coals. Every time he dropped the heavy cast iron cover, the bang shook through us. Then just as the dark got as black as the inside of an Angus cow, the whole goddamn sky began to split up with flaming cracks of lightning. Suddenly what had been stillness itself broke into a wild and windy motion. It was every man for himself. We scrambled for holes, for a rock to hold onto, for a chunk of brush to tie our roots to. Afterward there was rain, tons of it, but that was just cold and wet. We'd been there before.

In a clear sunny morning we surveyed the wreckage. Sougans were scattered over the grasslands. A spool of barbed wire had been unrolled like a spindle of thread. Sill insisted that his dutch oven had been lifted and set down ten feet away from what had been the fire. The only thing missing was Barney. "By god, we won't even need a casket," Burt said. "Old Barney's been swooped straight up into heaven like that old guy Elijah." But we found him. When we looked down the slope from the hill back of camp, we could see him standing right in the line of the fence we were making. Mont said, "Is that Barney or a post that isn't wearing a hat?" "That was a goddamn powerful wind," Burt said. "Not only picked him up like a log but drove him half way into this rocky ground." Seems the wind didn't do it. Seems Barney was running for cover in the moving darkness when he stepped into a posthole. His boot shoved all of the way to the bottom. There he was. He couldn't pull his boot out of the hole, and he couldn't pull his foot out of the boot. Had him anchored so well even Elijah's whirlwind couldn't have budged him.

He sure as hell was a sight to see. Only God knows where the old brown Stetson had flown to. Every snap on his dirty blue shirt had been yanked apart. We circled round some to get the full picture. "We can try to pull him out," Mont said, "or we can let him be. Just string the wire along and put in a few staples." Barney grinned through the whole show, and when we finally yanked him out, first the leg and then the boot, he sort of hopped around the hole for a last admiring look. "That son of a bitch would hold tight a section post in hell itself," he said. "And by god I believe I dug her myself."

They were all good guys, and some of us in this goddamn shitty world would miss them. If I ever got out of this place before they hanged me, I would hold that service, even if I had to do it all by myself, even if I was mourner, preacher, and rememberer all rolled into one. Maybe I could even sing a few lines from "The Cowboy's Last Dream." All of this made me sad, hurtfully sad. I couldn't cry. I had forgotten how to let my feelings loose.

I was just about ready to bust up inside when I heard again some sounds outside my window. I could make out what seemed the scrape of a stone bumped by a boot. Then I could hear muffled voices. Out of the mess of words that were not words suddenly rose a short string of meaning, like the sound of the preacher against the stir and whisper when the starting time has come. "Be quiet, goddamnit. He'll hear us." Then I listened as hard as I could as they quieted as hard as they could. The short wait was broken by a song, or what was supposed to be a song. I could make out the words and even the four different voices that had ganged up on the tune. "Oh, if I had the wings of an angel, over these prison walls I would fly. I would fly to the arms of my darling, and there I would be willing to die."

I pulled the cot close under the barred window, and standing on it I could almost see the dark that crowded against the outside wall below it. "You crazy living bastards," I yelled.

There was a bit of silence. Then a voice spoke. I could tell it was coming through the brim of his hat. "We are not living," it said. "We are ghosts. We are the ghosts of brave riders who once rode the range."

"Bull shit!," I yelled back. "Double bull shit."

Their laughing faded, and then all I could hear was that goddamn barking dog. I lay back down on the cot. But I found I was laughing too. That was just about the worst singing I had ever heard, but it was sweet sweet music to my lonesome ears. I must have gone to sleep smiling to myself. Knowing I wasn't going to be hanged was comforting, but all that was loosely in the future. Hearing those crazy bastards serenading in the darkness was like a glass of good whiskey in a stove-warmed room. I could almost feel the tingle of the morning sun.

The tingle I first felt was the closing of the jailhouse door. Turning I could see Turly big as life putting down the old tray on the oak table while he took down the key.

"Brought you some breakfast," he said.

While he unlocked the cell door, I sat up and studied the tray. After a good sleep I was hungry enough to eat a set of sardines can and all. But there were no sardines. Instead of a can there was a bowl, and alongside the bowl a cup of what I hoped was coffee. "What's that good-looking stuff?" I said.

"It's wheat mush," Turly answered. "Made it myself."

"You make the coffee too?" I said.

"Tried to," he answered. "At least she's brown. And once this morning she was hot."

It was a long way from that bowl of mush to the plate of eggs and sow belly I would have chosen, but I wasn't yet doing much choosing. "You could just turn me loose," I said. "You could give me back that dollar and those three nickels and I could go spend the whole works on a breakfast you didn't even have to try to make."

"Can't do it," Turly answered. "Case ain't solved. The law has got to run its course."

"Suppose I tell you where the bodies are," I said.

"Won't make a bit of difference," Turly answered. "Besides I already know where the bodies are."

"But if they aren't dead bodies," I said. "If they aren't genuine corpus delicti."

"It don't make a bit of difference," Turly said. "The case ain't solved until it's solved. The case ain't solved until I know exactly how it happened."

"How what happened?" I said.

"How the bunkhouse murders happened," Turly answered.

"But they didn't happen," I said. "There weren't any murders. There was just a lot of blood."

"I know that," Turly answered. "I saw it. I smelled it. And until I can account for every goddamn drop of it, there's an unsolved case. There's more to the law than murder. There's the crap piled up by a bunch of goddamn cowboys."

Turly was stirred up. He had that empty notebook. He had all those dusty miles on the Harley. And he didn't have even one hacked up body that was waiting for burial. All he had was the steel-trap logic of his trade.

"Still going to hang me?" I said, smiling in the hopes that the investigator would see the fun of it.

"I hope so," he answered. "But that's not my business. That will be up to Judge Bascom. He comes through the day after tomorrow."

"You mean I have to wait here feeding on those goddamn sardines for another two days?" I said.

"And maybe longer," Turly answered. "Depends on the judge."

"What's he got to decide?" I said.

"If there's been a crime committed," Turly said.

"What kind of crime?" I said.

"Murder, for example," Turly answered.

I started to protest. "That will be for the judge to decide," Turly said.

"How about bail while we're waiting for the judge to decide?" I said.

"Judge will have to decide that too," Turly answered. "Besides, it ain't usually the rule to grant bail in capital crimes."

"But you haven't got a capital crime," I said.

"Judge will decide that," Turly answered.

It was no use. It was like arguing with a phonograph.

Turly left and I struggled through the bowl of mush and the cup of coffee. Both were now cold as a sack of last night's rain water. But I figured I had to keep my strength up some. I had to stay alive at least until that judge came through. I had to be alive in case he wanted to hang me.

Sometime about the middle of the morning I was counting the match marks on my cell wall when I heard familiar voices and the jail door opened to let in the late quartet in person. How come a cell door thick enough to keep out a buffalo is locked with a key big enough to lock the gates of Hell itself—and the door to the jail is left unlocked as the swinging door to an all-night whorehouse? Burt, Sill, Mont, and Barney stumbled in and stood in a ragged line, all of them grinning broadly, as if they had just watched the preacher's wife take her Sunday bath. I just hoped they wouldn't break into song.

"Howdy, Mr. Prisoner," Barney said.

"How come you ain't wearing no ball and chains?" Burt said.

"I'd say from your looks," Sill said, "the law is feeding you well. You be sure and get their recipe for bread and water."

"Nice place," Mont said. "Safe and quiet. I'll bet a guy can do some real good thinking here."

Grinning back, I watched them through the bars of my door. Finally I exploded. "How come you bastards are out there and I'm in here?"

"Because we didn't commit no crimes," Mont answered still

grinning. "Especially since we didn't commit no murders."

"You crazy bastards," I yelled again. "You guys get me out of here. There's the key to this goddamn cell. Right there. Right there on that hook." I pointed to the ring with the key hanging back of Turly's desk.

"Sorry, we can't do it," Sill answered. "That would be aiding and abetting. That's serious. That would even make us accessories to the crime." Sill like to show off his learning.

"What crime?" I said.

"If you didn't commit a crime," Mont said, "how come you're in there?"

"Aw, come on," I said. "We're all in this together."

"No, we're not," Burt said. "You're in there, and we're out here. You're a prisoner, and we're free citizens of a nation dedicated to liberty, equality, and the pursuit of happiness."

"Bull shit," I said. "Bull shit with four aces."

They'd had enough fun for one visit. "We'll drop in this afternoon during the regular visiting hours," Burt said. "What are the hours?" He looked around. "What the hell kind of jail is this? No posting of the visiting hours. What does Turly think he's running? Some kind of twenty-four-hour whorehouse?"

"Any time," I said. "Any time the door is open."

"We'll be back," Mont said. "In the meantime you might start digging your way out. See if you can find a loose stone and then go on from there. You might even come up inside the Pinville Land and Lending. Then they could hang you for bank robbery too."

They left as they had come, straggling in single-file, four dumb bastards who should have been on horseback. Barney was the last one out the door. He turned and waved. "Tell the bedbugs to wait. Tell 'em there's better eating where you come from."

So I was back to counting the match marks on the cell wall. Then I found myself studying how many match marks would add up to a sack of Bull Durham. I was about ready to tote up the sacks when the jail door opened and Turly pushed in. "It ain't suppertime," he said, "but I thought you'd like to know that your expected visitors won't be in."

"They have a change of feeling?" I said.

"Don't know about that," Turly answered. "Could say something changed their feeling. I didn't see this directly, but I can say I learned it pretty much firsthand. Seems your buddies in the game were lined up at the Sidesaddle Bar having an easy beer when this big man, limping a little bit but wearing a high Stetson, comes in and without even coming to a full standstill yells out plain as the preacher on the second coming, 'What under God's pretty blue sky has happened to the world? I hire a bunch of goddamn cowboys, and the first time I turn my back they've run off to Pinville looking for beer and women.' 'It ain't that,' someone says. 'They been murdered.' 'Murdered my ass,' he says. 'You don't need a schoolteacher's bifocals to see that these lazy bastards ain't bleeding a bit.' So they ain't coming in this afternoon during visiting hours. They've gone back to the ranch. You might say they hurried back to the ranch. The last thing that man in the Stetson said you could have heard all the way to the suburbs of hell itself. 'All right. I don't give a good goddamn how many of you guys have been murdered. Hacked up or whole, I want my cowboys to take care of my cows. Now you boys bind up your wounds if you have any and get the hell out there and take care of those cows."

"But they are the witnesses," I said. "They are the witnesses to their murders that never happened. I got to have them talk to that judge before he puts me up for hanging."

"Don't worry," Turly answered. "I figure those guys will be back in time. Once Pulley sees his cows are chewing their cuds again, he'll let up some. Once he sees you need some witnesses, he'll probably haul them in in his own pickup."

"I always knew he had a respect for the law," I said.

"It ain't that," Turly answered. "He just figures he can't afford to lose a good cowboy."

Along about sundown, Turly came back with his tray of sardines and coffee. "You get these sardines cheap?" I said. "I buy 'em by the case," he answered. "You buy this coffee by the gallon?" I said. "No," he answered. "I got a bag of beans and my ma's old grinder."

I had been looking forward to that afternoon visit. I could even look forward to another nighttime serenade. Now I just had the whole long night to get through. So I guess I hung on to Turly a little.

"You ever spend a night in jail, Turly?" I said.

"You mean did I ever commit a crime?"

"That's not exactly what I asked you," I said.

"Once spent a night in jail," he said. "Matter of fact that same cell you're locked in."

"What did you do?" I asked. "Rob the stagecoach, or did you shoot the driver?"

"I just wanted to see it from the inside," he answered. "I just wanted to study the whole setup. I figured if I couldn't find a way to escape, nobody could."

"You find a way?" I said.

"No," he answered. "They had to let me out in the morning."

"What did they give you for breakfast?" I said.

"They didn't give me breakfast," he answered. "I had to fix that myself."

When he had gone and I was alone again, I kept thinking about old Turly having himself locked in so he could study the ways to get out. He was thorough all right. He made that fellow named Holmes seem as indifferent as a hog man buying beef.

VII

I waited through another whole day with nothing to disturb my peace and loneliness except Turly and his trays of mush, sardines, and coffee. I kept thinking that maybe the boys would suddenly appear or maybe sing me a song through the window. I figured once the cows were settled and Pulley had proved that he was boss he might say, "You boys get the hell into Pinville and tell that goddamn Turly to turn my cowboy loose." He might even offer the use of his pickup.

But the boys didn't come and after supper and the darkness that soon set in, I was about ready to confess I had slaughtered the bunch of them, mowed them down with a scythe or stabbed them one at a time with a hat pin I had stolen from the Pinville whorehouse. Hanging seemed a whole lot better than sitting in that cell trying hard to hear the sound of something. If I couldn't hear a woman laugh, I was ready to listen to that goddamn dog, no matter what he had to say. I saved myself by remembering. I lay on that cot and went over again how we almost got into the movies. I played all seven reels, sometimes turning it down to slow motion when the parts were good, sometimes hurrying it along when the plot got bent and crappy. I must have fallen asleep with one of the good scenes flashing on the inside of my tired eyeballs, or maybe I added a scene of my own. It would have been a great touch to see that voice coach jump bare nekkid into the wooden pool and get a sliver an inch long in the enameled skin of her precious ass.

I was awakened by the usual morning sound of Turly closing the jailhouse door. "Good morning," he said, coming to the cell carrying the tray of mush and coffee. "Eat heartily," he added. He seemed in hearty spirits himself. I realized that this would be a big day for him too. With all the authority he carried behind his badge he would bring a prisoner before the judge. It would be Turly's show. It would be almost as good as leading the Fourth of July parade on his Harley.

Reluctantly I took the tray. "I want you to promise me one thing, Turly," I said.

"What's that?" he answered.

"If that judge decides to hang me," I went on, "I want you to promise me a final breakfast of bacon and eggs. Cook the bacon until it's brown and crispy, and turn the eggs—all three of them—over lightly."

"Wait till we hear what the judge has to say."

"What does that goddamn judge have to do with my breakfast?" I yelled. "He doesn't tell me when I need to piss."

"I wouldn't talk that way if I were you," Turly said. "If the judge could hear you, he might want to hang you twice, once for murder and once for contempt."

I quieted down to eat my mush and drink my lukewarm coffee. Turly left, saying he would come back and get me just before ten. "By god," he said, "you better be on time, or that judge may want to hang you a third time, for being late."

As I ate that shitty mush, I kept thinking to myself, if there was just some little part of all this I could enjoy, I would store it away in memory, and then when my grandkids got down and moody I would bring out the fun of it and we would all laugh until my wife, if I ever had one, would come into the room and say, what

The Bunkhouse Murders / 215

the hell's going on here? Did your granddad have his upper plate fall out?

Well before ten Turly returned. He opened a closet in one corner of the room and after pawing around a bit came up with some leg chains and a pair of handcuffs.

"You mean you're going to put those goddamn things on me," I said.

"That's right," Turly answered. "A murderer has got to come into the court clinking and clanking a bit. Otherwise the judge and the audience won't see the seriousness of the charges. You wouldn't want to come in cheerful and happy, wearing a new shirt and a pair of lizard-skin boots, would you? That wouldn't look right, would it?"

I wanted to say that it would be fine with me, especially the lizard-skin boots, but I had sense at the time to stick with Turly's rightness. He fastened the leg chains to my ankles, reminding me when he stood up and straightened the campaign hat that there wasn't a hell of a lot of length in the thing. "If you want to escape by running," he said, "you'd better remember to take short steps or you'll end up ass-up in the street dust." Then he snapped on the handcuffs. "What I really need is a clean shirt," I said. "That judge is going to smell me and hang me a fourth time for being a public nuisance." Turly ignored my suggestion. "You're ready," he said. Then he took down a shotgun and said, "Now I'm ready." "What you going to do with that shotgun?" I said. "Standard equipment," he answered. "I meant what you going to shoot with it." "Whatever's necessary," he answered. "Might even be a rabid dog come charging down the street."

We went out into the street, and I hobbled along toward the meeting hall of the Pinville Third Chorus of Zion, where Judge Bascom would set up camp for the cases at hand. We got a lot of comment along the way. "He looks mighty mean, Turly," someone said. "I think I'd play it safe and put another chain and collar on." My ankles were already getting sore when someone else called out, "He sure as hell can't run much faster than a hobbled bull, but how's your shooting arm, Turly? Been hunting ducks lately? I remember Sheriff Tooker. He couldn't hit a bull in the ass with a handful of wheat. Close up, that is." Turly didn't pay much attention. I couldn't see his face, but I could guess that he looked straight ahead from under the campaign hat, his eyes having all the seriousness the law needed.

We entered the front door, and I worked my way down the center aisle toward the front of the hall. The place was mostly filled. Things were always slow in the pool hall in the morning. The bowling alley didn't open until noon. The court, when it was in session, was the best show in town. In fact it was the only show. If you got tired of hearing the lawyers argue, you could always watch the well-dressed members of the Pinville Tea and Tatting Society, who sat with their work in hand on the front row. You could tell that they didn't know a habeas corpus from a hog in a windmill, but they seemed to enjoy themselves, and you could say that they added a bit of feminine culture to the reign of justice. Turly pointed to a chair behind a long table. Already one chair was filled with a fat woman brought in from Turkey Town about six miles down the river. "What'd she do?" I whispered to Turly. "She shot her husband," he answered, adding, "used an old shotgun he kept loaded for skunks. The skunks kept eating his sweet corn. Said they'd taken every goddamn ear." "But why did she shoot him?" I asked. "It's alleged," he answered, "mind you I said alleged, that when he went out at night hunting skunks, he usually came back smelling like the perfume bin of the Pinville whorehouse. It is alleged," he went on, "that she said, 'Now I'm going to use this gun to shoot a skunk of my own.'"

When we were all seated, there was a period of waiting while we watched the empty judge's chair. Then a shriveled little fellow with a high-pitched voice hurried in from a side room and said, "Will you all stand while the judge leaves his chambers." He squeaked a bit, and the audience smiled and snickered. Even the Tatting Society exchanged a tight-lipped grin at the part about leaving his chambers. We stood, and Judge Bascom, looking as mean as he could, stiffly walked to his chair. You could tell he was sure as hell trying. You could guess that when he left home this morning, his wife said, "Ernest, why don't you judges put on a robe and wig the way the British do? You look too much like a preacher. Remember, Ernest, you're in the business of hanging people, not baptizing them." I didn't much care. I remembered what a late friend once said to me, "Watch out for a smiling judge. He'll yank out your balls as a kindness."

A big oak chair had been moved into position right in front of the pulpit. The judge took his place in it and looked us all over. With that pulpit as a backdrop you had the feeling he was studying us for the signs of sin. Even the tatters stopped and squirmed a bit. The fellow with the high-pitched voice turned out to be the bailiff. When the judge was ready the bailiff gave him a large gavel. You could have banged a steer between the eyes with that gavel and he would have crumpled like a wet tent when the pegs are pulled. The trouble was that it was too heavy for the judge. He had to put two hands to it. Then there was the further trouble. He didn't have anything to bang it on except the floor, and you had the feeling that if he hit the floor hard enough the whole goddamn place would cave in.

Everything finally seemed ready to go. The judge held his gavel like a batter waiting for the first pitch. The bailiff stood at attention nearby and squeaked the formal announcement. "Hear ye, hear ye. This is the court of Judge Ernest O. Bascom. First case for hearing: the state versus Henrietta Jimson Deever. Charge: murder by means of a shotgun, 12-gauge, goose-size pellets." Already I knew enough to translate that goose-size into skunk-size. The bailiff went on: "Will the defendant rise." Mrs. Deever struggled to a standing position. "How do you plead, Mrs. Deever?" the judge asked. "I shot the son of a bitch, your honor," she answered, "but I don't agree it was murder." "You'll have to plead one way or the other," the judge said. You could tell he didn't like getting into the ifs and maybes. "Then I'll take innocent," Henrietta answered. "I'll go with my feelings," she added. "I sure as hell don't feel guilty for putting all those pellets into that unfaithful fucker of wanton women." The judge coughed as if he had swallowed his upper plate. The tatters sucked in their shocked breath in unison. "Mrs. Deever," the judge said, "let me remind you that you are in a court of law. And let me remind you further that this court of law is meeting in the hallowed hall of the Third Chorus of Zion." "I ask your pardon, your honor," Henrietta said. "I just get worked up every time I'm reminded of that lazy goodfornothing turd of a man, if your honor will pardon the expression." The judge seemed anxious to set a trial date. He probably sympathized with Mrs. Deever and so he wasn't in a hurry to deliver judgment. My guess was that after the proper legal flurry he would send her back to Turkey Town, with the warning that shotguns were for rabbits and other varmints, not for wild and straying husbands. "I'll accept that plea of innocent," the judge announced, "and set trial for two weeks from today in this court." She sat down, and what pleased the judge most of all, she fell into a pudgy silence.

So now it was my turn. The bailiff had to make two starts before he could get his voice going right, but finally he declared to the court that the next case was the state versus Andrew Monroe Pickens. Charge: the murder of four cowboys in assorted ways and places. "Will the prisoner rise," he said in conclusion. I rose and looked straight at the eyes of Judge Bascom. I wanted him to know at the beginning that I wasn't the evasive and sneaky sort. "That's a hell of a lot of killing," the judge observed. "I can't remember when we had that much killing on the docket."

"I'm innocent, your honor," I said.

"I haven't asked you to plead," the judge answered. "No point in your coming in ahead of the question. Just confuses the whole established procedure."

"Yes, your honor," I said.

"Well, then, how do you plead?" the judge said.

"Innocent, your honor," I answered.

"You got a fair amount of evidence, Mr. Sinker?" the judge said to Turly.

"A fair amount," Turly answered. "Only thing missing," Turly started to say.

"Is what?" the judge asked.

"The bodies," Turly answered. "The corpuses delicti."

"You mean we've had all this killing and we don't have a body?" the judge said. "Somehow it don't seem right."

"Yes, your honor," Turly answered.

The judge scratched his mostly bald head, and just when he seemed ready to give birth to a high point of law there was a commotion in the hallway. I could hear the shuffle of boots and the push of sucked-in laughter. Then I heard singing, sad singing, a number of voices sort of mashed together. "Oh, bury me not on the lone prairee, where the coyotes howl and the wind blows free." The door pushed open and a strange procession entered, three men carrying a wooden door on which lay a figure covered with a sheet. On one side marched Burt and Sill. On the other staggered Mont. The corpus on the door I figured was Barney. They were all as drunk as a herd of sun-struck hoot owls.

As they proceeded up the aisle, there was a strange kind of silence. Even the judge seemed surprised into a startled respect. But then something happened to the right-hand pallbearer. He stumbled or he was tripped, and while he struggled to keep his balance he lost his grip on the door. The bier dropped like a chute and Barney shot like a bundle to the floor. There was the body thump and a loud "goddamn." Still covered with the sheet, the corpse staggered to its feet and, blinded, bumped its way on down the aisle. As it approached the defendants' table, Henrietta began to rattle her chair, and by the time it came into the open she went into action. "Oh god, oh god," she cried. "It's my Stanley. The son of a bitch has come back to get me. Where's my shotgun? Where's my shotgun? Somebody get me that shotgun or I'm a goner." By then she had knocked her chair over on its back. Her whole fat body was churning with action. If she could have stopped for a moment of scheming, she could have seen the chair itself as a weapon. It would have been damn near the end of Barney if she had brought the whole of that furniture down across his hatless but sheet-covered head. She spotted instead the judge's gavel. Before he could get a proper legal grip on it, she had pulled it from his hands and was already getting the swing of it as she chopped and slashed the air around her. "Come on, you dirty lying son of bitch," she yelled to the corpse. "You get any closer to this decent person and I'll knock you flatter than a bull that's been rammed between the eyes by the ass-end of a pickup truck." Barney could probably hear all of this, but he still couldn't see which way to jump. Luckily he slipped at the most dangerous moment. His legs must have failed him. He shot head-first under the table just as Henrietta brought down the gavel on the table top. You could have heard the smash all the way to the next county. Even the judge squinched a bit in the face as if he had been shot in the withers.

When the dust cleared, I was pretty much back to where I had started that morning. The leg chains were gone. The handcuffs were hanging on the rack. But I was still behind bars. I didn't have even a sniff of that time-honored freedom to ride the unfenced western range. Who cares? I said to myself. Who gives an honest shit? Who wants to ride those goddamned ranges anyway? In fact I was feeling happier and happier. Especially I wasn't lonely. It was a bit crowded in the cell, but there we all were, the whole outfit celebrating the fun of being together again.

When that dust cleared and the wreckage could be surveyed with a cold legal eye, the judge threw the whole bunch of us in the slammer. He might have included Mrs. Deever as well, but on further meditation he fell back on proprieties. Besides, the cell would have bulged like a branding chute filled with a big cow ripe with calf. And if the judge had not been able to reclaim his gavel, that cell would have been the scene of enormous pushing and pounding. Even when the sheet came off and Henrietta could see that Barney wasn't Stanley, she wasn't ready to join the tatters. She seemed to have a thing against men. If she could bang one more of the species, that would somehow ease the hurt in her innards.

I yelled to the judge, "But your honor, you can seen now that I didn't commit any murders. I didn't kill these men."

"Right now I almost wish you had," the judge answered.

So we were all locked up together. But Turly, when he checked out our possessions, didn't check our boots, and Mont and Burt each had a pair of pints slipped down inside the shafts. I was the only one who had any catching up to do, and that was easy after Turly slammed and locked the door. Burt pulled out a pint and I took a long drag. Then I stopped, remembering. I lifted the pint high in the air. "I think we ought to drink a toast to Henrietta. Poor old Stanley probably had it coming. I drink to injured womanhood. I drink to the scatter of her righteous shotgun. I drink to the power of her pounding gavel." "Hold it," Mont said. "We've got to have time to catch up. We've got to have time to honor that pile of spiritual shittings."

"What we need is a song," Sill said. "What we need is the harmonious beauty of man's voice lifted in the sweet tones of an old melody of the range."

"What we need," Burt said, "is a sad song."

"The saddest song there is," I said.

"A song that would make old Bascom weep at his mother-in-law's funeral."

"Then it's got to be 'When the Work's All Done,'" Sill said. "That's about the saddest song in the cowboy's repertoire."

Most of us didn't know a repertoire from a ring-tailed raccoon, but we were willing to go along with Sill's suggestion. He was, you might say, our cultural leader.

"All right," Mont said. "How does she go?"

"I remember how she starts," Barney said. "A group of jolly cowboys, discussing plans at ease."

"I mean," Mont interrupted, "I mean what's the tune she goes by?"

"Goddamnit," Barney answered. "I was singing the tune."

"God," Burt said. "She's got to have more tune that that."

"What we need to do," Sill threw in, "is grease our strings. Then maybe we can come up with a more dulcet harmony."

"Piss on the harmony," Mont said. "Let's get on with the greasing."

Digging in their boots, the boys came up with a couple more pints, and we earnestly went to work to oil our dusty singing chords. By the time we had passed the pints around to the empty, we had almost forgotten the name of the song, but Barney came up with the first line again, and from there we rode up the trail together. We probably didn't have any more tune than a corral full of newly branded calves, but by that time even Sill couldn't tell dulcet from dinkum. Sometimes we sang the same line. Sometimes we sang a set of lines. It didn't seem to matter. Somehow we came out pretty much together, and when we finally arrived at the point we had struggled toward, we couldn't seem to let go of the words. "And he'll not see his mother when the work's all done this fall." We played it over and over again like a phonograph stuck in the last sad groove of the record. No one who wasn't listening in the outer wilderness will ever know how many variations we gave to that line. Someone would hold *mother* while the rest sang the whole line. Someone would hold *fall* while we went back and gathered up mother again. And once we sounded *fall* together and held on until we all exploded in desperate sucking of the whiskey-scented air.

How long we filled the Pinville jail with song I cannot honestly remember. No doubt we sang until we had no more oil to keep our tonsils humming. No doubt we sang until poor Charlie wished in his grave that some dumb cowboy had never heard about him, let alone write a sad song about his wanting to see his mother in the fall. No doubt we sang until poor Charlie's mother, wherever she was, might have cried out, "Please, boys don't torture the air anymore tonight. I haven't got another tear in my tired old eyes."

I don't remember how we slept in that crowded cell with one old cot. After all that drinking and all that singing, we probably fell on the floor like a patch of dead timber hit by a whirlwind. The snoring that followed was probably worse than the singing.

The first sound I recognized was the familiar closing of the jailhouse door. I could open one eye enough to see Turly and his eager tray, and when I pulled both eyes open I could see my customary breakfast multiplied by five. Turly banged a spoon on a cell bar, and from the commotion it caused you would have thought he had fired a short-barreled .44 in a cast-iron piss pot. I was probably the best off of the bunch, but if the bang of that spoon had been just a tinkle louder my head would have cracked open from my hairline all of the way to my belly button.

"Breakfast is served," Turly announced, as if we were the tatting club in person.

"Hope those bowls are filled with eggs," Mont said. "The rawer the better."

"Mush," Turly answered. "Good nourishing mush."

"God," Mont said. "You find a man when he's almost gone, and then you finish him off with mush."

"I'll tell you what," Burt said. "Let's donate these bowls of mush to charity. I'll bet that tatting society keeps track of things like this. I'll bet they know a set of hogs that ain't yet been finished off for market."

We left the mush for charity, but we managed to finish off the coffee. In the state we were in, a cup of coffee, even cold coffee, looked like the juice of life. When we finished and let the bitter wetness soak in a bit, we could at least tell the difference between upright and across though we couldn't have read a fancy brand if our noses had been rubbed on the scab itself. If someone didn't bang another spoon on a cell bar, we would recover into upright sometime before noon.

About nine the jail door opened and Turly marched in. He didn't even bother to slam the door shut. We were thankful for that.

"I'm going to unlock this cell door," he said, "and you fellows can march out. You're free. You can march out to that waiting pickup. You can all climb in the back, and I hope I never again have to hear a song about seeing mother when the work's all done this fall, or any fall for that matter."

We marched out and crawled into the bed of the pickup. You didn't need to look hard to see who was doing the driving, and you didn't need to ask questions to know that if we survived all the jolts on the ranch road we would be lined up on Sill's porch and listen to a cussing that would make a drill sergeant blush with envy.

What had happened to turn us loose? Seems when Pulley found his cowboys all gone, he turned the pickup and roared into Pinville. Seems Judge Bascom was just shutting up court on his way to supper. "I've had a hard day," he said to Pulley. "I don't think I've ever had a harder day. If I had known days like this could happen, I would have stayed out of the law. I would have herded sheep with pleasure."

"I've got to have my cowboys, your honor," Pulley said. "I would be glad personally never to see their hides again, but goddamnit, Judge, the cows can't do without them. Think of the cows, your honor."

Seems the judge was already doing some thinking. "I'll tell you what, Pulley. I could keep those rowdies around a bit longer and then I could hang the whole bunch, but frankly I'm not up to it. Suppose I just go ahead and sentence the whole gang to hard labor on the Pulley ranch. And how would it be if I threw in a cook, a Mrs. Deever? She's mighty handy with a shotgun and a gavel, but I think if you tame her down a bit, she could rassle some pots and pans."

"Sorry, Judge," Pulley said. "I don't need another cook."

We rode out to the ranch with the driver staring straight ahead and watching for every rock and hole he could jar us with. When we finally pulled up in front of Sill's porch, you could barely tell the living from the dead. But we crawled out, flapped our wings weakly to get off some of the dust, and lined up.

"God," Pulley said. "God. What has the cowboy come to!"

VIII

When Mr. Pulley is really steamed up he explodes like an old leaky boiler, but the pressure soon goes down, and finally he takes a long sigh of relief. He even begins to feel fatherly toward his wayward cowboys. "You boys have done the goddamnest things. You have got yourselves into the goddamnest situation." He stopped to let all that sink in. "But as far as I can tell, the cows are still in reasonably good shape. Through no fault of the men who are supposed to take care of them. That's what I like about a cow. She's got sense to take care of herself no matter what happens, no matter how filled with froth and shit the cowboys get." He started to leave, and then he turned on the heel of his boot. "Sill, you get the hell in there and cook these boys a decent meal. They look like they been fed on dried prunes and hog slop. And make the coffee strong and hot."

After Mr. Pulley drove away in his pickup, Sill dug around in his grub box and got a stew going. Then he ground some beans and started the coffee boiling. The rest of us just sat there smelling.

"God, does that aroma do a man good," Mont said.

"That Sill is some cook," Burt added. "Course that Henrietta might be even better. We don't have anything that even looks like a gavel, and we could keep the shotgun locked up in the bunkhouse. We sure as hell wouldn't want to start another round of murders."

"She'd be different to look at," Barney said, "especially when she bent down to reach the bottom of the grub box."

Sill just grinned his own sweet grin of contentment. He knew we loved his cooking as we loved our mothers. He knew he could out-cook Henrietta even if he couldn't use a shotgun quite so well.

When the stew was done we filled our bowls, then filled them again. Barney said it for all of us. "Goddamn, this sure tastes good. I don't know what's in it, and I don't care. You could boil up an old sock, Sill, and it would still taste good."

Then we sat around the table enjoying the coffee that Sill poured out of that old pot. You could take a sip and then wait while it gently warmed and soothed the places where that snakehead whiskey had left its bite. You couldn't have found a more contented bunch of cowboys in the whole wide West.

Soon after dark we were both pooped and piled high with pleasure. If a stampede had come straight toward us, we wouldn't have bothered to turn it. Someone would have said, "I feel too good to move. Let's just lie low and trust that no goddamn steer is going to put his foot in my happiness."

Finally we moved to the porch and spread our bedrolls. The bunkhouse was no longer haunted by murder, but it was still spattered with blood, and sleeping with all that dried blood, even innocent blood, might start up some active nightmares. Besides that old porch had become a special place in our special home. We liked the feel of its boards. We liked the view out across the feed yard. At night we liked the chance to watch the stars. We liked too the handy place to take a leak. After all that coffee there might be considerable coming and going.

We settled down in a soft almost silent sighing. Burt suddenly spoke the benediction. "God, don't it seem peaceful. Don't it seem blissful after all those murders."

We slept late the following morning. There was no schedule of work for the day. Pulley had us in place, but he had dictated no immediate jobs to be done. If we suddenly heard the charging approach of Pulley's pickup, we could come to alert, pull on our boots, and be ready for orders or whatever cussing the old man had stored up for our ears.

So we were surprised in our drowsiness when we heard the sound of a motor which had none of the mechanical outrage of Mr. Pulley's pickup. Listening, we could easily make out the sputter, and long before the soft churn of dust pulled up we could recognize the driver.

"By god, it's old Turly in his Harley," Mont said.

"Probably driving out to thank us for our help in solving all those murders," Burt said.

Burt was wrong about the investigator's motives. The Harley stopped, belched its last gasp, and Turly pulled himself off the saddle. Then he stood for a minute pounding dust with his gloved hand.

"Mr. Sinker," Burt observed, "seems to me that if you rode in the sidecar you could keep away from the dust some. That Harley ought to know its way out here all by itself."

Turly wasn't amused. He straightened his already straight hat. Then he reached down into the sidecar and pulled out his notebook.

"Must seem good to have the case all closed," Sill said.

"Case ain't closed," Turly answered. "Ain't closed at all."

"But you found out there weren't any murders," I said.

"I found that out," Turly said, "but that don't close the case, that don't solve the mystery."

"What mystery?" Sill asked.

"The mystery of the murders that weren't murders," Turly answered. "You could call this the case of the unmurdered murders. We don't yet know how it happened, or how it didn't happen."

"I'll be goddamned," Mont said.

"Until I've filled this notebook," Turly went on, "and until everything in this notebook gives me some final answers, the mystery is not solved. The case is not closed."

"You want us to answer some more questions?" Burt asked.

"I don't want to ask you fellows some more questions," Turly answered. "I've heard all the shit an investigator can stand to hear. I'm going to leave you jokers right here where you can enjoy the shit and sun. I'm on my own. I'll find my own answers." With that he marched off toward the bunkhouse.

"As I said, that Turly is a regular Mister Doopin." It was Sill speaking for the bunch of us.

We watched Turly enter the bunkhouse, closing the door behind him. Then we simply waited, listening for whatever we could hear, which wasn't much. That Turly, like all good detectives, was a quiet one. Once we caught a small thump in the air, but we couldn't make out whether the investigator had bumped his head or pulled a dead porcupine from an upper bunk. After what must have been an hour, he came out of the bunkhouse, stopped to write something in his notebook, and moved off toward the hay yard. He seemed to be studying the ground closely, with his head out and down a bit.

"He walks just like a goddamn bloodhound," Mont said.

We sat most of the morning watching Turly work. Much of the time he was out of sight, but occasionally he would appear from behind a shed or a clump of greasewoods. Then we would study the way he examined the ground, picking up what seemed to be twigs or crumbled horse turds. We sat back and admired the doggedness in which he went about his task.

"Pinville's own A. Doopin," Mont said. "By god, it makes you feel good just to know he's out there snooping around."

Knowing we were getting a little weak from all our watching, Sill slipped inside and got up another fresh pot of coffee. When it was ready he brought it outside alongside a set of cups, and we leaned back some more, sipping our coffee while we followed the comings and goings of our faithful August Doopin.

Sometime just before noon, Turly worked his way through an acre of greasewoods and pulled up in front of the porch. He was dusty on the leggings and a little red in the eyes. Looking at enough sunny patches of alkali brings on a bit of snow blindness. He carried his notebook open, and since his pencil was still in his hand we guessed he had stopped somewhere in those greasewoods to make a note or two. He seemed to study what he had written, then he poked the pencil into his shirt pocket, and with a fancy flourish he closed the notebook. There was a distinct pop when the pages hit and a faint puff of dust.

"She's done," he said. "She'll all tied up. She's tighter than a schoolmarm's corset."

"You mean the case is closed?" Burt said.

"I mean the case is closed," answered Turly.

"You mean the mystery is solved?" Mont said.

"I mean the mystery is solved," Turly answered.

"Well, I'll be goddamned," Mont said.

Turly leaned over and tucked his notebook somewhere deep in the sidecar. Then he pulled on his gloves and threw his right leg over the Harley.

"Hey, wait a minute," Sill said.

"I'm finished," Turly answered. "I'm ready to start on the next case."

"But you're not finished," Sill said. "You haven't told us how it happened. You haven't explained the mystery."

"If the judge asks me, I'll tell him," Turly answered. "My guess is that he doesn't want to know."

"But you can't end the mystery without the explanation," Sill persisted. "The detective always goes through the whole business pointing out where wrong guesses went wrong, where good clues were false clues, how the butler only had a lifelong habit of sleep walking, especially on moonless nights."

"Yeh, you haven't told us what the butler had to do with it," Barney said.

But Turly had had enough with this set of delicti. "This mystery has a different ending," he said. "This time the murdered have to explain their own murders." With that he stomped the old Harley, let her sputter a bit, and then with an exhaust explosion that filled the air with blue smoke he turned his cycle and chugged off up the hill.

"Kinda like the hero riding away into the sunset," Burt said. "I think I'll miss old Turly. However dumb he looks, you'd have to say, by god that old Turly is a straight arrow."

"I'll go with that," Mont said, "and up the ante too."

"But what are we going to do about the case of the bunkhouse murders?" Sill said. "We can't leave it hanging like a dusty question mark in the western sky."

"We can't do anything," But said. "We can't do anything unless you want to bushwack old Turly and steal his notebook from the Harley."

"Personally," Mont said, "I don't think that notebook proves a goddamn thing. Personally I think he finally made a lot of it up. Made it look tight and finished, but like an old saddle blanket I'll bet it's got more loose yarns than a blindman's doily."

"So it comes down to finding the truth ourselves," Burt said.

"We may still have to hunt a little to find it," I answered.

It seemed sort of logical to everyone that since we had been in the center of the mystery we might know something about it. We didn't have anything better to do. The cows didn't need us. After what had happened Mr. Pulley probably preferrèd to believe that we were all out on the fence line armed with hammers and staples.

Sill turned out a batch of sourdough doughnuts and a fresh pot of coffee, and we leaned back on the porch to enjoy the unfolding of our mystery.

"It's better than going to some goddamn movie," Barney said.

"That's cause we're in it, not somewhere back in the dark watching while we munch on popcorn that's been buttered with lard of an old boar pig."

It seemed logical to start at the beginning, with the first murder being explained by the first murderee. This meant that Burt would ride point, but Burt had ridden a lot of things in his time, and taking the lead in the grizzly business would somehow suit his character.

"But we need some rules," Mont said. "At least we need one big rule. No shit. That ought to do it."

So we opened with the bloody murder of Burton Sullivan, remains never found or discovered.

Burt jumped right in. "It was pig's blood," he announced. "Plain old pig's blood. I had seen a movie just the night before I stopped off at the Pinville Butchering and Tanning Shop. I needed to see Pod Beaner, who worked there. He had a real way with a dead hog. I've never known a man who had more real talent with a dead hog."

Mont pounded the porch floor with the heel of his boot. It wasn't a gavel, but it did bring Burt back on track.

"I must have had blood on my mind after seeing that movie," Burt went on. "It suddenly struck me that Pod was mostly letting it go to waste. I saw a gallon honey bucket nearby, and the next time Pod let the blood gush out I slipped that bucket into place. Damn near filled it to the top. Then I found a lid and pounded her down tight. 'What the hell you going to do with all that blood?' Pod asked. 'I was thinking of making a big blood pudding,' I answered, but blood pudding was really the last thing I had in mind. I knew I could have some fun with it, maybe liven up our lives with a good old-fashioned murder."

Burt went on telling his bloody story. Seems he came back to the ranch, hid the honey bucket at the bottom of his bunk underneath his bed roll, and waited for the night and the snoring to start. Along about midnight, he decided we were all beyond wakening. Even a close-up shot would have caused us only to turn over. He slipped on his boots, pried the lid off the can with his belt buckle, then poured and slopped the blood over his whole sleeping place. Carrying the empty bucket and his denim jumper, he then left the bunkhouse and headed up the ranch road toward Pinville.

"I knew I was leaving some pretty plain tracks in the road dust," he said, "but I figured those tracks wouldn't last long when things got started. I figured you fellows would notify Turly right off and that old Turly would come chugging right out on his Harley. I knew Turly had to drive in the left rut to let the sidecar have a place to go, so I stayed in the left rut. Long before Turly began hunting for tracks, he had already ploughed them up with his Harley. It was a long walk, but I had a big breakfast when I pulled into Pinville. And then I had time to go down near the jailhouse and watch Turly when he climbed on the Harley and headed out for action."

"Some points may need more proof," Mont said, "but for now she stands more or less logical."

It was funny how that word logical had become just about as common as beans and saddle blankets.

"It's sort of like buying a cow that's been fed too much green hay," Barney said.

"Nevertheless, we move on," Mont said. "We take up the case of Silliman Sanders, murdered in cold blood, remains never recovered."

"It wasn't pig's blood," Sill announced. "I can't stand the smell of the stuff. I couldn't even carry it in a bucket. I'm a beef blood man. Probably comes from working with so much raw meat. When I saw the way old Burt had got the story going, I knew I had to go to the bloody route, but I wasn't about to go hunting another bucket of hog juice. It just happened that I had two whole steer livers hanging on the north side of the chuck house in a flour sack. They were a bit past good eating, but they were still alive enough to give up a mess of redness. I put them in an old leather nose bag, pounded them a bit, jumped on them a couple of times, and squeezed out a cup or two of stuff that looked like blood. It was piss-poor blood, but I figured you fellows wouldn't know the difference, especially Turly. I sprinkled it around in my bunk."

Seems he was ready to disappear into the night when he saw how we had closed up Burt's resting place with his saddle blanket. Sill keeps a long-bladed knife extra sharp for some of the old bull beef he has to cut. One hard stroke of that knife opened a slit in Burt's blanket a fox could have jumped through. Then Sill left. He knew he couldn't just walk up the road. Turly had too many tracks on his dogged mind. So he made for the pole fence around the feed yard, climbed astraddle, and worked his way around to the other side.

"The aspen poles weren't so bad," he said, "but then I hit a couple of dry fir poles. By the time I was ready to jump off I had about seven dozen slivers in my ass. Some of them are still there. They didn't make the walk to Pinville a damn bit shorter."

"Could be the judge will want to see those slivers," Mont said. "Real hard proof of how you did it."

"Could be the judge won't want to see those slivers," Burt said. "Next to Henrietta swinging that gavel like a miner's hammer, the last thing the judge probably wants to see is Sill's bare ass, no matter how many slivers it may have in it."

"Except for that part about the liver I'll go along ," Mont said. "But I want to add this warning: under threat to your very life itself don't ever put any liver, whatever the color, liveliness, or breed, on my plate for me to eat. I never did like liver, and now I'm off it for good."

Sill seemed touched a bit. He had always been proud of his liver and onions. "I still think that cooked right a liver can add a zest to life, maybe even stir up the old manhood."

We had come to the third case, the murder of Montgomery Masterson, no signs of bloody violence, just disappearance in mysterious circumstances.

"I decided not to take the bloody trail," Mont announced. "Burt and Sill had played that game. There wasn't much left in it for me. Besides, I didn't have any blood, and I'll be goddamned if I was going all the way into Pinville just to get a package of red stuff to spread all over my bed roll. There isn't any good way to wash blood out of a bed roll. About all you can do is let it sink to its rest in the watering pond. So I decided to do a disappearing act. I decided to be murdered without making a bloody mess out of it."

Seems he had some old moccasins he kept tucked into his bed roll, just in case he didn't want to pull on his boots to step outside the bunkhouse to take a leak when there were lots of thistles

232 / *The Bunkhouse Murders*

on the ground. So when he decided to walk up to the outhouse and not come back, he took along the slippers he had won in a poker game with a Paiute citizen in Pinville. While he sat comfortable in private seclusion, he slipped on the moccasins. Then he eased out the door and made off through the garden of greasewood.

"God, I should have practiced some," he said. "Those Indian shoes are as flat as a shoe tongue under a ton of baled hay. When I started to walk, I damn near fell over backwards without my boot heels. So then I leaned forward and hoisted myself into normal position with my moccasin heels about two inches in the air. It was a delicate balance, and the goddamn ass-ends of the shoes kept sliding down, but I managed to tippy-toe across the landscape. No wonder Turly couldn't track me. What I left in the dust must have looked a lot like bear paws. I can imagine old Turly spotting those marks and saying to himself, 'By god it's a bear walking in a funny way, and the son of a bitch doesn't have any toes on his feet.'"

Seems Mont finally decided he could stop, sit down, and pull his boots on as he headed for Pinville. He didn't say what he did with the Indian shoes, but our guess was that he shoved them down a badger hole, saying, maybe you guys can use these for hauling rocks next time you want to dig a hole.

That left one last murder, the case of Bernard M. Tullus, another disappearance without blood and in mysterious circumstances. Sill sighed as if he was sorry the inquest was about over. "Seems to me," he observed, "that we have so far piled it up a bit. Still I like to believe that the world is better off for knowing some of the truth."

"There wasn't any plan to it," Barney announced. "I could see that Turly couldn't tell blood from grape juice. It was tracks that got him going. The bodies kept getting away. Old Turly kept sniffing around like a goddamn half-breed fox hound. There just had to be some tracks. Unless the bodies flew. But old Turly didn't even look up. He knew goddamn well that everything was moving down here on the ground."

Seems Barney didn't have any Indian shoes. Seems he would rather step on burrs and thistles than put his feet in one of those unnatural contraptions. He played his game loose, and luck was with him. When he got to the feed yard back of the baled hay, he saw that the old brindle cow had wandered in for a nighttime snack. She had put her head through one of those stanchions where we could move a bolt-hinged two-by-four and put a headlock on whoever might be eating. The old girl must have been hungry. Barney sneaked up, pulled the bar, and dropped the stop in place. The old cow could pull and squirm, but she couldn't back out, not at least if she kept her head on.

"I knew I couldn't ride that old cow anywhere," Barney said, "unless I had a rope across her withers. I saw this chunk of lariat hanging on a corral post. I slipped it under her brisket and pulled it up over her back. God, did she fight and squirm! But I held my ground and tightened up a sort of bucking strap. Then I slipped a leg over her and worked my fingers under that rope. Without gloves it was going to have to be a short ride or I was going to be as fingerless as a chair leg. When I was set I reached up over her ears and yanked the holding block. Her head came out of that stanchion as if it had been sucked by a fence stretcher. I could have said to her, take a minute to find out what the hell is going on, but she wouldn't have been interested in anything but moving out. She didn't even twist her head around to look me over. We just went. She didn't know a goddamn thing about bucking, but she had mean old legs that chewed up that feed yard ground like a country race track. We headed for the river pasture throwing shit in six or seven different directions."

"I don't know whether you would call that an explanation or a fabrication," Sill said. "Could be the witness threw a little in the telling."

"All sounds logical to me," Burt said. "I know that old cow some too."

That was the end of the mysteries. That was the end of the tidying up of all the little puzzles that had kept the story going. We could sit there on Sill's porch working on another pot of coffee while we could smell the beans and beef a-stewing. It was pleasant to know that nothing was lurking, that peace was soft in the evening air.

"Could be that Turly has put together another story," Sill said. "Could be that Turly's truth is not the same as ours."

"That's fine with me," Burt said. "As long as Turly's happy."

"Could be that judge will want to do some comparing," Mont

said. "And it could be he won't want to hear about murder in the bunkhouse ever again."

"Could be that somebody will want to make a movie," Sill said. "Could be that they'll want to do it right here, with none of your fake front porches. Could be they'll want to get Paul Newman to play old Turly."

"And of course you'll want to play yourself," Burt said.

"Well, I'd be willing," Sill answered, "if the money's right. I could give it what they call authenticity. Of course I'd want to add a new pot or two and maybe some spoons with colored handles."

"And if the money's not right?" Mont said.

"They can maybe get Mr. Hoffman or Mr. Redford to do the part."

"God, that would be a special kind of truth," Mont said.

"It would, wouldn't it?" Sill answered.

AFTERWORD
SOME CRITICAL REFLECTIONS
ON THE WORK JUST CONCLUDED

The title *The Bunkhouse Murders* may suggest the conventional murder mystery, curiously set in a bunkhouse instead of an English country house or in the random compartments of a train speeding from Calais to Istanbul, but nevertheless assuming the persistent presence of an investigator of some sort asking pointed questions and sweeping the field of crime for crumbs of evidence. There is no compelling reason why Maigret, having faithfully attended a murder hearing in Tucson, should not be drawn into an investigation of a mysterious death at the Sundown Ranch near Pleasant Valley.

The title may likewise suggest a conventional Western, with the murders not so much a mystery to be solved as acts of intrusive violence which reveal the presence of evil forces seeking to maintain a tyranny of power or exclude a peaceful settlement of moral and civil right. In the conventional terms of the genre, the murders might be the violent efforts of a range king to scare off the little rancher who has legitimately presumed to establish his own fiefdom. To deal with such a situation, we of course need a special kind of hero: not a quiet pipe-smoking Maigret, but a master of the six-gun in the image of Shane or Matt Dillon or one of the many fictional versions of Wyatt Earp.

The work just concluded, however, does not use the conventional features of either genre, although clearly these features are sometimes a part of the total context of reference in which the work has been conceived. To be sure, there is an investigator, and there are cowboys. But although the investigator is centrally involved and occasionally touched with refrain-like allusions to Auguste Dupin, he is not a masterful detective in the traditional mode. The cowboys, although they are involved with cows and thus have or recall authentic range experiences, are not the standard cowboys of popular fiction. They do not carry guns. They do not engage in walk-downs. They ride with no high mission of restoring right upon the grasslands. And yet it should be clear to the reader that neither the investigator nor the cowboys are parodies or anti-heroes. A parody or a spoof requires an explicit comic burlesque of recognizable characters and patterns of action. It should be easy to call up the prime model of a Belgian-sounding detective named Harvey Peeperiot. Mrs. Christie had the pleasure of parodying herself in her mystery-writing character, Mrs. Oliver. It should be easy to see the shaping background presence of the Virginian and others in any of a herd of comic Westerns from *Maverick* to *Cat Ballou* and *True Grit*. But it should ultimately be argued that whatever the delights such parodies may provide, the higher artistic achievement lies not in mockery but in imaginative affirmation. John Mortimer's Rumpole, however rooted in the historical personalities of the old Bailey, is not a parody. His eccentricities, in which we delight, come within the believable comic probabilities of realistic characterization. Rumpole is not a cartoon on which certain exaggerated touches have been stroked. He is a man whose integral humanity is comically but realistically established. Max Evans's Dusty, in *The Rounders*, however related to the historical cowboys Evans has known, is not a parody. With all of his comic features, he is his own man. We believe in him not because we see a historical authenticity patterned in him, not because we see an inversion of the mythic hero, but because he lives convincingly on the pages of Evans's novel.

The writer of the work just concluded would like to claim a similar affirmative existence for both his detective and his cowboys. Turly Sinker is related to Dupin in a series of allusions, but any reader who knows Poe's detective will not be tempted to see Turly as his parody. Burt, Mont, and Barney on occasion do cow work. They wear boots. They can recognize cow and horse shit when they smell it. But they do little, in mockery or otherwise, to carry on the heroic traditions of Tom Mix and John Wayne. They do not ask to be compared with the Virginian and Shane. Such comparisons would make no more sense than comparing a Jersey bull with a docile Angus steer. They affirm their own right to exist in the living space on and beyond Sill's front porch.

Their way of imaginatively existing does however raise important questions. These questions follow easily from the unabashed

Afterword / 237

persistence of certain literary features. The work just concluded seems to have no solid ground of authenticity. The writer may seem to be uncertain about the nature of what many critics and historians call the Real West. The historians may be made particularly nervous by the occasional, indeed sometimes frequent, anachronisms, or what, assuming a specific historical time frame, may seem to be anachronisms. But there are still other features: one might suppose that cowboys as literary characters are individuals not only by the particular size of their boots and hats, their preferences for color and height in the horse they ride, but also in the manner of speaking and in the personal experience out of which the speaking may issue. In the work just concluded, it may be difficult to distinguish Burt speaking from Mont speaking. Sill may more often refer to pots, pans, and food, but he is not a character conceived as cook in any deep and significant way. When he participates in the voicing of range experiences, his idiosyncracies, if he has any, tend to be lost in a community of remembering and telling. Furthermore, there is ultimately no way of checking on the reliability of what is being reported. Mont may corroborate what Burt has said. Barney may corroborate what Mont has said. But it may be equally possible that Mont is adding to Burt's range fiction and that Barney is adding to Mont's. What finally seems evident, if anything seems evident, is that satisfaction comes not from realizing that a telling matches exactly some objective perception or action, but from the pleasure of sharing a fabric of telling that may be, if assayed by the sociologist and historian, a tissue of lies. There are tall tales here, but they are tall tales with a difference. When the buffalo chases Bemis up a tree in Mark Twain's *Roughing It,* we all know that we are well along the way in what we might call an amusing literary lie. Mark Twain give us certain clues so that we need not be wholly taken in. However open-minded he hopes we are, he does not suppose that we are naive enough to accept a literal-sounding report as a version of reality.

Since Mark Twain's time, the problem of literary reality has become increasingly complicated. We can continue to believe in an objective world of things, rocks, grass, bones, and hardpan, but for almost a century we have been more and more uncertain about ways to perceive and reliably report this world. And even when we have established some confidence in our ways, we have lost confidence in the artistic value of what we can report. If we could restore our faith in naive realism, we would lack appreciation for the reality it gives us.

No body of fiction in all of literature has so stubbornly kept faith with the epistemological assumptions of naive realism than has the literary Western. Again and again we have been told that the authentic character of the cowboy is found in his work. Thus if he uses a rope of the right length ("right" being determined by experienced observation) to catch a calf for branding with the right iron heated to the right hotness, then his realness is established. The embarrassing aura of his fictiveness has been somewhat dissipated.

As readers, however, we have been only faintly moved. We admire the skill involved, but we know that if we want the real thing in its pristine realness we had better go to the rodeo arena. Words, even when they are used literally, tend to blur reality. Thus if we are given the cowboy of naive realism, we have the comfort of seeming to hold on to reliable facts, but we have little to give us delight and pleasure. And worst of all, we have the strong suspicion that there must be more to literary reality than ropes, brand smoke, and dung dust.

Almost by definition the literary cowboy has been tall and taciturn. To be sure, the Virginian talks a good bit, but except for one line we are likely to remember him as a grinning Gary Cooper rather than as a voice filling in the spaces of a fictive world. Even when the cowboy has told a camp fire tale, that tale has been only a relatively brief oral moment in a world which remains curiously nonverbal and unarticulated even when we find it in the pages of a book.

In the work just concluded, the reader may if he wishes gather up a whole Western junkyard full of things which can be authenticated. Some of these things can be documented, although the writer has done no research to prove their rightness. But the world of Sill and Burt and Mont and Barney is a world which they create by their remembering and telling. Questions of objective validation are irrelevant. We do not need to ask, is Barney's account of an event true to the facts which may seem to harden the historian's world? Barney is not a historian. He is a man with a voice, adding his telling to the oral world which has its central geography on Sill's front porch. It is easy to say that Barney, like his friends, is a good liar, but when we have made that observation we are not likely to find much comfort in our pious factuality. However, if we mean by goodness that Barney and his friends have shared with us their honesty and comic pleasure, if their voices (seeming often to be one voice) have drawn us into their special brotherhood of thought and feeling, that is another matter. That is another sort of dimension of human reality. Thus the cowboy, conventional symbol of man alone, can sometimes help to redeem our human loneliness.